CATS
and other
PEOPLE

by Tay Hohoff

Doubleday & Company, Inc.
Garden City, New York
1973

Geneva Public Library

ISBN: 0-385-02295-6
Library of Congress Catalog Card Number: 72-92403
Copyright © 1973 by Tay Hohoff Torrey
All Rights Reserved
Printed in the United States of America
First Edition

This is for Arthur and my grandfather.

❀ AUTHOR'S NOTE ❀

These records were begun when the present didn't bear thinking about. Nearly three-quarters of a century lay behind me—why not take refuge in the past? Not an original idea, but one that had never occurred to me before.

My memory for names, faces, dates is poor. The very thought of burrowing in memory and expecting to come up with anything but blanks was laughable. But it was a challenge.

To my amazement, I discovered that memory was alive and kicking. Concentration and association are abilities most people develop almost without realizing it. The trick I had to learn was how to guide them. Theoretically, I knew that nothing is, in fact, forgotten, merely neglected or, by choice, lost sight of. Remembering became an adventure, like uncovering ancient cities or hacking trails through a jungle or raising sunken treasure ships.

Whatever I found had to be subjected to interpretation— my own—of personalities, events, places. I think I have been honest with myself—which isn't easy—and I know that the major facts, situations, and characters are essentially as I saw and understood them. But isn't what we call "real" like a prism, changing color under the light of each separate mind?

Dialogue is admittedly reconstructed or fictional but in tune with the speakers, few of whom are still in a position to quarrel with it for being off-key. The liberties taken in translating the emotions and physical sensations of the characters belonging to species other than the human will, I hope, be forgiven;

they spring from observation and a sympathy that has, at times, risen to empathy—or so I hope.

My original intention was to delete entirely my personal history. However, a considerable experience as an editor of work by more talented writers, soon warned that, while this was desirable from my point of view, it would result in a sequence of chilly reports lacking even the excuse of scientific value. There must be reasons for the actions, settings for the actors, a bit of scenery, even some background music. I threw away what I had written, silenced my noisy self-consciousness, and tried to tell these stories of the tyrants I have known, without fear or favor.

T.H.

CATS
and other
PEOPLE

ONE

Cat Nap became a member of our family about three months before I did. Our cats were usually introduced to new arrivals immediately, but Nap waited for me to take the initiative. Climbing to the second floor of the house on West 149th Street would have interfered with his sleep.

Nap had cried at the door late one evening when my grandfather, absorbed in some book, was alone in the living room. Nobody cried at that door for long if anyone was within ear shot. When the door opened he streaked in, crouched in a corner, and hissed. Out of the wind that was blowing up snow, he could afford to assert himself.

He was a true Maltese, but his coat was weatherbeaten and his flanks were caved in. He and my grandfather inspected one another carefully but at a distance.

"I think," said my grandfather conversationally, "there's some beef stew left over. The girls have gone to bed. Come along with me and let's see what we can find."

After a pause, to think over the proposition and to save his dignity, the gray cat followed down the stairs. A plate of warmed-up stew and a bowl of milk were set before him. My grandfather went upstairs; it isn't good manners to watch a strange cat eat. He wanted to go to bed, but he waited. After a while, the cat appeared. Watchful and close to the door, he washed vigorously. A gust of wind shook the windowpanes.

"You can sleep here," my grandfather said, "if you want to. I'm going to bed."

There was a family story that I once boasted, "*All* animals understand *everything* my grandfather says to them."

No one knew better than he that this childish faith was unfounded. Yet he went right on talking *as if* they could understand. He only rarely used anything but his ordinary voice, which was pleasant and unaffected. When pinned down he explained, with a touch of embarrassment, that perhaps it helped them to know your real intentions towards them. We call certain species "dumb" because they can't speak our language and we can't understand theirs, but the ratio of stupidity to intelligence among them is no greater than among us.

The theory, if that's what it was, broke down, he pointed out, under some conditions: blind panic, serious injuries, what in elephants is called "musth," rabies, congenital insanity. As he had lived and worked with animals most of his life; bred, raised, and trained race horses, what he mockingly called his theories were solidly buttressed by experience.

The Maltese stayed and in the morning was discovered, looking considerably plumper and sleeker, asleep in my soon-to-be mother's favorite chair. It wasn't the biggest chair in the room, but it was softly cushioned, with arms high enough to keep out drafts and deep enough to be comfortable for a rather long cat. My mother was never able to call it "hers" again.

Nap was his name and Nap was his nature. My grandfather said he must have led a hard life for a long time and was catching up. Food, warmth, and especially plenty of sleep worked a miracle in his appearance. The picture indelibly printed on my infant mind—and the first I can recall—is of a large gray object that lifted its head and opened blue eyes when I touched its back.

I had just learned that my legs would hold me up and that if I moved them in a certain way they would carry me vast distances before letting me down with a thump. My grandfather watched me wobble over to Nap. Would I yank the tail hanging over the edge of the chair or poke an exploratory finger into an eye? He always said I committed none of these crimes, but he was a prejudiced observer.

Whenever Nap decided to wake up, he displayed an extremely amiable disposition, and a large bump of vanity. He groomed himself assiduously; it was his most frequent and vigorous form of exercise. I seem to have a misty recollection of sitting on the floor in front of him and watching the entire process. Red tongue scrubbing away at whatever it could reach, paws rubbing ears and face with marvelous dexterity, the Statue of Liberty pose of one hind foot straight in the air while the head swivels around to clean the rear and the bulk of the tail which can be reached in no other way. And then, the toilette completed, the smug gaze of self-congratulation.

Affectionate and friendly when awake, Nap's somnolent habits overshadowed other facets of his personality. But he was, as my grandmother said, "very restful to have around."

At the turn of the century, my grandparents were in the process of moving the combined family home to Brooklyn. The twice-a-day trip from Harlem to lower Manhattan was rough. Public transportation, if any, was a farce. Sometimes the men drove (two horses were stabled nearby), sometimes they rode. Occasionally they fell back on the New York Central. Because their children had been slow in arriving, my grandfather was already elderly—and my father was a sybarite. A house big enough for everybody had been found near Prospect Park, not too far from Brooklyn Friends' School where I was already enrolled. There was never any question (then or later) about splitting up into two families.

Soon after the decision to move had been made, a complication arose which bothered the younger generation more than the older. My father—a lawyer specializing in property and estate work—was sent to Rio de Janeiro to settle a large estate, very important to the firm in which he was then a junior partner. It promised to be a long job and he took his wife and daughter along. They consoled themselves with the thought that they were at least removing a lively two-year-old from under their elders' feet.

Thanks to my grandmother's unruffled efficiency, moving day arrived with every possible emergency considered and solved in advance. And then, as the first van pulled up at the gate, with the predictable unpredictability of felines, Cat Nap disappeared.

The search was intensive and thorough, from cellar to attic, cupboards, closets, trunks, bags . . . Neighbors were alerted, passers-by accosted, the moving men joined the hunt. At last, in desperation my grandfather said the men had better start taking furniture out to the vans; perhaps in denuded rooms they would find Nap tucked away in some forgotten corner. It had been arranged to put Nap's chair where it would be unloaded first. Placed out of the way in the new living room, it would help him feel at home. So the last thing to go on the first van was Nap's chair.

The nearly empty house echoed to a yell. My grandfather ran to the living room. Nap, under the loose cushion, yawned and then spit. Somewhat unceremoniously, he was bundled into the box specially designed to carry him in comfort.

"I've seldom seen thy father really cross," my grandmother wrote, "but this time he *was*. I thought myself it was rather clever of old Nap."

After that everything went like clockwork. The house seemed more spacious with the furniture in place. The lilac bush in the back yard would be lovely in the spring. My grandfather badly missed the horses, but to keep them would be an unnecessary extravagance and renovating the house had cost more than had been expected. The buyer was a man he knew with a stable of his own and so . . .

"He doesn't say anything," my grandmother reported to her daughter, "but it hurts. It had to happen sooner or later, and everything will be all right when you come home." Nap, she went on had settled down and was sleeping on top of the cushion again, "like a Christian, although," she added, "some habits of the early Christians have always struck me as peculiar, to say the least."

On a blustery evening with icy snow hissing against the windows, they were reading comfortably near the cannel-coal fire, and sometimes nodding a little. Suddenly my grandmother looked over at Nap's chair.

"Thomas," she said, "there's something wrong."

By the time they crossed the room, Nap had gone, without a sound or a struggle.

In the morning, my grandfather dug a hole in the frozen ground under the lilac bush. Rose and Mary came from the kitchen, pulling shawls over their heads. They were used to the family's heathen ways, and each had brought her rosary. So Nap received a proper burial.

In Rio, a doctor vaccinated me with a dirty needle, blood-poisoning developed, and in a panic, my young parents used charm, pull, and bribery to get passage on the next boat. Their fright was excusable, for the doctors they called in were more embarrassed by their colleague's carelessness than hopeful for its victim's recovery. Apparently my father's clients moved heaven and earth to help, and somehow we were shoveled into the last available cabin on the next ship sailing for New York. He would return later and alone to tie up loose threads.

There was a theory that the ship's doctor saved my life, but the details were vague. He must have had his hands full, poor man, on the stormy voyage, what with seasick passengers and a small girl who was alternately delirious or unconscious, and probably dying. (I wonder what became of the doctor who vaccinated me? A good cat, like Nap, might have taught him to appreciate cleanliness.)

There is no doubt that my grandfather saved me from the miseries of a sickly childhood. Night after night, in the hours after midnight when vitality falters, he would hear me cry, he would get dressed, order my mother and grandmother back to bed, brush aside my father's frantic protests, and carry me the three blocks to the trolley line that ran all the way to Coney Island. It must have been a cold spring for I distinctly remember the warmth of the pot-bellied stove in the middle of the car. There was always a group of women—Poles, Lithuanians, Germans, probably—going home after cleaning offices, I suppose.

Sometimes one of them would say, "You tired, sir, leave me hold her," and I have a sort of in-and-out memory of strong arms that knew how to hold a sick child and of an unfamiliar, pungent smell compounded, I can guess now, of lye soap, disinfectant, and sweat and a clear impression that I liked it.

Gradually the car emptied, and the fresh breath of salt marshes seeped in, overpowering the heat of the stove, the subtle stench of candy wrappings, cigar butts, vomit perhaps, for there might be a drunk or two among the passengers. Then the conductor would sit down near my grandfather for a talk, and the motorman would chime in when he could, and I remember the sound of the men's voices as good and somehow healing. The deep voices and the salt air sent me to sleep.

At Coney Island was the ocean from which life came. At first, my grandfather had to carry me along the sea's edge; then I could walk. Then run. As strength returned, so did independence; I wouldn't be carried, and so we were often late for the scheduled start of the last trip back. The crew would wait, swing us aboard and say, "Gee, Pop, she's doin' great."

Why did he put himself through all this? I prodded him about that once, until he was embarrassed and stumblingly told me that these "little jaunts," as he called them, had occasioned the one and only quarrel he and my father ever had.

"He was angry, really angry," my grandfather said as if that still surprised him. "He kept saying he was younger, stronger, and thy father. It was his duty and his right, he said."

"Well, thee couldn't deny any of that."

"Of course not." He squirmed like a small boy caught throwing spitballs in class, but I looked at him insistently and he finally said he had pointed out that the very fact that my father was young, gay, exciting might hinder more than help. "I told him, 'Thee's everything she wants when she's well.' I said, 'I'm not exciting, I've taken care of dozens of sick animals. This is a sick animal. Leave her to me.'"

Getting well, and therefore cranky, I began to complain about no cat, and my grandfather picked *Alice in Wonderland* off a bookshelf.

"There's a cat in here," he said. "A special kind of cat."

The beginning pleased me well enough, but then came the magic words:

. . . flashed through her mind that she had never before seen a Rabbit with either a waistcoat pocket, or a watch to take out of it . . .

The spell was wound up.

Any child learns early when to turn the page in *Mother Goose*. While he read—and read again and again—I kept my eyes glued to the page. Sometimes he dozed. I was a spoiled brat, but I loved him and I let him snooze a little. But, oh dear, there was Alice with the key on the table out of reach, and the rose garden, the croquet game, the Duchess, clever, funny

Father William (*Do you think I can listen all day to such stuff?—Be off, or I'll kick you downstairs!*) I had the rhymes fairly well by heart, but there was all the rest, all behind a locked door. Somehow I must find the key. Alice had got into the rose garden, hadn't she? Well, so would I.

There were a couple of Globe-Wernicke travesties, responsibility for which was repudiated by everyone. I suspect a door-to-door salesman had given my grandmother a hard-luck story. The general rule was open bookshelves, openly arrived at. There were no Forbidden Areas. To this day, I can feel my sense of outrage when a well-meaning relative gave me a "prettily illustrated" volume containing novels by Charles Dickens "carefully selected and edited for Young People . . ." But that came a little later.

At the time, the Cheshire Cat left several conflicting impressions on my unformed mind. Its engagingly sinister grin only heightened my desire for a similar companion. But in some way, perhaps by inherited instinct, I caught the essence of Mr. Dodgson's Cheshire Cat. Its arbitrary choice of periods for retirement just as Alice most wanted him to stay, its equally disconcerting reappearances, its ironic interest in the world below, and royal indifference to approval or disapproval are, of course, authentic insights into the psychology of the Cat.

Unable to formulate my reactions to a portrait I intuitively understood and recognized, a feeling of uneasy kinship stuck in the dough of premature introspection. The Cheshire Cat was not admirable. Was I like that? Were cats really like that?

Such undigested lumps of awareness may have reconciled me to the advent of Pudge.

Not long before my mother entered her glamorous teens, she was given a pug dog from the Prince of Wales' kennels. Just how this canine aristocrat ended up on a Hudson River farm,

I never bothered to find out, but possibly by way of a relative who had been a Beauty in Victorian England and a popular Shakespearean actress. Judging by a faded photograph, his build and heft were like an English bulldog, but his face and nose looked as if something heavy had squashed them, and his popeyes were gentle. It was a humorous and likable face and from all accounts bespoke his character. To my knowledge, I have never seen one of his breed, and assume that these large pugs may have been victims of a fashionable vagary.

When my mother set out to find a suitable present to celebrate my full recovery, *toy* pugs were high style. It was natural that a miniature version of the pug she had loved and still mourned should appeal to her as an appropriate pet for her small, skinny daughter. Pudge (her name for him) was not only a toy pug, he was a puppy, and in size and weight comparable to a kitten. He was very beguiling, with his tan body coat, darker head, rear and tail, his bulging brown eyes that shone liquidly out of his funny, squashed-in face. His little tail curled in on itself over his back, like a fancy Polish sausage.

He was a perfect plaything. Nothing bothered him. Did I want to dress him up and put him in a doll carriage? Fine. Teach him tricks? Splendid. His tiny body was big with love and good will for all the world. One afternoon I was summoned to meet an acquaintance of my mother, but not told that she had brought with her an elderly, large, and not very amiable dog, so I entered the room with Pudge trotting at my heels. My mother, who said later she had simply forgotten that Pudge would show up with me, was nervous. So was the visitor. So was I. Pudge bounced on his nearly invisible legs straight up to the big dog's muzzle, barked with obvious friendliness and in an absurd little dance suggested a game —any game his guest would like. The stranger rose majestically to his full height and made for the doorway. Pudge scampered after him, saying, "Oh, do you want to see the place? Well, come right along with me . . ."

Pudge had serious difficulty with his curled-up tail. He was happy and to prove it, naturally wanted to wag his tail. But try as he would, nothing happened except a sort of mad contortion at the end of his spine. Acting on the principle that practice makes perfect, his little backside was seldom still. When we laughed at him, he was so pleased with us and himself that he would dash around among us, barking shrilly with delight, his tail quivering like jelly.

The abundance of his affection spilled over everyone in the family. He knew I must come first, but my mother led the field. She always found time for him, whereas my energy ran out and all too often I rejected him in favor of a book. Depending on his mood of the moment, he would either settle down with me or demand to be carried downstairs to my mother.

The stairs in that high-ceilinged house were long and steep and the steps were too high for him to negotiate. If none of the family was at home, I would take him all the way down to the kitchen where Rose and Mary made much of him and gave him forbidden tidbits. One afternoon he had been very good and quiet, not teasing me to play with him, but lying with his chin on his paws and his liquid eyes shining up at me. As I got up to light the gas he jumped eagerly after me, and remorse struck my heart. I picked him up and cuddled him.

"Look," I whispered in his ear, "you've been good as gold. I think I heard Mama and Nana come in. Suppose I take you down and just as soon as I finish this chapter, I'll come too and we'll play hide and seek in the library. Will that be all right?"

His wet nose nuzzling my neck said it would be fine, and we had a kissing match, a game Pudge always won.

He was a featherweight and I had carried him up and down

those stairs a hundred times, but somehow on the top step I lost my footing.

We fell. Instinctively I clutched him tightly in my arms. When we reached the bottom of the long flight, I was bruised, but Pudge was dead.

The noise had brought my grandmother and mother at a run. Rather dazed, I lay on the lowest step still holding Pudge. Somehow I knew what had happened. Perhaps it was his silence and his stillness, perhaps the feel of death in one's arms is unmistakable.

Temporarily unhinged by the sight of the tiny, inert body, and presumably by discovering that I was comparatively undamaged, my mother cried furiously, "Why didn't thee let him go! He'd have been safe . . ."

Certain moments from one's early childhood remain vivid for a lifetime. I even remember her eyes, which I believed were the most beautiful in the world, blazing down at me without pity.

My grandmother gathered me up in her arms. As she carried me away, she said through my wild sobs, "It was natural to hold him. Thy mother is just frightened and upset."

After a few days, my grandfather led us back to talking about Pudge, but I wouldn't join in. Pudge had not been my only loss that afternoon.

Kindergarten and association with other children were new experiences about which I had mixed feelings. The gentle but firm disciplinarian methods of our Montessori-trained teacher didn't bother me, but the conventional activities bored me and were often coolly ignored. The girls both bored and terrified me, but I made friends with two boys who were to be my classmates and friends until we all graduated from high school.

Two things did bother me: School interfered with reading—

in which I was becoming adept at skipping over words I didn't understand if there was no interpreter available—and I was still "cat hungry," as my mother said.

Flotsam and Jetsam, when they showed up, were an amusing and pleasant pair so alike in appearance and behavior we had to guess which was which, but as we never saw them separately that wasn't important. They had first appeared for no obvious reason. They came and went without notice, treating our home as a hotel, returning after an absence of several days, or even several weeks, with equally erratic periods when they graciously accepted our bed and board. This upset Rose and Mary.

"But why?" my grandmother demanded. "It isn't as if you had to get dinner for them. They'll take anything we have."

"'Taint natural," Rose maintained. "Just when we get used to having them around, off they go again. Save up a nice bit of steak or roast lamb off a plate—and find they've taken off."

"The truth is," my grandmother remarked later, "the girls miss a cat we can call a member of the family as much as someone else who shall be nameless."

Flotsam and Jetsam seemed to know about weekends when my father would be home. They may have felt a kinship with him for, like them, he was a born wanderer. Or they might, my grandmother suggested provocatively one Sunday evening, pity him for his present state of domesticated bondage.

My father laughed and looked affectionately at the two cats curled up at his feet. He had just returned from a rather lengthy stay in a lumber camp in Canada, I think, where a client had sought help in solving some labor trouble. He had had to leave my mother behind, and he had been horribly uncomfortable. "You don't know when you're well off," he informed the Identicals, who purred.

The two cats interested my grandfather. He said he had never actually known two cats to stay together unless they were mates, and even then the circumstances were usually rather special. Flotsam and Jetsam were males, handsome blacks with similar white markings, and they apparently prowled together. At least, they always left together and arrived together. The problem bothered him.

"Come on, fellows," he coaxed, "tell us the story."

We laughed at him, and my grandmother remarked placidly, "Takes thee down a bit, doesn't it, sweetheart? Live and learn."

For a few months we had a guest, a gorgeous white Persian. (During this time Flotsam and Jetsam were conspicuous by their absence, a fact carefully noted by my grandfather.) She belonged to a couple of my father's theater friends who were signed up for a long tour and leaped at his casual suggestion that they leave Precious with us.

Precious was arrogant, self-centered, and stupid. She had won several blue ribbons and she was beautiful. She frequently forgot how long it took to reach the back yard, to the shock and despair of Rose and Mary; but when she was presented with a properly equipped pan, which she was used to as an apartment-house cat, she coldly rejected it. She liked foods such as crabmeat, calf's liver, white meat of chicken, and lobster. These being rated as "special" on our menu, she put up with leftovers, chopped beef, or boiled haddock, but made anyone who fed her feel like the dust beneath her chariot wheels. She was still young, her figure was perfection, yet she never played or responded to attempts to entertain her. She set herself in poses.

"She makes me think of a cloak-and-suit model," my father remarked at dinner one night when Precious had chosen a side chair in full view. "All beauty and no brain. Empty," he added, looking at Precious, "except for a lot of expensive food."

My mother asked how he knew so much about cloak-and-suit models. "Oh," he said, raising an eyebrow, "lawyers can't always pick and choose."

My mother detested Precious. "Don't bring another of them home," she warned. "If Precious isn't out of here pretty soon, *I* will be."

When her people came at last to take her home, she yawned in their faces.

Flotsam and Jetsam returned the following evening.

Change was in the air. We were going to move to the country. Flotsam and Jetsam seemed to know and transferred their patronage to another hotel. Rose and Mary spent most of their time crying; they wouldn't go with us, they were afraid of the country, there were family ties in the city, and friends and the church. My grandmother finally uncovered the real reason.

"They're going back to Dublin," she said, waving her hands. "Why couldn't they just say so? They've saved up a nice little nest egg and there's a small pub they can buy cheap. All this fuss and feathers!" she exclaimed crossly. "Making us feel sorry and responsible for them."

Life without Rose and Mary was hard to imagine, and when they said good-by *everybody* cried. However, I was cheered by becoming a center of attention at school. I was moving to the country, I would ride to school on the elevated railroad, there was a real barn on the property, big trees, lilac bushes, spirea, a wisteria vine, grass . . .

"Now you can have a dog," one of the boys said wistfully.

"I suppose so, if I want one."

Hard as it is to believe now, in the early years of the century Richmond Hill, Long Island, was still thought of as "country." In fact, it was a suburb, but I think the term was considered somewhat derogatory. Our new house was big, with generous grounds, and my grandfather, I know, thought of horses; maybe just one. But, for once, common sense prevailed. I am equally sure my mother dreamed about a dog, or maybe two. It was a simple dream, yet I never heard her mention it, except indirectly, and why she did not have her wish has been a puzzle to me ever since.

For that matter, I don't know why we moved. I was told it was on my account. Better air; I would be out of doors instead of spending hours with my nose in a book; companions aside from schoolmates; and so on. Probably all that did enter the picture, but I suspect the underlying reason was the family's itching foot. My grandfather had spent years at work that took him all over the Eastern Seaboard before he returned to the family farm. My father was constantly on the go; if he could find no professional excuse for traveling, he and my mother—and often, I—would be off in a cloud of dust. It's hard to be sure about my grandmother. She had shared many of her husband's varied and sometimes wild experiences, and sometimes talked about them. Nostalgically? Yes, I think so. A move from Brooklyn to Richmond Hill was no real adventure—but it was a change.

The place was a great success, which is nice to remember for it was the last time we would have a roof of our own. The house was square, comfortable, covenient; the grounds were spacious and "workable," as my grandfather said. I was in heaven, sharing the top floor and a bathroom only when there were guests. To stop me from reading at night, someone had to climb the stairs, which obligingly creaked.

Within a few days, however, I discovered that I also shared my room with a mouse. I had gone to bed with a book and a plate of crackers and cheese on the bedside table when I heard an odd scratching noise and looked up to see a tiny bit of brownish fur half in and half out of a small crack between the wall and the floor. I was more familiar with Alice's Mouse than the flesh-and-blood variety, but I recognized it immediately. My first thought was, "Granddad will be upset." With his almost fanatical insistence on cleanliness, he had had the entire house closed and fumigated before we set foot inside. He thought he had eliminated any chance that rodents or other unwelcome habitués might survive. That this insignificant creature had fooled him, made me giggle. The mouse vanished.

While I waited hopefully, I slowly and silently nipped off a piece of cheese and set it on the floor at a little distance from the bed. Having dipped a tentative finger into ancient history, I named my roommate Hannibal—the only pronounceable name I had found. I continued to wait like a cat at a mousehole, but with kinder intentions, and had almost given up when he appeared again. Then he went into a sort of minuet, advancing and retreating with lengthy hesitations, and now I could see him fairly clearly in the light from the bed lamp. He (or she) was not as small as I had thought and he was more gray than brown. His little nose twitched in the direction of the cheese. I held my breath. A flashing scamper, the cheese was caught, and he nibbled. He must have been hungry or perhaps he was too young to have learned suspicion. Dinner over, he left for home and finally, with even more reluctance than usual, I turned out the light.

My increasing appetite for cheese attracted some desultory attention and a slight effort was made to educate my taste. "Try a little Camembert, darling, it's just the right consistency," or, "The Liederkranz isn't quite soft enough . . ." But I was positive that Hannibal had less exotic tastes whether I did or not. I explained that plain American was better for eating in bed than the gooey kinds. This was the first time I had seriously practiced to deceive, and my prevarications were overelaborate.

Hannibal became confident of his safety and would sit beside the bed nibbling happily and waiting for more. I held whispered conversations with him which at first startled him back into his hole. When nothing came of this except more cheese, he would listen with his little head cocked a bit and his eyes bright, with such an air of doubtful interest that I was hard put to strangle the giggles that might reach my mother's sharp ears.

When he first took the cheese from my fingers, my sense of triumphant accomplishment almost got the better of my discretion. And now I wonder why I felt I must keep little Hannibal a secret. I had never had a secret from my family before, and perhaps it went to my head. When one night came, and no Hannibal, and then another and another, I found my grandfather alone, weeding the vegetable garden, and told him. I tried not to cry; a girl big enough to keep a secret should be brave enough not to cry.

I said, "I told him about cats. And dogs and traps. Of course, I knew he didn't understand. It just made me feel better, as if I might be helping him."

He pulled up a bunch of crab grass and said thoughtfully, "Hannibal may be a female, thee knows. He—she—may have simply gone off to start a family. Or, if thee is right about his sex, he may have found a mouse who means more to him than friendship." He turned his back on me for a moment, and then added, "If thee named him right, he'll survive, I expect."

They were a funny lot, my family. They turned me loose in a library that included almost everything from Pliny to Plutarch, Shakespeare to Byron, Jane Austen to contemporary trash; they answered any question factually; they never whetted my curiosity by accident without satisfying it—and when I worried about the possible demise of a mouse, protected me by offering possible, legitimate alternatives.

Probably it was an odd family altogether. You might as well expect the unexpected from them, because that's what you would get. When my grandfather, through no fault of his own, lost the rich old Farm in the Hudson River Valley, he had returned without bitterness and with no apparent regret to a position in a real estate brokerage firm in the city. His closest friend was my father, many years his junior. That he was also my father's closest friend is perhaps another oddity. They shared innumerable interests, among them a passion for New York City. Now I come to think of it, I wonder why they decided to live in Richmond Hill? Because its urbanization was just beginning and they wanted to watch it happen? It seems far-fetched, but they were unpredictable.

I don't know how long we had lived there when Bagheera came. Black from nose tip to tail tip, without a white hair, big and friendly and intelligent, what else could he be called? Steeped in *The Jungle Books* as I was, recognition was instant, and even my mother admitted it, with a laugh. He came to us out of nowhere, stood at the kitchen door asking with polite insistence to be allowed in, ate, washed thoroughly, said "thank you" to my grandmother and Gerda (the daily substitute for Rose and Mary), and then, "rather tentatively," my grandmother reported, stretched out in front of the stove. When she told him it was all right, go to sleep, he lifted his head and she saw that his eyes were emerald-green.

There are cats who avoid children, often from bitter experience, but Bagheera adopted me on sight because I was the smallest human being around. He was the companion I had been hungry for. He never pushed or crowded or made demands at the wrong moment. He slept on my bed and opened his amazing eyes when I said something like, "Oh, Bagheera, what does *inconsequential* mean?" and looked on while I made a check in the margin to remind me to ask the nearest authority when I woke up.

In addition to all his other virtues, Bagheera was a warm, loving cat who demonstrated his affection by rubbing, kissing, snuggling, purring, patting my face. He loved to be rubbed under his chin and even more, to be scratched vigorously behind his ears. He was a great one for kissing and his rough red tongue would tickle my face, hands, arms, until I laughed. I was very happy with him.

Him.

One day when the early spring sun felt deceptively like summer, my grandfather picked me up at school, although I was now allowed to travel without escort, and as the train rattled past the roofs and windows of tenements, stores and warehouses, he said, "I think there may be a surprise waiting for thee at home."

"What?" I demanded.

He shook his head. "It's a surprise."

In a box behind the kitchen stove, out of the draft, were six tiny kittens, each one black from nose tip to tail tip. Bagheera, purring like a steam engine, looked at me proudly. Newborn kittens should not be touched, but I could look my fill. Six miracles . . . seven, counting Bagheera. Superb in her maternal pride, supremely content, she lay at full stretch, accepting congratulations and admiration as her due, while the kittens wobbled and fell and staggered to reach her milk.

But quite soon, I made some excuse and ran upstairs to fling myself on my bed and weep tears of relief. For what seemed to me a long time, I had been worried about Bagheera's increasing girth, his odd shape, his alternating sleepiness and restlessness. I had thought, "If no one, not even Granddad, sees anything wrong it must be my imagination," and had tried to shut my eyes and my mind against a possibility I couldn't face. It had all been needless, and the world was right side up again.

Perhaps adults should think twice before treating themselves to the pleasure of "surprising" a child.

The kittens went from phase to phase of growth at a pace I found unbelievable. I arrived home in the afternoons—not loitering in the playground these days—breathless with anticipation. I was never disappointed. The other children could come and look, which they did with a regularity that drove Gerda nearly out of her mind, but why should I go and play when six kittens were putting on a new circus act every few minutes?

Gerda said, "Miss Tazie, I take whip, beat you out of my kitchen. I promise. Yah. I tell my lady so, too."

"What did she say?" I asked, removing one kitten from the back of a squealing brother—or sister, it was too early to tell.

"She laugh," Gerda said ruefully, and laughed too.

Strictly speaking, the active performers were five. My grandfather said that in most large litters there would be a runt, the one who got kicked around, pushed away from the mother's teats, buried under a pile of fat, well-fed, aggressive siblings, the one who was always out of line and out of step. He picked up Bagheera's runt and looked it over carefully.

"Nothing really wrong," he said. "Well-shaped. I think it's a male—look at that head, wide between the ears, broad in the jaw, or would be if he had enough to eat." He put the kitten next to Bagheera who gave it a casual lick.

I said, "Bagheera doesn't seem to like the—the little one as much as the others . . ."

"I've seen that before. We had a sow on the Farm who killed all her runts—rolled on them. But I've seen the other kind of mother, too. You never can tell. And I've known runts who turned out to be the best of the lot, given a decent chance."

The fame of Bagheera's kittens spread beyond the nearby families. "*All* black, there's not a white hair on any of them."

As the weather warmed and they grew, they were moved out of Gerda's way into a small room used as a catch-all, and this became a Mecca for children of all ages, many of whom I had never heard of. An occasional parent would trail along, but I suspect less to see the famous kittens than out of curiosity about my parents whose parties and comings-and-goings were watched by our neighbors with intense interest. Neither was snobbish, they genuinely liked people, rich and poor, high and low, black, yellow, and white. They chose their friends according to their own tastes, not by the rule book. In a close-knit, conventional community, they were conspicuous and misunderstood.

My grandmother's experience with similar, and uglier, situations, as well as pride in her children, made her sensitive. In the presentation of the five kittens (one would stay with us), she saw an opportunity to soothe ruffled feathers and mute, if not silence, criticism, without, as she put it, "committing us in the future."

"It's unlikely," she said, "that there'll be the excuse of five black kittens again."

"We could mate Bagheera with one of her sons," my grandfather suggested and touched off an argument that ranged from throwbacks to insanity; Egyptian pharoahs and other royal houses; animal inbreeding for specific purposes; the inbred communities in the New Jersey hills, the Ozarks, and eastern Europe. When a foray into botany threatened, my grandmother reversed the talk full circle by mentioning an article she had recently read dealing with future similarities between urban and rural societies.

I was too young to appreciate how cleverly she switched the runaway discussion back on the track, but on later occasions I was to hear and marvel, and watch my grandfather's eyes glow with awareness while, under the mustache that tried to hide the sensitive mouth, flickered a smile that I could not read but made my heart turn over.

Weather permitting, the party would be held on the lawn. She and Gerda would take charge of refreshments and extra help, folding chairs, tables, and so on. My mother would collate and organize the lists of guests each of us would prepare, and send the invitations because "she's the only one of us who writes a hand anyone can read." The date? Oh, yes, July 3, a Saturday.

"That's Tazie's birthday," she went on, "but we won't confuse matters by mentioning that if she doesn't mind."

"I've been telling you for years and *years* I hate birthday parties—this will be fun."

"So thee has," my grandmother said. "At least, ever since the fat boy ate more cake than even he could hold. This year . . ." she continued serenely, "Ernest will give the kittens to the proper people—the children, of course—and thee must be sure not to get them mixed up. And say something graceful each time, but not long and try not to be too clever."

My father grinned, and said he would try.

"Don't I have anything to do?" my grandfather asked.

"We'll talk about that later. I have some ideas."

His eyes danced. "I was afraid of that."

The party was a dizzy success. My mother set out to charm the women—she didn't have to worry about the men—while my father operated in reverse order. By the time it was over, the entire family could have danced the cancan in front of the Methodist church during Sunday services without a blot on its escutcheon.

We were tidying up the living room, for of course the party had spilled over into the house, when my mother suddenly broke the weary silence by turning on me with a demand to know why she hadn't been consulted about which kitten we were to keep. "After all, *I* have to live with it too." Generosity was all very well, she rushed on, but in this case it was unnecessary, and selfish too, because I hadn't taken her into consideration, she hadn't even been *told* until it was too late . . .

I saw my father's right eyebrow go up as he looked at his "two girls." His wife could do no wrong—but neither could his daughter.

I tried to speak, but her voice rose. "Giving the cream of the litter away to strangers," she cried, "and keeping the *runt!* It's just plain stupid."

For a moment no one moved. Then I felt my spine stiffen and my eyes go hot.

"He's mine," I said. "Not thine." I marched stiff-legged to the doorway. Then I turned on my heel and faced her. "I'm going to take him upstairs with me," I told her. "He'll be lonely without the others."

I remember I left a dead silence behind me as I walked down the hall.

❊ TWO ❊

Carrying the kitten downstairs next morning, I thought about Bagheera. After the kittens were weaned, her behavior became, I thought, odd. She was away for days and nights at a time, was pleasant and affectionate, but as if her mind was on other things.

Gerda had Sundays off and I found my grandmother in the kitchen preparing breakfast. After giving the kitten some milk, which he attacked with enthusiasm, I said, "Where's Bagheera, Nana?"

She turned the sausages and said vaguely, "Goodness knows. I expect she'll be back, when she gets good and ready."

"Doesn't she love us anymore?"

"She doesn't *need* us anymore."

"Has—has anything happened to her?"

"I don't believe so. Not in the way thee means. She has a restless nature, Bagheera." She laughed a little. "Runs in the family, thee knows." She pushed the pan to the back of the stove and sat down. "Come sit on my lap. Thee's getting enormous but not too enormous for that." She was silent for a long moment, watching the kitten and holding me rather tight.

I suddenly realized how small she was. I said, "I am getting too big for thee, darling. I'm getting too big for anything but a man's lap, I guess."

"Well, not quite yet," she said seriously. "That will come, though, and then thee may understand a little more about Bagheera. She's as female as anyone I've ever known. And clever. Beautiful and lovable and clever. It's quite a combination. I don't worry about Bagheera. If she needs us again, she'll come back." While I was trying to digest this novel view of Bagheera, she went on thoughtfully, "It will be interesting to see how this one turns out. He hasn't had anything his own way. Now he will. What will it do to him? Or for him?"

I buried my face in her soft mass of sweet-smelling hair. My world was steady again. I whispered, "Thanks, darling," and slid off her lap. "What shall we call him? Nana, *thee* name him, please."

"Impo," she replied promptly.

I shrieked with laughter. "Impo! Why?"

"Because the Imp o' Darkness cannot be Imp o' Light."

I dashed off to meet my parents coming down the stairs. "Nana's named him," I cried. "Just listen . . ."

By early autumn, the runt was bigger, stronger, far more handsome and amusing than his brothers and sisters. His superiority irritated two mothers whose children had made their own selections out of the litter. We had, they claimed, kept the best for ourselves. When this allegation reached our ears, my mother was the first to laugh.

She nicknamed him Puddah. It was exactly the sound he made when he ran up and down stairs. We all slipped into it, and he answered to either. Even in early youth, his character was complex. When he was affectionate, playful, or mischievous, he was Puddah; when he chose to be regal, austere, scornful, annoyed, or bored, he was Impo.

While he was still small and scrawny, I dressed him up and put him in a doll carriage. This performance bored him extremely, but he put up with it, usually. It bored me, too. Unfortunately, someone had given me the idea that the kitten would be a perfect substitute for the dolls I detested—and if a little girl didn't want to play at being "mama," something was very wrong. This aberration didn't last long, and I don't know whether Impo or I was the more relieved.

Bagheera never returned.

Plans for the summer got underway by the end of the year. They didn't please me very much but, as my mother said, it did no good to pout. A client was insisting on my father's concentrated attention in, I think, Cuba, for "as long as necessary," and that meant my mother would go with him. He would not, however, have both his "girls." The advanced age of eight presented problems with which my mother had no desire to contend, and quite rightly. If I could be satisfactorily disposed of, my grandparents could be alone and take a much-needed rest. I would, therefore, spend the summer with some cousins who lived on part of the old family property. One of the children was a girl three or four years older than I; the other two were even older twins—a girl and a boy. I had never laid eyes on any of them.

"Thee knows Cousin Nicholas," my grandfather said consolingly.

"I know he has a nose just like thine, and a lot of white hair —not a bit like thee—and a white beard and he's getting a little deaf, and sometimes he spends the night on his way to Washington to testify for the Department of Agriculture and he's the other cousins' uncle and has an 'experimental garden,' whatever that is, and he keeps bees."

"Well," my grandfather remarked mildly, "that's quite a lot."

In mid-June, he took me to the *Mary Powell*'s berth on the New York side of the Hudson. We were promptly taken up to the Captain's quarters where the two men plunged into talk about the old days and gossip about the decline and change in River traffic (the West Shore Railroad had cut deep into freight and passenger business), while I drank milk and nibbled cookies, sniffing the new smells of tar and bilge water and brass polish. There was a typewriter on a table.

"Ever try one of those things?" the Captain asked.

"In my father's office. It's fun."

"It's yours for the trip. Just come in when you get tired of watching the River." He chuckled. "If you're anything like the rest of your folks, you won't be. Hey, Tom?"

My grandfather said, "In a way, I wish I was going with you. But—I'm a coward, Cap'n."

"Bosh! Stuff and nonsense!" He turned back to me. "Ever hear anything about the *Mary's* bell?"

"Only about a thousand times," I replied pertly.

"Want to help pull the rope when we come in for a landing?"

What a question!

The bell of the *Mary Powell* was famous. People who should know have called it the most beautiful river-boat bell in the world. For close to a century, it sang and echoed over the River country. For every landing, large and small, its voice hovered like a blessing on cities and towns, villages and hamlets.

That day of introduction to the River was unalloyed happiness. I had the run of the boat from the pilothouse to the engine room—or at least I was allowed a closer look than most passengers at the shining brass rods and pistons that moved with a powerful rhythm that always seemed to me consciously happy.

Several of the deckhands and all the officers, except the young purser, knew my grandfather, saluted him as he left, and asked questions when they cornered me. "Doin' all right? Looks fine. And how's Mrs. Thomas? Miss Ann?"

"Miss Ann, your mother," one of them told me, "was the purtiest girl I ever set eyes on in all my life. And I never forgot the way she laughed, almost good as the *Mary*'s bell, and so friendly and treatin' everybody alike."

"She's just like that now," I assured him proudly.

Around the middle of the eighteenth century a shipbuilder whose Yard was on the ocean side of Long Island—apparently tired of being shot at and burned out by pirates, casual marauders, and the French—obtained a royal grant to a fairly extensive tract on the west shore of the mid-Hudson River and moved there, lock, stock, and barrel. Barn, houses, a mill were built, other settlers followed, and so, in due course, did the American Revolution. The British circumvented the iron chains America had slung across the River near West Point and sailed upriver firing at towns and hamlets. Twelve miles above Newburgh they cannonaded Forefather Edward's settlement. Most of the shots went wild, but one ball hit the Mill, demolishing a wall and setting a fire which was easily brought under control. One of Edward's sons fished the ball out of the ashes. It remained in the family until, mercifully, the heavy, unlovely object rolled off a moving van and was lost. My grandfather felt sad, but his womenfolk callously rejoiced.

All this I knew when the Captain led me down the gangplank to Cousin Nick waiting on the dock. Yet when the reality *I* saw came face to face with the reality my grandparents had given me in vivid detail, it had the illogical logic of Alice's worlds down the Rabbit Hole and behind the Looking Glass.

The region, with its steep, stony, sun-washed hills, was still "copperhead country." We were not allowed to go barefoot in the fields and pastures. When my cousin Gifford tried to tell me how to know a copper when I saw one, I informed him scornfully that I had already been taught all that by someone who knew more about snakes than he ever would. Nevertheless, my first, and I think my only, sight of one gave me a real, if never admitted, fright.

Seen in a zoo, behind thick glass, it is possible to appreciate the beauty of their coloration and the subtlety of their markings, like a divinely conceived and executed batik. The narrow head, hypnotic eyes, and the flickering tongue may seem like the personification of evil, but a copperhead, like other equally beautiful snakes rightly feared by man, doesn't know it is evil. I suppose there is a tenable theory to explain why fear and hatred of the reptile is so general among humans, but I have never heard one.

My meeting with a copperhead took place in the proper setting: a hillside pasture thick with stones of assorted shapes and sizes where I had gone in search of wild raspberries for which I was greedy. When I tripped over one of the stones, falling to my knees, I may have disturbed the copper's midday siesta for it partly emerged. My eyes were level with the snake's as we stared at each other. Then it slithered back under the stone, and I left the pasture with no further thought of raspberries.

For some reason, I was rather ashamed of this encounter and never told my cousins. My grandfather said, "The snake was more frightened than thee." I was sitting on his lap as usual, and his arm tightened around me, but that was all he said.

Copperheads were killed whenever opportunity presented itself, but the useful or harmless snakes were plentiful and safe except from cats, dogs, and bloodthirsty boys. At Richmond Hill a pretty little garter snake would sometimes be seen in the garden, but garden or grass snakes were new to me. Pencil thin, and long, they slid unmolested through the lawns and gardens like animated lengths of green silk ribbon, their sustenance the infinitesimal bugs that destroy plant leaves.

There were three ponds on the old place: the Round Pond, the Long Pond, and the Mill Pond. Between the Long Pond and the Mill Pond were a dam and a sluiceway running sharply downhill. When the water in the upper pond reached flood level, the sluices would be opened, the water rush to the Mill Pond and down again under the lane into a stream that meandered through meadows and eventually found its way to the River.

The ponds were rimmed by trees, many old and tall with branches that hung over the water. Cousin Nick taught me to row the old, slab-sided, flat-bottomed rowboat, and I spent hours dreaming in the dappled shade of trees, among the bullfrogs, the dragonflies, the skater bugs, and (at the far and shallow end of one of the ponds) a couple of snapping turtles. Cousin Nick said they wouldn't hurt you if you didn't bother them, but I caught a good glimpse of open jaws and decided neither of us would have a chance to bother the other.

The boat was not always used to dream in. On hot afternoons, the water snakes liked to sleep on the overhanging branches. They were harmless and lethargic but sizable in length and thickness. On the first hot afternoon, my cousins took me for a row. As we slipped under the mass of heavy, leafy branches, one of them stood up and lazily swung an oar. Several snakes fell into the boat. My reaction was disappointingly casual. However, that countryside always attracted summer visitors from New York and even more distant cities, and having learned how the game was played I joined with enthusiasm.

Two or three young visitors, including at least one girl, would be invited to come for a row. I wasn't big enough to be trusted with the operative oar, but I could keep the clumsy boat in position and help distract the guests' attention with, "O-oh, there's the biggest bullfrog I ever saw!" or, "Did you know dragonflies can sew up your eyes?" while the snakes were dislodged.

The one thing the snakes wanted was to get out of the hateful boat, but they were too stupid to learn from experience and there was a lot of slithering and slipping, yelling and even hysterical screams before they were all heaved overside. After I had described this as a new game, my grandfather chuckled and said, "Well, there *are* new things under the sun, but that isn't one of them."

Unlike many country people, my cousins' midday meal was not dinner, but lunch. Cousin Henry, the children's father, seldom came home at noon, and Cousin Nicholas disliked "stuffing" himself at any time, which may explain why he could outswim and outdive any of the younger generations. Sally and I had happened on some wild strawberries that didn't know their time was past, and I was trying to resist temptation while doling them out in separate dishes, when the telephone rang our signal. Sally answered and a heavy voice came into the room. Sally said, "Sure, no trouble at all. About four?"

The caller, a well-thought-of farmer, wanted to know if Mr. Thomas' granddaughter could come over—he had something he thought Mr. Thomas would be interested in.

Having washed up the dishes and prepared the dinner vegetables, we woke up the elderly mare, Susan, and backed her fat, reluctant body between the shafts of the open, one-seat wagon, Sally handed the reins to me, whereupon Susan swiveled her head around with a look of such disgust that we fell into a fit of giggles. Sally was the kind of cousin every little girl should have. If she was bored or annoyed by having a younger cousin underfoot all summer, she never let me know it. She taught me the mysteries of living in a house without plumbing, how to clean and fill kerosene lamps, what did and did not go into the Springhouse, where to find the best mud for a yellow jacket sting, and a hundred other items of vital information. She would never be a "pretty" girl, but she radiated love, kindness, instinctive wisdom, and humor. In the true sense, she was beautiful, and as she grew into womanhood she was blessed, or cursed if you wish, with the sexual appeal men can no more ignore than a bee can fly away from a nectar-filled flower.

The farm looked prosperous, with a big field of feed corn near the main road, a well-kept lane leading up to a white-shingled house, a number of outbuildings, and a large red barn. The heavy-set man in the barn doorway came forward to help us down.

"Leave her here," he said. "Bit of grass and shade. If I know Susan, she won't run away."

The barn was even larger than it looked from outside, and apparently empty. In this weather, the livestock would be at pasture, but Sally said afterwards there was room for at least ten cows and we noticed four roomy stalls. With the steady, unhurried gait of a working farmer, our host led us to the last stall at the far end of the barn.

"Here we are," he said.

There was an adolescent rendition of a bellow, a rush of hooves on straw-covered wood from the back of the stall, and I found myself staring up into a coffee-and-cream colored face with a white exploding star on the forehead. A Guernsey bull. The head belonged to Greek mythology, young Zeus, already up to his tricks. The air around him was electric with vitality, it was almost visible. Perfection met without warning struck me dumb with awe, and I moved a little closer to Sally. Her blue eyes were wide and sparkling.

"Whee-ee!" she breathed. And then, practically, "You won't be able to keep him in there much longer."

The farmer laughed. "Don't mean to. His own place is ready, but he gets lonely without the other critters." He looked down at me. "What do you think?"

I stammered. "I—I don't know."

"You're Mr. Thomas' granddaughter. Got his blood. What do you make of Ahab?"

"*Ahab!*"

He looked pleased, as if he had won a bet. "Know about Ahab, huh? All right, tell me what you think Mr. Thomas would make of him."

Suddenly my shyness blew away. "I don't know. *I* think he's a Greek god in disguise. Is he . . . But it's all so long ago."

"You mean, is he in Ahab's direct line? Well, in a way, yes, he is. My dad bought a calf sired by one of Ahab's get. Yeah, it's a long time ago. We tried to keep the strain as clean as we could. But this one's like a throwback. I remember Ahab, and this one—well, it's like . . . What do you call it?"

"Reincarnation?" I ventured.

"That's right. Ever see pictures of Ahab?"

"Oh, yes, but you know what those old photographs were like. I guess I'm going by Granddad's description, the way he talks about him."

The young Ahab was not getting the attention he expected. He whuffled in his nose and pawed the floor impatiently. He could just get his head and neck over the stall. I put both hands on the stall and pulled myself up. We looked at each other. Then I kissed his nose, and dropped down. "I'll tell Granddad about you, Ahab," I promised.

To my astonishment and dismay, the farmer's mouth was quivering.

"Thanks, Miss Tazie," he said. "That's what I wanted to hear."

Old Susan, of course, was happily dozing. The farmer said, shyly, there was some homemade chocolate cake up at the house, and ginger ale or milk. Would we? We would, naturally. The kitchen was cheerful and spotless, the cake delicious. He had made it himself, lived alone now and his dad had been sick so long, he'd learned a lot about cooking.

Sally said reflectively, "This is better milk than we get. They're adding Holsteins to the herd."

I interrupted their violent agreement on the subject of Holsteins. ("Milk's good for cheese," he said with an air of giving justice where justice was due. "Ha!" said Sally. "Who makes cheese around here? Except potcheese, of course.") "Do you," I demanded, "know anything about the time Granddad drove Ahab down to the village?"

He leaned his chair back against the wall and laughed. "Do I? *I was there.*"

Influenced perhaps by chocolate cake and pure Guernsey milk, Sally forgot her strictures against listening to "those old yarns," and joined me in teasing him to tell. "Well, Mr. Thomas would have told you, and Miss Sally's likely heard it, too, people still remember . . ."

Shamelessly, I pulled rank. "Too bad," I said, loftily. "Granddad will be sorry not to hear it from the other side. I don't believe he ever has." (This was certainly not true, but *I* never had.)

"We-ell," he admitted, "maybe I did see some Mr. Thomas didn't. It was a Saturday afternoon, you know. I don't remember now why Dad and I had come over, but I remember everything else as if it happened yesterday. The village was bustin' with folks, kids in from the farms an' wimmin doin' last-minute shoppin' for Sunday an' the men shootin' the breeze an' the Reverend whippin' up trade for Sunday services an' the old geezers on the hotel porch gettin' in practice for Sat'day night." He was quite relaxed now and looked companionably at Sally. "*You* know how it is. Ain't changed much.

"The Post Office was jam-packed with folks who weren't expectin' a thing except mebbe a Sears catalogue. I was about Miss Sally's age, I guess, and I was runnin' in and out, busy as a bird dog, you know the way boys are. That's how I happened to notice hoofbeats comin' down the road. Nothin' surprisin' in that, 'course. Later some o' the men claimed those hooves didn't sound right, but I dunno.

"We-ell, somebody let out a yell—from the hotel porch, I guess—an' there was Mr. Thomas comin' 'round that sharp bend by the hotel, in the sulky but he wasn't drivin' Nell—he was drivin' a godamn—a bull. Funny how things stick in your mind. I can see right now those hotel rockers swingin' back an' forth with nothin' in 'em but air.

"Wimmin were screechin' an' yellin', doors were bangin' shut an' windows crashin' down an'—it's takin' a lot longer to tell— in two shakes of a lamb's tail the village looked empty as the one some man wrote a poem about.

"Crowd in the Post Office was millin', not knowin' what to do. I stayed on the steps. I guess I was scared, but I couldn't take my eyes off Mr. Thomas." He stopped short, and when he began again the words came more slowly.

"Funny thing. My dad used to say Mr. Thomas knew so much about horses, he might's well *be* one . . . And yet, well, Main Street was lined with rigs, horses tied to the posts. First thing I thought of—and my dad said he did too—was panic. Jee-*sus* . . . Excuse me."

I think I banged my fist on the table. "Go on," I ordered. "What about the horses?"

"Well, they were nervous-like. Tossin' their heads. Shiftin'.

Ears pricked. Mebbe pawin' a little. But nothin' like when the circus comes to town . . ."

"Oh!" Sally exclaimed. "Talk about the horses later. Tell about Cousin Tom and Ahab." She cut herself another piece of cake. "You tell it better than Uncle Nick or Dad. But they weren't there."

The farmer laughed and tipped his chair back again. "We-ell, I watched Mr. Thomas get outa the sulky, hitch the bull to the post, run a hand down his nose like you do to a horse, and come up the Post Office steps. He said hello to me, and my dad saw him come in, calm as a summer day, look around, say, 'Afternoon' to the crowd, get his mail, riffle through it like you do, tip his hat to a coupla wimmin starin' at him like rabbits in front of a snake, say, 'Afternoon' again an' walk out real easy. Anybody else," he added parenthetically, "mighta been lynched right then an' there." He drew a deep breath. "I hadn't budged, couldn've if you'd paid me a hundred dollars. He gave me that little quiet grin under his mustache like he's enjoyin' a joke he might tell you some day, 'less somethin' funnier comes up . . ." He glanced at me. "Still do that?"

I couldn't speak. For the first time, I was homesick.

"We-ell," he started again, "Mr. Thomas goes down the steps, unhitches the bull, climbs into the sulky, says, 'Giddap, boy,' whirls the bull around in a space mighta held a silver dollar an' . . . an' off they went up the road." He leaned forward and poured himself a glass of milk. "That's it," he said. "That's what I saw. Takes a long time to *tell* things, don't it?"

We could hear the wall clock tick away a few seconds. Then Sally sighed. "Now you can talk about the horses," she said. The farmer looked at me.

I shrugged. "He says wild animals, even in a circus, smell different. And after Ahab was broken to harness, he drove him around among the horses on the Farm. So I guess he was pretty sure." I hesitated, wondering if it would be disloyal to go on. "But he did say once, 'It was a fool thing to do and I was old enough to know better.'"

The farmer nodded. "Sounds like him. But *why?* You must know why he thought of breakin' that bull."

"He said he just wanted to see if it could be done. Ahab was brighter than most bulls, and gentle. There was a fire, you've heard about that. About the only thing left was this almost newborn calf and Granddad bought him. My grandmother says Ahab thought Granddad was his mother, he fussed over him so."

"Yeah, I know. But that's how, t'ain't why. Tell you what my dad thought. He and Mr. Thomas used to talk a lot, and *he* thought Mr. Thomas did it to show some o' these geezers dumb critters ain't so dumb if they're handled right. He's so gentle-spoken, Mr. Thomas is, folks think butter wouldn't melt in his mouth, but my dad saw him grab a stablehand—twice as heavy as he was—by the shoulder, swing him around, and knock him flat. Know why? The damn fool had kicked a cow in the udder. Seems she'd knocked over a full pail the way they will sometimes. Makes you mad, but you don't kick her. Anyway, not where Mr. Thomas might see you."

The kitchen clock struck six. Sally and I got up and the farmer walked us down the lane. We woke up Susan, and we said good-by and thank you for the cake and the story. He looked at me anxiously.

"You'll tell him, sure? We still miss him around here. I think about him and my dad . . . they were real good friends . . ."

We were very late for dinner.

Without Sally, I would have made some bad mistakes that first summer. There was a plethora of relatives in the area, and I had to meet them all and keep them as straight in my mind as I could. Following Sally's lead, I liked almost all of them. Like or dislike, our youthful judgments were positive and, undoubtedly, often wrong. Cousin Lottie, for instance, fooled me for a while; I thought she was "interesting." She was, but not quite in the way I meant it. When she saw which way the wind was blowing, Sally, with a wisdom beyond her years, sat back and waited.

Lottie, with her mother, Henrietta, lived almost in the back yard. Their compact little house perched on the hill a few hundred yards away. This was close quarters, in those days. Cousin Lottie, then I suppose in her late forties, was a very tall woman, very large in every way. She had the whitest, softest skin I ever saw, and she never wore anything but white. With her pale blue eyes, white hair, bulk, thick white skin and pale lips, the effect was a weird combination of the celestial and the gross. I soon learned that the younger generation abhorred her. No one under twenty could do anything right (she had taught grade school for years), but neither could anyone escape her wet, flabby kisses and the clutch of her strong arms. She had read widely and talked well about books I had not yet read but wanted to, but when I caught her viciously berating her gentle, weak-minded mother, I ran from the house, sick with a protected child's horror at wanton cruelty.

We met on the road a day or two later, and she smothered me in kisses. Unable to breathe for the odors of lavender sachet and flesh, I broke away by main force and ran home where I pounded up the stairs to my room, poured cold water into the washstand basin, and scrubbed her touch away.

But Lottie in the flesh was not so easily disposed of as the sensation of hot wet lips. Between the Old House and Cousin Henrietta's there was an almost constant running in and out. Everyone was fond of Cousin Henrietta and sorry for her. She, too, was a tall, large woman, but her cowlike eyes held nothing but resignation and affection. Sally's mother was forever "just running up" with some treat for Cousin Henrietta, or to take her a new magazine or a detective story from the library. She was an avid reader of this genre and there was ferocious speculation among the younger generation about her plans to make use of the lethal methods described, as well as unanimous agreement that we would assist in any way we could.

Lottie, in turn, came down the hill bringing flowers from her fabulous garden, or to ask Cousin Nick for advice about some ailing plant, or "just to borrow a teeny bit of butter" or a cup of heavy cream. It was therefore no surprise when Sally and I came home after a swim in Long Pond to find Cousin Lottie ensconced in the most comfortable chair on the cool front porch. Greed for iced tea and cupcakes lured us up the steps.

The moment we caught the gist of the conversation we nearly fled, but rules of polite behavior were strictly observed in that household so we settled down on the top step with iced tea and as many cakes as we could get away with.

Lottie was holding forth on the subject of the graveyard. ". . . actually *hear* the children shouting." She glanced over at us. "They seemed to be playing a game of tag—right among the graves."

Cousin Nick murmured that he had played there and so, he believed, had his father. "Before that," he continued thoughtfully, "I don't know. Maybe there weren't enough stones to make it interesting."

Cousin Lottie seethed visibly and Sally's mother hastily remarked that really the children shouldn't make so much noise that it disturbed poor Cousin Henrietta.

"That's not the point," Lottie said. "It's disgraceful for a sacred place to be used as a playground for children."

I don't know how long Cousin Lottie had been there, but long enough for Cousin Nick to become thoroughly exasperated.

"Sacred?" he repeated. "A majority of our friends and neighbors wouldn't agree. That ground has never been hallowed by bell, book, or candle, thee knows."

"Thee's quibbling. Thee knows perfectly well what I mean."

"Oh, I suppose so," he admitted. "I'll tell the children not to be so loud. Still, I don't quite see why thee's fretting so. Thee's not there, yet."

"That isn't funny," Lottie said furiously. She set her empty iced-tea glass on the floor and rose to her feet, an irate colossus. "And I will promise thee that when my poor, dear mother is laid to rest, *measures will be taken.*"

Cousin Nick stood up slowly. He was as tall as she. He said in a gently inquiring voice, "What does thee think Henrietta will do?"

We all watched in silence as she turned off on the short cut to the road.

"Poor Lottie," Sally's mother sighed. "She hasn't a grain of humor."

"She's a beast," Sally said, without emphasis. "May we get some soda pop out of the Springhouse, Mom?"

Of all the new joys I discovered that summer, the Springhouse came near the top of the list. The spring that flowed through it had not failed more than twice in almost two centuries. Through open louvers under the deep eaves rays of sunlight fell on the water and were reflected against the whitewashed walls. It had a smell you could taste—a little sweet, a little pungent, with a hint of something almost sour that came and went. It was the summer refrigerator, primitive and efficient. Then there was a communal, or family, icehouse, filled every winter with ice from the ponds. The simple requirements for all the ice any of the family needed were a strong back, a wheelbarrow, and a couple of pieces of sacking.

Carrying our soda pop—a new-fangled delicacy we thought delicious—Sally and I by common consent headed for the graveyard. From the lane that led eventually to the barns, we turned sharply to the left and up another rise, then hard right to the opening in the stone wall where iron gates hung hospitably open, sagging on their ancient hinges. The shade of the towering locust and chestnut trees fell on us like a benediction. Only an occasional hot-weather cheep from a bird or a fluttering of wings and our own voices broke the gentle silence. The many flowering bushes and the gay flowers planted casually along the stone wall did not go untended, nor did the uneven ground covered with Virgina creeper. Cousin Nick took care of that, but they were left unmanicured, comfortably homelike. (However, heaven help the child who left bottle caps or paper lying around, for Cousin Nick would not.)

Some of the older stones were tilted at various angles, but the effect was not of slovenliness but of a sort of happy abandon. Most of the stones were simple straight-sided slabs inscribed only with name and dates. And yet, almost in the center of this Quakerish austerity rose two tall shafts, each topped with a carved Union soldier's cap. They were not really very tall—from the square bases to the top they were the height of two tallish men: the Ketchum boys. One was killed at Gettysburg, one dead of fever in Libby prison.

If any objection had been raised against these memorials, the fact was lost in kindly reticence. On every Decoration Day, until her death, Great Aunt Martha Ketchum, their mother, had come from her home on the other side of the village, in her buggy drawn by veterans from the vicinity, followed by marching men and a band, up the hills to the Quaker graveyard. While her strength lasted, Aunt Martha alighted, planted an American flag next to the base of each shaft, and stood while neighbors and family placed their flowers, the band played "The Battle Hymn of the Republic" and an aspiring politician spoke not too many choice words. After a few silent moments someone blew "Taps," the old lady was helped into her buggy where she sat bolt upright, and the whole procession returned to the village for the customary celebrations of the day.

Soda pop, perhaps because we still weren't used to it, acted as a soporific, and Cousin Nick, taking the back path to the Big House, found us both asleep under the big chestnut and scolded us roundly. "I'd a lot rather have you yelling and *ramping* around," he said. "Ground's damp under the trees."

He asked if we wanted to go with him. Sally said she'd better help Mom with dinner, but after a moment's hesitation, I said yes. The Big House had been my grandfather's birthplace and home and I had been there only once during the summer. It was no longer the place he had loved.

"Well," said Cousin Nick reasonably, "thee could hardly expect anything else." With a rare gesture of affection, he put his hand on my shoulder and squeezed. "Don't be a sentimentalist. Thee'll give thyself a lot of unnecessary wounds."

The ancient path between the houses was overgrown but passable, and the view at its end over wide lawns to the simple, dignified house was charming. But the gardens were gone, the grass was ragged, there was a clothesline handy to the back door, the trees needed pruning. The place was too much for the farm family who lived there. I had been taken through the house against my will, because the people were so pleasant, so excited, so insistent, but I had not gone again.

On the way back, I said, "Is Granddad a sentimentalist?"

He laughed a little. "Got under thy skin, did it? Well, yes.

And no. He wouldn't have lost the Farm if the whole answer were no. He didn't *have* to keep up his father's crazy pattern of giving away property to his old retainers. Le Grand Seigneur . . ." He was silent for a moment. "As a matter of fact," he went on, "I don't know if I'd be so fond of him if he weren't such a cussed mixture. I'm a bit older than he is, as thee knows, and I used to think he should have been a doctor. He never let his sentimentalism get the better of his good sense when it came to taking care of his people and his stock." He chuckled. "Farm stock, I mean. When it comes to finance, he's always been a babe in arms."

I told him about the trolley rides when I had blood poisoning. He hadn't heard much about that, and he was interested. "That's it," he said. "He knew what thee needed and he saw that thee got it. In many ways, he's a great man. People around here still hold him up as an example, talk about him a lot even now. He had influence, and as far as I know, he never used it for anything but good. Or what he believed was good."

We had reached the graveyard gate, and he looked in. "Only thing about all the rampin' around, couple of those stones might be knocked over and someone might get a broken leg or arm. Oh, well."

I said, "Cousin Nick, one of the stones, I've forgotten whose, says, 'Dust thou art, to dust returneth.' Does thee believe that?"

He shook his mane of white hair—which badly needed cutting, as usual. "Same answer. Yes and no. Sure," he slapped his thigh, "this carcass goes to dust, eventually. And a good thing, too. Leaves room for you youngsters. But there's something—not only in thee and me and Lottie, but in everything that lives—that *isn't* dust. Although," he added parenthetically, "there's nothing wrong with dust. Necessary part of the universe. But there's something. I wish I knew what it is. I wish

I knew what happens to it when the heart stops beating, the blood doesn't circulate, the brain stops working." He leaned down for a piece of grass to chew, and slapped a hand on the stone wall. "Thing is, there are as many answers as there are religions, and that's a lot of answers. I've read a good many, as thee will, and maybe only the East Indians come closest to satisfying me. But not close enough."

He turned to go down the hill. "Dust isn't entirely lost. Does thee know that? Transmuted, maybe, changed, gone beyond our vision, but not lost. Not *gone*." He put his arm around my shoulders and gave me a hug. "There's Sally," he said. "We're late."

Sally was standing on the back porch. She made a megaphone of her hands. "Uncle Nick! Tazie! Dinner's on the table. Hurry up."

❁ THREE ❁

During the summer, long weekly letters from my grandmother had kept me up to date on what she called the "Progress of the Imp o' Darkness" and—from what I could decipher, often with Sally's help—Impo seemed to have been well named. Letters from my grandfather were shorter but more legible. I was warned that I would find a cat no longer in the kitten class. Nothing was said that led me to believe he would remember me, and I girded myself to accept the probability that he would not.

It was a waste of energy. It was I who hardly recognized him. There are few things in life more heart-warming than to be welcomed by a cat. I didn't expect it then, and I have never quite learned to take it for granted. Demonstrations of affection come easily to the canine, but the feline nature is different, more reserved, more sensitive to its own dignity, more egotistical. Stress is laid on the hardship he has suffered by your absence. (Of course, you have turned yourself and half your dearest friends into nervous wrecks in the effort to keep his life as normal as possible. He then insults the Angel of Mercy by turning his back after eating and settling down for a long winter's nap. "He" is used loosely; any of them will do it.) I had had no experience with that parenthetical comment when I came home that autumn, but I expected the worst.

Impo went all out to show me that his world was now complete because I had returned to it. There were no hard feelings. He followed me from room to room, he purred, he sat in my lap—it was like holding a young panther—he came to bed with me in the usual place, at my feet. The first night I rather missed my lumpy country bed and the whispered talks Sally and I had when we were supposed to be asleep, but Impo suddenly got up, walked the length of the bed, kissed me, purred in my ear, and went back to his own place. The timing was perfect, even if accidental.

What my grandmother hadn't attempted to convey in her letters was his physical development. He had been handsome enough since he left off being a runt; now the only word for him was "magnificent." His coal-black coat shone like highly polished leather. He carried his long, luxuriant tail like a banner or swished it like a dueler's sword, twitched the very tip in moments of concentration, and waved it like a flag in a high wind when he was excited. When you learned the language, his tail was a fairly accurate index to the momentary contents of his active mind.

He was as clever as a monkey at opening doors, pails, boxes. If interrupted, he would walk away, only to return when interference had subsided. He had very little discrimination about "mine" and "thine." My father had brought back from Cuba a pair of fine, soft, handmade gloves which he liked very much. So did Impo. He absconded with one, but when my father surrendered and tossed him the other, he merely sniffed at it contemptuously.

Someone sent my mother a delightful little pillow from Belgium with a fine lace slip over a pink-covered cushion rather strongly scented with expensive perfume. Impo apparently decided the smell was deadly poison. He would sit for long minutes silently regarding the pretty object with baleful green eyes. Everybody, except my grandfather, thought this was amusing and my mother teased him by rubbing the pillow under his nose and then snatching it away. He made no attempt to grab it with his claws. He simply pulled his head back and continued to look.

"I wouldn't do that," my grandfather said, "if thee wants to keep the thing."

One morning she came into the living room to find lace, pink cover, and cushion in ribbons and shreds on the floor. Impo was crouched beside the wreckage. Enraged, she chased him around the room, shrieking imprecations and half crying, until Mr. Thomas, standing in the doorway, said quietly, "Better save thy breath to cool thy porridge, daughter."

Cats, in general, are dramatic animals, but I have never known another who dramatized the ordinary acts of everyday living with such gusto. If he wanted to go out, he would stand at a door—preferably one as far from any of us as possible—and scream. "Hurry! Hurry! If there's an accident, it won't be *my* fault!" Sometimes he chose to be suspicious of his food, looking over his shoulder and hunching himself, nibbling thoughtfully: "Poison? Stuff been around too long?" Another nibble. "Doesn't taste quite right. Tricking me into something new, are they?" Then getting down to it: "Oh, well, a fellow can't live forever."

He worshipped my grandmother and whenever she sewed, he would sit in front of her, watching every motion of her hands, and purring. While I was in the country, Impo had taken to sitting on my grandfather's lap, and when I came back with every intention of reverting to this lifelong habit, Impo was annoyed. He flounced, he glowered—or, if that was the way I wanted it, why couldn't we *both* be there? We compromised: when I was away, he sat there, when I was home, I did.

All young cats, and many older ones, play special games of their own. Impo ran the gamut of emotions while chasing, losing, finding, tossing, a small rubber ball or a piece of crumpled paper. When someone brought him a catnip mouse, his excited activity was so excessive my grandmother wearily suggested that we all move out and leave the place to Impo until the catnip smell faded.

The instinctive urge to dramatize, to play up to a situation, was not lacking in any of us except my grandfather (and even he had broken Ahab to harness and shown him off in public). Impo was in his natural environment. The one whose need for drama surfaced most frequently was my mother, who had first rejected him.

Any intelligent cat will show shades of difference in its treatment of the individuals it lives with, and Impo made the distinctions particularly plain. He understood that he and I belonged together. He wasn't unhappy without me, but with me he was content and complete. When I came home from school he was waiting. When I was hounded by commands to "go outdoors and get some exercise," he went with me. When I read he sat on my lap; my father speculated on what he was absorbing from the books that rested on his back. I've never known a cat who didn't love to sit on papers, and I did my homework under difficulties. The games we played sometimes turned rough, and as he had the more efficient weapons I often went to school with scratches on my hands and arms and even my face.

The older teachers took my wounds calmly, but a new teacher became extremely agitated. She was young, conscientious, and this was her first real job. I had been a thorn in her flesh from the first day and my scars did nothing to soothe her. I must have looked especially bloody the day she interrupted a lesson to interrogate me. When I explained that I had merely been playing with my cat, she turned white.

"A cat!" There was such horror in her voice that the boy behind me gleefully punched me in the back.

Pulling herself together, she told me to see her after class, and ignored me. That suited me down to the ground. I was tired of saying yes, I'd read that and being met with a cold look of disbelief. I wonder why she didn't speak to one of the other teachers about my "lies," for any of them could have set her straight. I suppose she was afraid to complain about one of her pupils, poor girl.

After class, I waited while she wrote a note to my mother, warning her of the dangers of blood poisoning . . . There were several other notes, complaining of my "falsehoods" and "showing off," until my grandmother made an excuse to have a routine interview as chairman of the Board of Trustees. Tactfully but firmly, she clarified the situation, although I can't say I ever became that teacher's pet. It was not the last time I would find it useful to be my grandmother's granddaughter.

That autumn one of Impo's brothers was hit by an automobile. He limped for several weeks and the incident stirred up more talk about ways in which the community was changing. Children were not allowed to play in the road, and there were rumors that it would soon be macadamized. Two families in the neighborhood had bought automobiles, my father was toying with temptation and my grandfather was egging him on, which surprised everyone, except his wife.

Horses, he said, did not belong on modern city streets. The hard paving damaged their hooves no matter how carefully they were shod. In icy weather they were always in danger of falling. All this was hardly new. His interest went deeper; he was strongly attracted by the new and the strange. A natural ingenuity had sparked a secret ambition to be an inventor, and some years later, he designed, built, and marketed a clever and practical window ventilator for which, characteristically, he neglected to obtain a patent.

That year it became a habit for me to dress in my best "city" clothes and have lunch on Saturdays with the two men. Feeling very grownup, I met them at the office they shared and then the day was ours. Once or twice my mother came along, but it seemed to me my parents and I did not make quite the happy threesome I had known as a small child. They had taken me to the theater when I was hardly big enough to see over the seat in front of me, and I can't remember when I first went backstage. Restaurants were fun, but nothing out of the ordinary and the cherries in the then-popular manhattans were my perquisite. The inclusion of a mere baby in all this riotous living did not go unmarked, but critics did not understand that to complete the *joie de vivre* that was an essential part of his temperament, my father needed both his "girls."

If there were indeed a small breach in our immediate family of three, nothing else in their gay life had changed. I was now a "big girl," as people kept telling me, and I tried to accept that as the explanation, as it had been the reason I went to the country instead of going to Cuba with them last summer. It was unsatisfactory and confusing, and the Saturday afternoons were balm for a hurt I could not speak of.

After lunch we went exploring. Never was a girl more fortunate in her guides to the city of her birth. They made me see below the surface and behind the facade to the builders, the owners, the winners, and losers, the entrepreneurs, the politicians. While I listened—and sometimes entered in—they talked to men laying new sewer pipes, to engineers at a building site who were in trouble with one of the hidden rivers that run through Manhattan's rock, to policemen, firemen, street cleaners . . . Sometimes my father would be reminded of a legal battle that could be made amusing for me, until my grandfather would chuckle and say, "Now, Ernest, thee knows that's an exaggeration," and he would join in the laughter rather ruefully, knowing his own reputation for making a good story better.

One cold day in November, with the streets still icy from a

storm a few days earlier, we saw an all-too familiar sight: a cart horse down on the paving, a crowd milling around helplessly. We stopped, and my father said, "Stay here with Tazie and I'll see what goes on."

He had a commanding presence when he chose, and the crowd made way for him. After a moment, my grandfather said, "Automobiles don't fall down and break their legs. Thee'd think I'd be used to this, wouldn't thee?"

My father came back and nodded. "It's broken. I've sent for a cop. Poor old bag o' bones will have to be shot. We'd better go."

"No," I said. "Please. I—just let's wait and be sure."

So we waited.

To distract me and perhaps himself, my grandfather gave me another lesson in dealing with traffic. The rules he laid down are out-dated, but one thing he said has stuck in my mind.

He said, "When there's a snarl—collision or accident, say— or even something like a child's balloon that's got loose, watch out for the horses. Horses sometimes panic, and it's bad. Takes a lot of skill and strength to handle a panicky horse, if it can be done at all. Automobiles don't panic."

No—but their drivers do. That possibility had not occurred to him.

A few blocks away there was a building my father wanted to show me. It was a business street, and it didn't need an expert eye to see that business had once been good but was now poor and getting poorer. We stopped in front of the tallest, widest, and most elaborately decorated edifice.

"It looks," my father said, with a flourish of his cane, "as if it had been through a war. And it has—the War of the Wills." A man stopped to stare. My father smiled charmingly at him, tipped his hat, and the man looked shocked and scuttled away. "There were a brother and a sister," he continued, "and a mother and a father. Both wealthy. A great deal of money and even more real property. They were killed in a railroad accident. Their wills were contradictory. Apparently neither one had consulted the other and yet, over a long life together, their separate properties had become inextricably entangled." He looked at my grandfather. "Does thee think I can make this clear?"

My grandfather chuckled. "It's never been done yet. Tazie will understand it as well as anybody, I suppose."

At first, the considerable number of lawyers called in regarded the case as a bonanza. It soon turned into a nightmare. Every twist and circumlocution the best legal minds could think up were worked threadbare.

"And yet," my father went on in his casually crisp voice, "if the two principal beneficiaries could have come to terms, some sort of fair solution could have been found. They wouldn't even speak to each other except through a phalanx of opposing lawyers, until, somehow, they were persuaded to have a meeting in this building that was the most valuable single prize in the package.

"Well, they met, if you could call it that. When they came out, all the pent-up fury and hatred they'd kept more or less under control, exploded out here, where we're standing."

Aunt Josephine and Uncle Archibald stood on the sidewalk, shaking their fists, dragging out all the dirty family linen—even their old childish quarrels (they were twins)—while their legal advisers, "including me," my father said with a grin, danced around trying to separate them, only to be brushed off like flies.

And, cowering against the building, weeping with fright and shame, were their children, all middle-aged, all helpless. The press had got wind of the meeting, and reporters and photographers formed a nucleus for a growing crowd of onlookers.

"A colleague and I finally rounded up a couple of hansom cabs and by main force got those two lunatics inside and told the cabbies not to spare the horses. That was when thee was a baby," he said. "I was just a fledgling lawyer."

His elderly superior had turned over the bunch of crackpots to him, hoping he might get one, if not both, to make some sense.

"Did thee?" I asked.

"I did not." He looked up at the building. "They might have been comfortable unto the third and fourth generation. Instead of which . . ." He shrugged. "What made me think of it," he went on, "two days ago I was present at the reconciliation scene. They wanted me to be there, for some reason, to see them kiss and make up. After all these years, and all the misery they brought on themselves and their children. It was very touching," he said, with a sardonic lift of his eyebrow, "but the timing was wrong. It was too late for a happy ending."

He pulled out his watch, and whistled. "I'll be late meeting my other girl." He took off his hat and leaned down to kiss me. "Thanks for listening, sweetheart. Next week, again? I hope so."

He tipped his hat to my grandfather, smiled at us both, and strode away, twirling his silver-headed cane.

I called after him, "If Mama expects thee to be on time, no one will be more surprised than thee."

He paused to look over his shoulder, scowled ferociously and, as he turned the corner, looked back to laugh and shake his cane at me.

My grandfather said, "Would thee like to do something else?" He sounded tired.

I said, "No. It's cold. Let's go home."

Five days before Christmas, my father came down with pneumonia. Three days later he died.

On December 26th, my mother, my grandparents, Uncle Charles and Aunt Cara Snedeker, and I crossed the Hudson to Hoboken. The Snedekers were not relatives but I could not imagine life without them. Uncle Charles was an Episcopal minister. He would not have considered it sacrilegious for me to say that he worshiped my grandmother. When he was young, lost in a maze of misunderstood emotions, intellectual confusions, and shaken faith, she gave him the thread that led him out to the light. *His* light. And because it was more important not to hurt Charles than to be married in Meeting, he officiated at my parents' marriage. It was right and natural for Uncle Charles to read the Episcopal burial service at my father's grave.

At Hoboken we piled into an overheated West Shore train and crawled through the winter countryside, with the Hudson on our right filled with ice floes jockeying for position on their race for the open harbor. Beyond the ice floes, the River was frozen from shore to shore.

At the station, a biscuit throw from the *Mary*'s dock, we were met by the local undertaker—and a limousine. He was in a flutter.

"I can't help it, Mr. Thomas," he whispered. "People round here *like* it."

My grandfather patted his shoulder and smiled. We waited in the limousine while Uncle Charles went forward to supervise unloading the coffin, then we were driven directly to the graveyard, or nearly so for the limousine couldn't make the turn from the lane, so we walked. A path had been cleared through the snow.

There was a smell from the north that my grandfather said meant more snow coming. In the graveyard, the snow was patchy, with brown earth showing through. The locust trees lifted bare arms to a gray sky. Uncle Charles had got into his surplice and stood at the head of the new grave while the undertaker's men pulled the long coffin by hand up the hill and through the open gate.

I saw Sally and her family and Cousin Nick's white hair blowing in the light wind. There was a dim impression of a great many people, standing silently. Who were they? It was very cold.

As the coffin dropped into the grave, my mother moved a step forward. Someone—Aunt Cara?—had talked her into wearing a heavy widow's veil, but as Uncle Charles's voice broke the silence, she lifted her right hand to sweep it back from her face and stood there tearless, proud, and straight as a queen.

When it was over, Cousin Nick walked us down to the Old House, where there was hot food, coffee, tea, cider. I kissed Sally and we took the train home.

1907. Someone said in my hearing that my father died because he was "worried about finances." I didn't believe it then, and I don't now. He had caught a cold—the worst ailment he ever suffered—and as usual it shamed and embarrassed him, and as usual, he ignored it. His losses in the Panic were, as my grandfather expressed it, no more troublesome than a mosquito bite, to be forgotten when it stops itching. It was the loss of his professional earnings that cut deep.

Dimly, I realized that "things" were not very satisfactory. But for me, only one thing had changed. I withdrew into myself like a turtle pulling in its neck, presenting an unyielding shell to family, friends, teachers. I made excuses—a cold, a headache, a stomach ache, an earache—to stay home from school and spent the hours alone in my room. My grandmother, with a despairing wave of her hands, said that I was "ungettable." My mother, drowning in the deep waters of her own agony, said pathetically, "Wouldn't it help to share it, dear?" My grandfather said nothing.

Impo stayed with me constantly, and I could endure him because he made no demands. All his activity was stilled. Even in my lethargy and indifference to anything but myself, I noticed his immobility. I'm not sure how long this state of affairs lasted, three weeks perhaps—a long time in the life of a young cat. When I took the trouble to look at him, I noticed vaguely that his coat wasn't as sleek as usual, his eyes looked strange, he wasn't washing. But I crawled back under my shell in a hurry, it was better not to see anything. Unhappiness makes an animal—any animal—vulnerable to illness. Impo was unhappy. I was hiding from him and it wasn't a game. He had lost me. He was lost.

One afternoon, my grandfather came into my room. I had been reading and crying alternately. He pulled up a chair but did not touch me.

"Would it help," he said, "to have Impo die, too?"

My eyes flew open. I sat up and stared at Impo, lying at my feet. His eyes were blurry; it wasn't because I had seen them through my own blurred eyes. I reached down to stroke him. Yes, he did feel hot, it wasn't imagination. He turned his head as if it were an effort and licked my hand. When had I last bothered to touch him?

Then Mr. Thomas took over. He read me the riot act in a level unexcited voice. He said things I needed to hear but would have listened to from no one else. Finally, he said he blamed himself for allowing Impo's condition to grow worse.

"Thee's been incommunicado, and Impo with thee. I've had

things on my mind. Now I'll see what can be done for Impo. I hope it's not too late." He stood up and looked down at me, almost coldly. "Thee is sick, too. But it's a sickness only thee can cure. I'll take care of Impo."

He picked up the big cat carefully and carried him downstairs.

The resilience of the young animal is nothing short of miraculous. Before the first snowdrops broke through the winter ground, both Impo and I were normal.

As soon as school closed, I went to the Snedekers' island in Penobscot Bay. The journey was complicated and long and I fell off the train into Uncle Charles's arms more dead than alive. He swept me off to a dock—he called it "wharf"—where several men as big as he lounged against bollards, smoking pipes, chewing tobacco, and spitting. Only waves against the pilings broke the misty stillness. A long way off, something mysteriously breathed in and out, in and out.

One of the men stepped forward. "Reverend," he said, "you ain't figgerin' on rowin' this—this young leddy out to the island tonight, be y'?"

"Why, yes, Jeff, I am." Uncle Charles dumped my luggage on the wharf. "Perhaps one of you men will help me stow this in the boat."

Behind a fog of tobacco smoke, another voice spoke up. "Storm comin'."

"We'll be there before it breaks."

"Better," said another voice, "ef y' want t' git thar a-tall."

The Rector of St. George's gave what we called his "clerical laugh," and said heartily, "The sooner we get started, the better. I'll agree to that."

"Where you goin' to stow *her?*"

"In the bow. The bags are pretty heavy—books, hey, Tazie?—and will ride best in the stern." He patted my shoulder. "She can act as pilot."

As Uncle Charles pushed away from the wharf, an arm reached out and dropped something yellow, rubbery, and smelly beside me. "Don't be skeered, Miss. The Rev.'s a good strong rower."

Bending to the oars, Uncle Charles shouted back, "Thanks. Put it on, Tazie. It will be wet outside the harbor."

Accustomed to the Hudson and Long Pond, I was considerably surprised by the size of the waves that rose before my eyes—and into them. Luckily, I knew the difference between port and starboard and was able, by a concentration of which I hadn't known I was capable, to give Uncle Charles the information he demanded. "Watch for a low spit of land to port . . . clump of pines by a beach . . . a cliff with a dead pine." There seemed to be no signals of human life to go by.

Time and distance had lost all meaning, when he shouted, "Well, here we are, safe and sound!"

We were in calm water. The boat grounded on gravel. It was pitch black. There was a whirl of something lighter than the darkness coming straight at me. A dog, barking. The bow and I seemed to be half a mile in the air. The dog kept trying to jump in. Uncle Charles shifted his weight, stepped out, the bow thudded down and I could see two eyes, two ears, and feel the dog's breath on my face. A wet tongue licked my wet cheek.

"For heaven's sake, Father," came a familiar voice out of the dark, "you must be crazy. We thought of course you'd stay at the hotel."

"Nothing to it," Uncle Charles said nonchalantly. "Bit rough. Tazie was a help."

The eldest Snedeker son swooped me out of the bow seat

into his arms. "Little Crazy Tazie." He grunted. "Not so little any more. That's Macgregor. Want me to carry you? I can try." He put me on my feet, holding me as I staggered on stiff, half-frozen, entirely wet legs.

I said, "Don't be silly, Karlchen, I can walk."

I wasn't as sure as I hoped I sounded, but pride kept me moving and with Macgregor on one side and Karl on the other I climbed up some steps to level ground, and Aunt Cara's arms, then the warmth and light of The Shack, and a plate of hot stew over which I fell asleep. And later Karl boasted that he had carried me all the way to the tent and I weighed at least five hundred pounds by the time he got me there.

The sounds of excited barks and an obbligato of baa-baas woke me. I got the tent flap open and saw Macgregor chasing a flock of flustered sheep. The sun shone, the water sparkled, a green hill rose gently against blue sky, and the air smelled of sunshine and salt and a faint whiff of fish.

Aunt Cara came out of the biggest tent. "Macgregor, bad dog. Tazie needs her sleep . . . oh, dear, he *did* wake you up! He can't leave those wretched sheep alone." She laughed and waved. "Breakfast in half an hour . . ." and the flap closed behind her.

I invited Macgregor to come in while I unpacked and dressed, and we discussed the behavior of sheep and that his people really didn't understand how important it was to keep them away from the tent area, and I said I had never been so hungry in my life and at the word he barked that he was too, and please hurry. As we left the tent, Karl came out of his.

"He's not allowed in the tents," he told me severely.

"I invited him."

"Oh, well." He shrugged. "I knew this sort of thing would happen."

Walking towards The Shack, I asked where Philip was and heard that the younger son was using his last vacation before entering Harvard to see something of the world, only he couldn't afford to get any farther than our own Southwest. That seemed like a good place to start, and I added that I honestly would try not to spoil Macgregor . . .

"But you will," Karl said gloomily, and tucked my hand in his.

Beach Island was a magic place. The Shack was living room, dining room, kitchen, and library, with a small ell curtained off for a wash room. Somehow the boys had never got around to putting down floors for any tent except the big one, which served also as Aunt Cara's writing room. This made life interesting in wet weather.

"I hope you'll get enough to eat," Karl said. "Mother's withbook, you know, and most of the time she's in the hills of Sparta."

We were at the door of The Shack, which smelled of pancakes and sausages, and Aunt Cara said, "That's a base canard, and if you don't mend your manners, I'll show Tazie over the Island myself."

"Oh, we needn't bother," Karl said airily, "Macgregor will take care of all that."

It was almost true. Except for the sheep, and the Snedekers and me, there was nothing that didn't belong there naturally. It was bigger than it looks on a map. There was the hill I could see from my tent, a spooky swamp, a pine forest (small, as Karl said, but select) with a fairy ring in its center, fields, and, of course, beaches—big and small, open and hidden, sandy or stony (the latter predominated). There were cliffs with mysterious caves with no visible entrances where the tides rushed in and sang to themselves, and on the east, running almost the whole length of the Island, a windswept beach where you could stand and look out at three thousand uninterrupted miles of Atlantic Ocean.

The ice water of Penobscot Bay masquerades as something to swim in. The "diving rock" was at one end of the west beach which was the practical, protected one, and Karl tormented himself trying to make me dive. I told him Cousin Nicholas had tried all last summer and if *he* got nowhere I thought Karl might as well give up.

"But it's so silly," Karl said. "You're not afraid, you'll jump, why don't you act like a normal human being once in a while?"

"Or a seal," I suggested. "Macgregor jumps too. Why don't you try to train him?"

"Maybe he would dive if you did," Karl growled. "You've cut me out, you've alienated his affections . . ." and he pushed me off the rock.

Macgregor immediately followed me. I got my hands into his wet fur and let him pull me a few feet, but only hard exercise could prevent a human being with no fur from turning into a cake of ice, and I climbed out on the sun-warmed rock, shivering. Macgregor loved the water, but he was my self-appointed protector—and goodness knows what sort of trouble I'd get into without him, so he came up on the rock and shook icicles all over us.

The collie was forbidden the rowboat, though I never could understand why. I loved rowing, but Macgregor's expression of distress as I shoved the heavy boat into the water and climbed in by myself nearly spoiled the fun. He would follow me along the shore, slipping and skidding on the stones, circumventing jutting rocks and cliffs, but never trying to swim out. If I landed on some forgotten beach, he met me, his tail wagging his whole body.

For compensation, he had the run of the catboat. The Ark was a sturdy, stolid, capacious affair, with a sail too big for her size. Even the natives admitted and admired the Reverend's prowess as an oarsman, but as master of a sailing vessel Karl had no rival in his family. Uncle Charles could no more grasp the simplest rules of sailing than I could force myself to dive. Karl claimed Macgregor knew more about sailing than his father did, and it would be hard to find anyone more nervous and distraught than the Reverend Snedeker if Karl asked him to take the tiller for a minute or two.

Except in bad weather, the Ark was used to pick up fresh vegetables, milk, and butter from the farmer's wife on Hog Island, a mile or so away. In fog or storm we went without. During a long foggy spell, we had run pretty low on supplies and Aunt Cara was worrying about proper nutriment, when she remembered that there was still a sufficient backlog of dried fruits in the dilapidated old building called The Store House. She sent me down to find the fruit and some other items that might be useful in the emergency. I opened the door which sagged drearily on its hinges, and stepped inside, waiting for a second or two for my eyes to adjust to the dark. There was a whrrr, and rush of sound and an owl flew at my face. I think I screamed, though Aunt Cara said she didn't hear it, and ran out into the benign, unterrifying fog.

I knew perfectly well there were barn owls in The Store House. There was no excuse for panic, but I can still shiver at the memory of those wings beating at my face. It was thoroughly shameful to be afraid, and I don't even know that it was fear I felt. But whatever it was, that owl put me off birds for ever, and I have never forgiven it—or myself. By the time I reached The Shack I had stopped shaking, and when Karl went down to get the fruit I went with him, feeling cowardly but safe. He didn't laugh at me, for which I loved him more than ever.

CATS AND OTHER PEOPLE

The Ark wasn't really needed for the short Hog Island trip, but came into her own when we went to Little Deer. I had been right in thinking that there was little or no human life on the islands between Beach Island and the mainland, but Little Deer and Deer Isle were, even then, hotbeds of population and civilization. Fishermen and farmers—usually rolled into one—lived an ideal life. They were cautious by nature, but friendly, and when you were *In*, there was no doubt about it.

Little Deer was our Post Office and the source of paper, ink, pencils, notebooks, magazines, and newspapers. There was one family the Snedekers were especially friendly with, who had a boy my age, and a team of white oxen who were in their way as perfect as Ahab the second. The boy was proud of them and I think I still have a faded photograph of him standing at their gentle, noble heads, with a look of shy proprietorship.

One day he showed us the farm's latest acquisition—a brand new litter of kittens. They were, I think, under the back porch, very snug. The mother was inclined to be nervous, and when Macgregor stuck his inquisitive nose between us, she was up and spitting, hair on end, yellow eyes blazing. It was not the sort of treatment Macgregor expected. Tentatively, he tried to smooth matters over by a friendly "woof." That did it.

An incandescent ball of maternal protectiveness, the cat jumped for him. He drew back but she got to the end of his nose. He gave a yelp of surprise, and ran. Perhaps equally surprised, the cat hung on. Blinded by the four-legged fury in front of his eyes, Macgregor went around and around the house, faster and faster with each lap, at a speed that would not have shamed a Grand Prix racer. And the faster Macgregor ran, the tighter the cat hung on.

Nothing stopped him. We stood in his way, we yelled, we

flapped our hands, people came running and *they* tried to get in his way. He simply swerved and went on. And on.

I remember shouting, "His eyes! His *eyes!*" and Karl shouting, "She's on the tip—of—his—nose. I think—it's all—right," and then taking off in vain pursuit. It felt as if the marathon went on for hours. I suppose it was at most two or three minutes. Long enough to attract an audience. When the inevitable happened and the cat lost her grip, Macgregor, unable to believe the demon had vanished, kept on running.

I am pretty sure I saw one man roll on the ground holding his head in his hands. When Macgregor skidded to a stop, I took his lovely, battered head in my arms, choking back laughter. His expression reminded me of Ed Wynn.

Mrs. Snow wiped her eyes and gasped, "Guess I'll have to bottle-feed those babies till the mother's milk comes back," and then administered first aid to Macgregor's scratched nose.

He was very subdued even after we boarded the Ark. What had happened? What had he done wrong? He stayed in the cockpit instead of stretching himself on the bow deck. He kept his head in my lap, now and then sighing deeply.

But the incident left a nagging doubt in my mind. Macgregor was coming to Richmond Hill with me to stay until the boys came home at the end of the college year. I took my problem to Aunt Cara.

She looked a little worried. "I don't know anything about cats. Ask Karl."

"Neither does he," I retorted, but I took her advice.

Karl said, "Won't it depend on Impo? It was the kittens that made the mother fly at Macgregor. I believe it's unlikely that Impo will produce kittens?"

I giggled. "Well, I thought Bagheera was a male. But," I added hastily, "I was much younger then."

"Of course. *Much*," Karl agreed solemnly, and I pulled his curly yellow hair until he hollered for mercy.

It is a common complaint of people who love Maine that its summers end too soon. By the middle of August we were beginning to "close up." Considering the simple life we lived, this seemed extraordinarily complicated. Between Uncle Charles's assumption that his opinions were as the laws of the Medes and Persians, Aunt Cara's absent-mindedness, my incompetence, and Macgregor's ubiquity, the brunt fell on Karl.

We were in a foggy spell, but the Hog Island farmer rowed across to say he'd come for the sheep the first good day, it wasn't no use lookin' for sheep in a mess o' pea soup. When the wind shifted one evening we knew the next day would be fair and Karl said it wouldn't be no use doin' chores in a mess o' lamb stew.

Uncle Charles said, "I just thought. This will be Macgregor's first sheep roundup, or whatever it's called. What do you suppose he'll say to the old sheep dog?"

"More to the point," Karl said, "what will the old sheep dog say to him?"

The farmer and two helpers arrived bright and early. After the ritual cup of coffee, gossip about weather and fishing, the hands went down to make the sheep-run "sheep-shape," Ha, ha. The farmer looked disgusted.

"Reverend," he said, "what do they say about puns?"

Uncle Charles chuckled. "The lowest form of wit."

"That's it. He does it all the time. Gets my back up."

My grandfather loved puns, especially his own, and I thought I had heard worse. The talk turned to the sheep who had had the run of the Island all summer and might be anywhere. It seemed the old dog wasn't up to it any more, and the young ones weren't to be trusted. Karl suggested that Macgregor might be useful.

The farmer eyed Macgregor doubtfully. "Purty fancy-lookin' critter," he commented. "Wa-al, we can try. If he gets 'em excited, though . . ."

That was a merry day. Karl and I tagged along, but Macgregor, told to "Go git 'em, boy," gave Karl and me one incredulous look, and then let nature and his heritage take over.

He found the sheep, pushed them into a huddle, and nipped at their heels when the bunch threatened to break up. He didn't waste breath on unnecessary barking, but the sheep, silly stubborn creatures, recognized a master's voice and—more or less—obeyed. The collie's sharp, authoritative yelp was not like anything we had heard from him before. This was his business and a long ancestry of Scottish sheep dogs told him exactly how to go about it.

It is always exciting to watch a master perform a complicated and difficult task, and Karl's tanned face glowed pink with pride. Macgregor had been born in a Long Island kennel, until this summer he had never so much as seen a sheep—and then he had been scolded for chasing them. In a voice shaking with emotion and excitement, I said solemnly, "It's Instinct, rising like a Phoenix from the ashes of civilization."

Karl burst out laughing, then hugged me tight. "Little Crazy Tazie. It *is* beautiful, isn't it?"

Was Macgregor, like the young Ahab, a "throwback"? A reincarnation of the Bob, Son of Battle the kennel people tried to claim was an ancestor? At that moment Karl and I would have swallowed any tall story. A change had come over the Hog Island men. From politely resigned condescension, to amazed disbelief, they had progressed to something like awe. As the flock scuttled down the hill to the level ground above the west beach, the farmer shouted to Karl, "Never see sech a thing in my life. Who taught him?"

"No one," Karl shouted back.

The farmer caught up with us. "Woulda taken us near pitch dark with my old Tibby, and she was pretty good when she was young." He was beaming. "Flock's in good shape, too. See the lambs? I'm sure obliged to you folks for lettin' me loan the Island for the summer." He wagged his head. "Now we'll see how he'll get 'em into the chute."

"He'll need help there," Karl said.

To keep the flock from flying off in all directions and to herd them one by one through the narrow gate to the run, took all hands, but Macgregor knew where he was needed and when. Uncle Charles and Aunt Cara came to help, and finally the last bleating sheep was down the chute and on the flat-bottomed boat. The day was over.

Karl and I took the hands cold tea and cake at the wharf and when we got back, Uncle Charles drawled, "Want to sell Macgregor, Karl? You've had an offer."

"Pay anything you ask," the farmer said expansively. "That dawg's worth his weight in gold. Not that I got any gold, but you know what I mean."

I looked fearfully at Karl. Adults are unpredictable. And I had to admit Macgregor would be in his element, watching his own sheep.

Karl was shaking his head. "No, thanks. I appreciate it, but no. Macgregor's had the time of his life today. Maybe he'll never have so much fun again but . . . I guess we'll be selfish and keep him ourselves."

The farmer argued a little, but he knew finality when he heard it, and we all trooped down to the wharf to see them off. Macgregor was there, bright-eyed and bushy-tailed, keeping a sharp eye on the flat-bottomed boat. Suppose, he seemed to be thinking, suppose one of them jumps overboard? Wow!

But none of them obliged, and the boats pulled away with

much waving and shouting above the racket made by the sheep and the happy collie. Macgregor and I stayed until the boats were lost in the gathering dusk. We could hear the sheep for a long time, and then everything was quiet.

By the first of September, the domestic paraphernalia of island living was so thoroughly wrapped up and stored away Aunt Cara complained she could hardly find a skillet to cook on.

His books and papers having been packed, Uncle Charles occupied himself by teaching Macgregor tricks. The collie was quick and biddable and learned almost too fast for Uncle Charles, who liked a challenge. "He'll forget as fast as he learned," said the Rector, out of bitter experience with parishioners and choir. "You'll have to keep him in practice, Tazie." I promised obediently, keeping my doubts to myself. Rather bored with the conventional, Uncle Charles thought up something more original. He would teach Macgregor to say Grace before meals.

The idea obviously struck Macgregor as unnecessary, illogical, and tiresome. Why roll over three times before he could eat, when he knew perfectly well he would be allowed to eat anyway? He was polite, indifferent, and as Karl said, "as stubborn as any Scot." Uncle Charles had found his challenge and Dutch bull-headedness met Scottish obstinacy with predictable results: stalemate.

Waiting for breakfast until the lesson had run its inevitable course, I said crossly, "Oh, Macgregor, give up! You *know* Charles Snedeker always gets his own way."

For a moment Uncle Charles stared at me in silence. Then he pulled out his chair and sat down at the table. "That is the judgment of a peer," he muttered. And said Grace, without bothering any more about bringing Macgregor into the fold.

✸ FOUR ✸

We sailed to the mainland, and Macgregor was happy for the last time in many hours. We took turns visiting him in the baggage car and he had an admiring audience, for the train crew made much of him, but he wasn't used to being tied and the noise of the wheels rattling over the tracks probably hurt his ears.

Karl and my grandfather had made careful plans for getting Macgregor from the station in New York to Richmond Hill. Karl had learned to drive the car belonging to a classmate who, by great good luck, lived on Long Island about half way between the Snedekers' home and Richmond Hill. Karl would pick up the car in the city, drive my grandfather, Macgregor and me to Richmond Hill, and then take the car to his friend's home. Even if there had been room for everyone, Uncle Charles refused to ride in an automobile driven by his son; the Long Island Railroad, he noted, was run by experts.

Macgregor was desperately unhappy. This was more torture. Would it never end? Karl growled that he didn't feel too happy himself during his first moments of uncertainty with the car. But finally we were off, with my grandfather beside Karl, while I gripped Macgregor's collar in the tonneau. He pushed his head down in my lap, and moaned.

My grandfather was in seventh heaven. His eyes shone like an excited boy's, and the smile under his mustache never disappeared. He directed Karl unerringly to short cuts and the best roads—how did he know?—and we arrived too soon for the two boys in the front seat. Not too soon for Macgregor.

He hated the collar which had been forgotten all summer,

he hated the noise, the smell, the horses, the other machines. He quivered and shivered. Had it not been for Macgregor, I might have enjoyed my first ride in an automobile. And I couldn't stop thinking about the meeting between Impo and Macgregor. My imagination ran riot, and I was almost sorry when Karl turned into the familiar driveway.

I begged Karl to wait, but he said hurriedly that it was getting late, and anyway he would just complicate matters, and anyway Uncle Thomas was there, and anyway . . .

"And anyway," I snapped. "You just want to get out of it, Karl Snedeker. He'll miss you." I was furious to find my eyes full of tears. "I guess I will, too."

He put down the last bag, laughed, and gave me a hug. "Drop that silly collar," he said. "He won't run away. Give my love to the family and stop looking mournful. This isn't a last farewell."

My mother called from the porch, "Karl! Come and have some coffee and a bite to eat."

But the machine sprang to life, he waved, and roared out to the road.

My grandfather said with a twinkle, "Probably afraid to take stimulants while driving that rig."

Macgregor at my heels, I charged up the steps for my homecoming welcome. "Where's Impo?" I demanded when I caught my breath. My grandmother pointed behind me.

Impo was sitting quietly, looking at Macgregor.

My grandfather put his hand on my shoulder. "Leave them alone," he said. "Thee'll have plenty of time for Impo."

Macgregor lay on his stomach with his chin on his paws. His tail wagged tiredly. He looked sadly at the black cat. I waited for Impo to notice *me*.

"Leave them alone," my grandfather repeated. "Impo's confused. Macgregor's exhausted."

"Confused? What's he confused about?"

"Macgregor." He sounded impatient. "Thee comes home in a noisy machine and stays outside with a strange dog. Why wouldn't he be confused? Let them work it out themselves."

But I kept running to the living room window where I could watch them. It seemed to me neither was ever going to move. I felt shut out, rejected. At last Impo stood up, stretched, and yawned. After a glance down at the collie, he walked to the front door. I ran to open it, kneeled to put my arms around him, and everything was all right with us. My mother remembered Macgregor. She called him indoors, making much of him, but he was shy.

Macgregor was supposed to sleep in the kitchen. On the first night, I half woke to hear him scratching beside my bed. Down by my feet, I could just see Impo's green eyes regarding me unblinkingly. I leaned over to rub behind his ears and got a quick kiss on my hand before I spoke to Macgregor, who knew he didn't belong where he was and was waiting to be told so.

There was tension in the room. I was both tired and sleepy, but I began to talk in an ordinary voice—about the Island, and what we would do tomorrow and I hoped Impo would be amused by the dried starfish and the shells and the stones I had brought back and there were almost two weeks before I had to go back to school and we could all have fun—and, now, please, wouldn't it be a good idea to go to sleep? I felt Impo curl around and rest his head on my ankle. I heard Macgregor sigh, yawn, and relax. The tree branch outside my window tapped at the pane. The room slept.

Does that sound silly? Romanticized? It was very simple. The center of Impo's universe had been absent for a long time and had returned with a strange dog who seemed to be getting the lion's share of attention. As for Macgregor, the world he knew was lost; I was all he had to cling to. Unknown places, unknown people, an unfriendly cat. What next? They were both used to my voice (Karl would have snorted, "They should be, they've heard enough of it.") and to hear me talking and talking away just as usual meant security, stability in a world that was mysteriously wobbling on its axis.

Sweetness and light did not prevail without interruption, but trouble spots were minor and often funny. Impo's flair for dramatization was at first incomprehensible to Macgregor, the down-to-earth type. When the cat pretended he heard a dreadful, dangerous sound at the door Macgregor rushed to protect the household, only to see Impo's hair smooth down, his switching tail relax and an expression of quiet satisfaction come over his face. The collie caught on quickly, and Impo had to think up new games.

Macgregor had never lived with a cat before, and the feline's dainty way of eating seemed to embarrass him, but before long, having gobbled, he liked to sit watching the cat push bits of food daintily around with a flexible paw, his silky head tilted and his feathery tail thumping gently.

Once or twice they raced around the house (I wondered if any memory of the Snows' mother cat lingered in his mind), but soon Macgregor found a friend in a white, short-haired terrier, and Impo's nose was out of joint. The collie's preference for the terrier was natural enough; Impo had a sneaky way of suddenly jumping off the course to the porch, using it as a short cut and landing ahead of the affronted canine. He rightly regarded this trick as a breach of good sportsmanship and would stalk away in a huff.

The Richmond Hill place had been sold. Plans for our future were taking shape, and Macgregor would return to Karl during the Christmas vacation. Like every creature who lives by instinct, he sensed a difference in the atmosphere. Once settled into his changed circumstances, he had enlarged his circle of friends, he had become independent and gregarious. He was welcome everywhere. Sometimes an entire day would pass without a sight of him at home.

Now all that changed. He became my shadow. When I was at school he stayed close to my grandmother. When I went upstairs, he galloped ahead to wait for me on the top step, his tail waving, his smile wide. When I read, he lay near by. When I went on an errand, he trotted beside me. There was nothing sad or lugubrious about all this, he wasn't unhappy, he was merely trying to make it plain that, separated or together, we were special to each other. And for as long as Macgregor lived, whenever I visited the Snedekers, this was the way it would be.

The lavish celebration of conventional holidays wasn't our style, at best, but we lived in a community of big families and hearty eaters who made the most of any excuse to serve giant roasts or turkeys with all the trimmings. The morning-after garbage pails were a sight to behold. These were kind people, and this year invitations to share Thanksgiving and Christmas with them were so many and so warm that I caught my mother crying over one of the letters.

"Thee doesn't want to go, does thee?" I asked in some alarm.

"Good God, *no*," she gulped. "But we—I haven't been very friendly. Not even very nice."

I sat down beside her. "Well, we gave a lovely big party. Even if it was a long time ago. And thee is so—nice. And so are Nana and Granddad. And I play with the children," I added with, I hope, unconscious arrogance.

She wiped her eyes, laughed, and kissed me. "Thee plays with them when one of us takes a whip and drives thee out of a book. Thanksgiving won't be so bad . . ."

I had an inspiration. "Look, on Christmas let's all go to the city and have dinner at—oh, at the Lafayette, maybe."

"Too expensive, I'm afraid." She hesitated. "After we move, I'll have a job. At the Hudson Guild. John Elliott promised me."

"That's wonderful, darling!" I threw my arms around her. "Something to look forward to. We'll be awfully busy, anyway, packing up. And Thanksgiving doesn't mean a thing to any of us."

It was Macgregor who made that Thanksgiving Day memorable. He was, to be sure, a little late.

On the morning after, my grandmother and I were washing up the breakfast dishes, when she glanced out the window over the sink, and exclaimed, "Look!"

Beyond the driveway and the strip of lawn that separated us from the next property, Macgregor was standing beside a big pail which was not quite big enough to contain the remains of yesterday's banquet. He looked comtemplative. And furtive. Garbage pails were strictly forbidden. We were invisible behind the curtains, but instinctively ducked as he looked towards us.

Apparently reassured that he was alone and unobserved, Macgregor pushed the pail top with his nose. It fell with a clatter to the frosty ground, and he jumped guiltily, but the temptation of the goodies now revealed was stronger than his conscience. The pail rocked perilously as he put his paws on the rim.

I said, almost in a whisper, "Should I call him? If he knocks that over, the mess will be simply awful."

"Oh, dear, I don't know. Let's wait a minute . . ."

We watched him nose the contents and then his head came up with the most enormous turkey bone in Kingdom Come between his teeth. The pail settled into equilibrium, and we both let out a sigh of relief.

And then I cried, "Oh, look, look, look!"

Macgregor had carried the bone over to our lawn. He laid it on the ground and sniffed it. There were gobs of meat still clinging to it.

And then Macgregor stood up, looked again at his prize—and lay down beside it.

My grandmother said, "But what in the world is he doing?"

"Watch. Just watch. Oh, Macgregor, you darling, you blessed darling!"

For the collie was slowly, solemnly, ritualistically, rolling over—once, twice, three times. He had been living with heathens for three months, but in his moment of triumph something reminded him that he was, after all, a part of the Episcopal Establishment and he was returning to it with his conscience clear.

My eyes were wet. "Uncle Charles tried to teach him to say Grace. We thought he hadn't learned it at all . . ."

My grandmother stared out at the happy dog guzzling his Thanksgiving treat. Then she ran fresh hot water into the dishpan.

"Macgregor," she said decisively, "is a gentleman."

As everyone knows who has done it, moving from a big place into a small one is physically, mentally, and emotionally wearing. What shall we do with this? Do we really need that? No, we simply cannot throw that out, if there's no room we'll knock down a wall. Where on earth did this come from? Remember when we got that? Throw away . . . Throw away . . . Give away, give away. When it's over a merciful fog shrouds the hideous memory and you wonder why you made all that fuss.

Impo was the only one who enjoyed it. After Macgregor went home with Karl, he looked around, sniffing, and occasionally made small noises in his throat. But the excitement of cartons and barrels served as compensation. There were new hiding places and dark corners from which to spring at passing skirts, and my mother wailed, "Macgregor may have been a nuisance while you were packing up at the Island—but at least you'd *see* him!"

Would Impo adjust to indoor life? He couldn't be allowed out of the apartment, if he got on the street he'd be run over, someone might steal him . . .

"Oh, for heaven's sake, stop worrying! Thee's always worrying about something, and none of it ever happens."

"I come by it honestly, anyway," I retorted. "Straight from thee and Nana." We were all on edge. Except Impo.

He took to apartment living like a duck to water. We were on the top floor of a building on a hill. There was a glimpse of the East River, plenty of sky, pigeons flapped past the windows and were, I believe, the first birds Impo ever paid attention to. He didn't even try to go out in the public hall, much less down the stairs.

The subway was almost brand new. The stations were clean, the cars clean and well-lighted. The trains weren't crowded and ran in an efficient, orderly manner, only stopping where they were supposed to. I loved it. But the trip was long, and three of us started out together very early in the morning and came home late. For much of the time, my grandmother was alone. "With Impo," she always said, when the subject came up.

But one day at breakfast, she looked around the table, and

said in a voice we had never heard, "All mah little birds gone off . . ."

My mother and I stared at her in horror. Had her mind failed? Her deep-set eyes were looking at something we couldn't see, her sensitive mouth quivered as if with suppressed laughter, one expressive hand played with the handle of the coffee pot. The floor of our world had given way.

My grandfather looked from his daughter to his granddaughter, and began to chew his mustache.

"Sarah," he said, "thee's a little devil. Thee's scared the girls. And Impo." He reached down and rubbed the black cat behind the ears. Then he began to chuckle. "I haven't heard thee do that imitation since Maryland. Virginia. The lumber country. What got into thee?"

She looked abashed. Then she put her hands over her face, and behind them she was giggling like a girl. "Thee remembers, Tom, that awful woman with the pigs and about two dozen children, and she kept caged birds. *Wild* birds she'd trapped. In a big, filthy cage. And she never knew who let them out."

He was leaning back on two legs of his chair. "Oh, yes, I remember."

She looked apologetically at the younger generation. "I'm sorry. I sit here and I start thinking back. Getting old. But, oh dear, how interesting it all was. Wasn't it, sweetheart?"

My mother said, "I suppose thee was the one who let the birds loose?"

She shrugged. "Well, yes. She was giving birth to her twelfth or twenty-fifth child—it was hard to say—and it seemed like a good opportunity."

As the three of us walked down the stairs, my mother said, "She's alone too much."

We went down another flight in silence.

Then my grandfather said, carefully, "No, it's all right. Don't thee worry. She's right, of course, we're getting old. We remember things we thought we'd forgotten. That was really teasing me. Those particular people were—well, potentially dangerous. Poor white trash, the worst kind. The War, for them, hadn't ended. I made a big fuss about those birds. She might have got in a peck of trouble." As we separated, he said, "Don't worry. Sarah's all right."

Perhaps. Except for marketing—which she whisked through with efficient celerity—trustee meetings and interviews at the school, she had little to occupy her time except reading. And thinking. The other occupant of the top floor was an old maid recluse who kept her door barred and demanded detailed identification before she opened it even a crack. What could Impo do if anything went wrong? My mother and I took to co-ordinating our social lives so that one of us would get home early, but it was difficult.

We didn't think much in those days about crime, and if there were drug addiction (as there probably was), it wasn't generally discussed. But there were maverick criminals then as there are now. There was a chain on the front door which my grandmother was supposed to slip into its notch when she was alone. She consistently forgot it. When the bell rang late one dark cold day, she trotted down the hall and flung the door wide open.

She stood about five feet two inches. A tall man looked down at her, his eyes shadowed by a slouch hat. She said pleasantly that she thought he must have come to the wrong apartment. He put both hands on the door frame and leaned over her. At the other end of the long, dim hallway, lamps in the living room glowed cheerfully.

The man put his foot over the threshold. "Don' wanta hurt any li'le old lady," he muttered.

She stood without moving as he gripped her shoulder. He started to swing her out of his way, and then everything seemed to happen very fast. With his free hand, he snapped down the hall light switch and in the dark she reached out to steady herself against the little table by the door and felt it shake under a sudden weight, although she had heard nothing and, momentarily blinded by the darkness, could see nothing. Then, by a trick of light from the living room lamps, she saw his eyes shift and stare and his hand dropped from her shoulder.

Out of blackness that was blacker than the dark hall blazed two vicious green eyes. The spell was not broken by a sound or a motion, there was only silence and the eyes.

With an incoherent exclamation, the man turned and ran down the stairs. She waited until she heard the street door slam shut. Then she closed our door—and put up the chain. With the hall lights on again, everything seemed normal. Walking regally towards the living room was just a black cat, a big cat, a very black cat, but . . .

Once in the living room, she sat down. "I don't know why," she said later, "but I felt a little tired. The whole thing hadn't taken seconds, after all." We had finished dinner before she embarked on a recital of "something that might have been rather unpleasant," and we listened in appalled silence, while Impo sat in his usual place on the sideboard, watching us through slitted eyes and occasionally nibbling at a bothersome claw.

"But really," my grandmother was saying, "I do wish you could have seen Impo. *I* could hardly see him until I turned on the hall lights and he almost scared me—three times his size and his tail . . ." She spread her hands exaggeratedly, "And it was lashing back and forth, like a whip. I could almost hear it crack. He was magnificent. I wish you could have seen him.

But," she added, "if you'd been here, it wouldn't have happened, would it?"

My mother and I looked at each other. *She had enjoyed it!* They didn't talk very much about those strange, dangerous years in the hostile southern mountains—could she possibly regret that they were over? We had an uneasy feeling that *we* had deprived her of the kind of life she wanted.

She said, speculatively, "I wonder what Impo would have done if the man had actually pushed his way in? What does thee think, Tom?"

My grandfather had listened without comment, almost as if his mind were on something else, but now he turned in his chair to look at the black cat. Impo had relaxed into a cozy, by-the-fireside position with his paws tucked under and only the tip of his tail twitching to prove he was still awake. As my grandfather moved, the emerald eyes opened wide to stare straight into the other male animal's face. For some reason, I shivered.

"Oh, well," said my grandfather coolly, "he might have flown at the man. At his eyes, probably. Good thing the fellow was a coward. Sarah, if there's any coffee left, may I have another cup?"

We moved to Brooklyn. It was better for everybody, my grandmother in particular. There were no stairs, the school and the Meeting—of which she was an Elder—were within walking distance. The neighborhood had changed, but it was here she had grown to womanhood, and we became used to finding her entertaining some old gentleman who had sought the favors of "the Brooklyn Beauty," and had not forgotten. My grandfather regarded these visitors with a twinkle and, we thought, compassion. After all, he had been the victor.

The apartment was sunny and pleasant, and in those days in a residential area it was actually desirable to be only a few feet above street level. Impo was the first cat I knew who became enamored of traffic. The window sills were wide and he would sit for hours with his nose glued to the pane. People began to look for him, children hung on the areaway railing and called to him. He swished his tail, washed elaborately, rose to his full height standing on his back legs. This called forth o-o-ohs and ah-a-a-hs. He was not above showing off.

College was not on the cards—or in the bank account. The owner of the business school so closely resembled a camel that one instinctively looked for a hump, but the similarity was confined to facial conformation and the way she carried her head, thrusting it forwards and backwards on her long neck exactly as a camel does. She was a martinet with a warm heart. I was by no means a prize pupil, but somehow she met my grandmother and after that went out of her way to be helpful. When I was offered a job a couple of months before the end of the six months course, she said, "Take it, my dear. If you find it's too much for you, come back." She was a tall woman, and she pushed her head forward to peer down at me with her dark, protuberant eyes. "Please remember me most kindly to your grandmother . . ."

Europe was consuming itself in the trenches on the Western Front, in open warfare and revolution in the east. There was no longer any doubt that soon the Yanks would be coming to set everything right. This was my generation's war, and it may have been just as well we didn't know there would be precious little peace in all the years of our life.

My grandmother took it very hard. The fires of her overactive imagination were fed daily by the firsthand reports and the photographs that filled the newspapers. People who couldn't stop talking about the war kept her nerves on edge, but were easier to endure than those who, as she said, behaved as if everything that was happening in Europe was an obscene smell it would be impolite to notice. Domestic help was hard to get and she took refuge in housework. Her standards were high and she wouldn't lower them by a single notch. My mother cried out in protest, "Stop pretending thee's Rose and Mary rolled into one! Thee'll kill thyself."

It amounted to that. A stroke paralyzed her vocal cords and left her nearly helpless. My mother had a good job with the city; her salary was important. I wanted to stay home, my job wasn't all that lucrative. We couldn't understand everything she said, but at the mere idea, her agitation was extreme and at first it had seemed best to give in to her.

During this interim period, whoever managed to get home first would find Impo close to her chair, and she made us understand that he had been "right there" all the time we were away. She pointed to her watch, running a finger around the dial—"every minute." Touching his head with one hand and her own face with the other—"watching"—she would smile at me and nod and then shake her head emphatically, which we took to mean that he was all right, he wasn't sickening as he had when he watched me hiding from the fact of my father's death. *She* was not hiding from anything—perhaps that made the difference.

Impo took it better than we did. One evening—the repetition of this scene became unendurable—I burst out to my mother that the lack of the little money I was earning couldn't matter by comparison with ending this horror, someone must be with her and I was electing myself no matter what anyone thought or said.

My mother said, "It's got past the point where I can argue. Thee's too young—but yes."

Impo was glad to have me. He still stayed near her and

when I had to go out on an errand, returned to his post at her feet.

One evening she seemed so alert, my mother and I became gay and made jokes, and she laughed. During that night she died, alone with her husband. We never knew at what hour it happened, or how. They were together, as they would have wanted it.

My mother and I had sometimes worried that my grandfather would be "lost" without his Sarah. "Sarah," he would call when he came home. "Where is thee, Sarah?" and she would answer, "Right here, sweetheart," and then they would kiss and cling together for a moment. It was a daily ritual, so commonplace that we hardly noticed it until it ended. I had a queer feeling that after her death he still called her and she still answered. He was not lost, the rest of us were.

At first, Impo spent days and nights searching for her. He made pitiful noises, or crouched beside her old chair, as if he were waiting for her and if my mother or I tried to console him, he rejected us. He turned to my grandfather for consolation, and found it. Impo was alone a great deal now that I was back at work. My grandfather was usually the first to get home, and I always believed he explained the beloved's absence to the mourning cat in some way that satisfied and reconciled him for, suddenly, Impo decided to act like a kitten again.

This isn't unusual in a healthy, middle-aged cat, but as might be expected, Impo went to extremes. I would come home to find my grandfather picking up torn scraps of the morning paper while Impo watched with a devilish gleam in his eye. Or he might be tossing a ball for Impo to jump at, and twice I caught them playing hide-and-seek around a chair.

"He insisted on it," my grandfather said defensively.

The big cat, whose size startled even people who were used to him, took to lying in my grandfather's patient lap, lazily playing with a loose end of his tie. If it had been in me to feel jealous of my grandfather, this phase of Impo's life might have brought it on. His attitude was sensible and right: having had to accept her absence as an irrefutable fact, Impo saw no reason why everyone could not do the same. But try as we would, my mother and I took longer to come back to normal, to put the long, agonizing months against the perspective of the longer, happy years. Of us all, only my grandfather's perspective seemed never to have slipped into distortion. He was perfectly natural. He neither tried to avoid talk about her, nor to seek it. He knew we were fussing about the chair where she had spent so many tormented hours, and said, "Don't throw it out. The frame is good, it's a nice shape. Needs a new cover, springs might be tightened up. You three women threw out so much when we left Richmond Hill, it's a wonder there's anything left to sit on."

❀ FIVE ❀

On the rebound from a love affair with a boy about my age, who looked like a Greek God and whom my mother detested with a fervency she might have put to better use, I became engaged to an acceptably older man she liked very much and thoroughly approved of. I thought I knew him quite well and liked him enough to imagine that we had—or could have—much in common. A minor physical disability had kept him out of the services (which it would not have done in the wars to come), and I saw a good deal of him. Emotionally battered, I had obtained what I believed I most desired: my mother's unqualified approbation.

After we were engaged, Lewis bought a house in the Chelsea district on a street that was favored by artists, writers, decorators, architects, and such. Renovated and painted, the houses were a delight to the eye. The apartment on Amity Street was dismantled, my grandfather would "visit around" until the house was ready for him, my mother leased a cozy little flat, and we moved in. With Impo.

There was a back yard which he regarded with some interest. There were cats on the back fence. They peered down at the huge, coal-black stranger with green eyes and a long thick expressive tail. I watched the proceedings nervously. Impo had not been face to face with another cat since Richmond Hill. He didn't *look* elderly, but he was. I conjured up horrors. After the first inspection, the neighborhood cats—a scrawny bunch but formidable in number—went quietly away. To talk over strategy, I thought darkly.

Lewis and Impo were polite to each other, but no rapport

developed. Nevertheless, the next day, a Saturday, when I came back from a necessary shopping excursion uptown, Lewis met me, doubled up with laughter. It seemed Impo had asked to go into the back yard and had immediately reverted to his country habits. Lewis considered that admirable and left him to it.

A while later, he heard a noise such as Hell must ring with and on looking out the living room window he saw a battle royal. The local cats' strategic plan had clearly been to mount a mass attack on this black, oversized interloper. I listened to his dramatic replay with growing alarm and had turned to dash for my beloved's mangled body, when Impo appeared in the doorway. He was rather rumpled and there were some bits of fur missing, but he was puffed up with self-satisfaction. Nothing on earth can look as smugly pleased with itself as a cat.

"My God," said my husband, the male animal speaking, "what a sight! You should have seen it. The old boy walloped the hell out of them. I thought I'd have to help one of them get up the fence . . ."

Impo ignored him and rubbed against my ankles, asking to be picked up and made much of. I hoped the ice between husband and cat had been broken for good and all, but it froze up again later although Lewis boasted happily about "our cat" to anyone who would listen. Basically incompatible personalities seldom get beyond a live and let live compromise.

My husband was an honest, upright man. He was interested in the aesthetics of architecture, painting, and other visual arts. He had humor and told an off-color story superbly. He had many devoted friends among his own sex. He was kind but lacked the sensitivity that lifts kindness above a pedestrian virtue. I was genuinely fond of him, but lonely. He cared nothing about music and knew less, he liked to "keep up" with the new books, he loved the theater and vaudeville (this was a real bond between us), and he deserved better than to have me for his wife.

We spent several months in Europe, had a marvelous time, and I came home happier than I had expected to be, and pregnant.

The area of Chelsea where we lived was part of the old Moore estate. Bishop Clement C. Moore had perpetrated "'Twas the night before Christmas, when all through the house/Not a creature was stirring—not even a mouse . . ." I think, though I'm not sure, that mice and rats won't live under the same roof. If so, there wasn't a mouse stirring in our house; it was infested with rats. The place was within gunshot of the waterfront, most of the houses were nearing the century mark, there was no cellar. The winter was exceptionally bitter, and I think that was one of the years when the dock workers struck and an unusually large number of freighters were tied up along the River. Did other houses in the block suffer a similar curse? It seems likely, and I suppose a primitive sense of social shame kept our neighbors silent—as it did us.

The beasts were annoying enough when they stayed inside the walls, but when overcrowded conditions (I suppose) drove some of them from their living quarters into ours, our attitude hardened. On the first morning after we moved in, I had come face to face with a large, stinking, grayish monster who was busy knocking over milk bottles in the basement vestibule. I stamped my foot and, if I remember correctly, said "Scat!" It snarled at me and, probably out of sheer surprise, vanished down a hole. Lewis had plugged one hole with thick, broken glass and now we tried to find other places to apply the same remedy.

Then we got in an exterminator. The rats laughed and the

house was almost uninhabitable for a week. Impo was a complicating factor; there was no way of knowing whether he was as immune as the rats proved to be. Short of moving out, we seemed doomed to live with the dirty brutes.

Very soon a new and much more serious complication was the presence of an infant daughter. I don't remember exactly when the rats' search for Lebensraum became a major force, but she was still small enough to sleep in our room where there was a Franklin stove that could be kept warm all night with cannel coal. But the warmth (more or less fictitious) of our room was mere camouflage for the real reason. John Elliott having commandeered me for volunteer work at the Hudson Guild the first moment I set foot in Chelsea, I had seen what rat bites could do to a baby. Lewis had not; his imagination was not prodded by visual memories.

The first time I heard Impo howling in the kitchen region, I ran downstairs barefoot, for he sounded *in extremis*. The rat he held between his paws was beyond *extremis;* it was thoroughly dead. Impo's tail was lashing with pleasure and pride. Shivering and giving a passing thought of wonder at the stupidity of a rat who would leave the cozy walls for this, I wrapped the ugly thing in a piece of newspaper and dropped it in the garbage pail, lavishing on the noble rat killer every loving compliment I could get past my blue lips.

It would be a wild exaggeration to say that the same scene was enacted every night—it just seemed so to me. He would howl like twenty demons until he heard me on the stairs. I kept newspapers handy and became adept at wrapping corpses without touching them. I told my grandfather (we were again under one roof) that I would be a splendid helper if the city were struck by an eighteenth-century yellow-fever epidemic. He growled that it wasn't much to joke about in this house; rats had carried the fever from the ships and could again. When I came back from these expeditions I would find that he had left his room across the hall and was leaning over the crib (Lewis slept more or less peacefully through most of these episodes), just "making sure," he would whisper apologetically; he knew it was silly but he felt better if he knew she was safe.

I didn't think it was silly. This was his first great-grandchild and he "fair worshipped" her, as my next door neighbor said, but he would have done the same if she had been a waif from one of the old-style tenements near the Guild. He said he thought Impo prowled through the house, but the cat was so silent when on the hunt, and so black, that he couldn't be certain. He rather wished Impo had continued to sleep in the crib—she had been really safe then.

On the coldest night of that winter I pulled the covers tight over my head and pretended I didn't hear the weird jungle cry from the kitchen. The air in the room, with the Franklin stove working overtime, felt frozen when you breathed it. The baby, I knew, was all right, under layers of blankets, and the crib tented over with a quilt. She wouldn't smother, her nose wouldn't be frost-bitten. *She* was my real responsibility and I would not—repeat NOT—go downstairs. I went back to sleep.

Perhaps the unwonted silence wakened me, for I was conscious when something heavy, smelly, and slimy hit me accurately in the middle of my back. I almost screamed. I couldn't turn over on top of the—the thing, so I knocked it on the floor and then looked down into a pair of blazing green eyes. Impo was furious. He spit. He spit at *me!*

I heard my grandfather stirring in his room. I got out of bed. It's difficult to be haughty when you're shivering from head to foot, but I tried. Making sure I hadn't pushed the ghastly object onto my slippers, I got into my dressing gown, picked up a piece of paper by the stove and, ignoring Impo, I rolled the rat in the paper and left the room. My grandfather, standing under the dim hall light, looked surprised.

I gestured at Impo, with the hand holding the body.

"He *threw* it at me," I told him through teeth chattering with cold and indignation. "He *spit* . . ."

My grandfather leaned back against the door frame, and laughed.

I was enraged. I stamped down the stairs—as well as one can stamp in woolly slippers—after Impo, who was halfway to the kitchen. I dropped the dead rat in the garbage pail, slammed down the lid, punched it tight. I don't believe in the resurrection of the body, but I wasn't taking any chances with this one.

When I got upstairs I found my husband, awakened by the ruckus, and my grandfather trying to smother their laughter.

I said, "Look at Ann. If her nose is blue it may be frost bitten. I think you put salt on it," and crawled under the covers as far down as I could get.

Two years later, a son was born four days before Christmas. He was a replica in miniature of my father, and when my mother saw him she almost fainted. The resemblance became less startling, but lingered.

My grandfather never saw him. He had died quietly, of what was called "old people's pneumonia," in his own bed, with his daughter and granddaughter beside him. We had sent the nurse out of the room. There was nothing she could do.

The waiting between each breath grew longer. We would glance at each other. Now?

Suddenly he sat up, his back straight. He smiled. His face was radiant.

"Sarah," he said clearly, "I'm coming to thee now," and fell back against the pillows.

Not half a block from our house, freight cars pulled by steam engines clattered along Tenth Avenue, carrying coal and other supplies to the factories and slaughterhouses farther—but not much—uptown. Neighborhood boys picked up pieces of coal as they fell and some bold spirits shinnied up the cars to push off as much more as they could before a slow-moving trainman made a show of chasing them away. Coal from the freights had augmented meager supplies in the adjacent tenements for several generations. The sweetish smell of the slaughterhouses was faint and soon forgotten, but the chocolate factory belched a saccharine stench from smoke that mingled with the less putrid smoke from the River traffic. Today's deplorable air pollution, which is probably compounded of more dangerous elements, has to reach a high danger level before I so much as notice it.

The freight trains didn't run on regular schedules, but after living near them for a while, it was possible to make an educated guess about when to expect them. Ahead of each train rode a man on horseback, waving a red flag. In good weather a small procession of mothers and children ran, walked, or toddled to the Avenue to wave at the man with the flag and watch the cars go by. From the time she could sit erect in her carriage, my daughter and I usually led the parade. From the first, I think the horse attracted her more than the flag; it was the second word she spoke. (The first was "Damn!" I can't imagine where she picked that up.)

Ann had recently learned to walk and was extremely independent about it, as she was to be about most things, so we had made an early start for the show and I was talking with a friend whose standards of entertainment were as infantile as mine and who was carrying an even younger baby against her shoulder, when I suddenly realized nothing at all was by my side. Looking back, I saw a honey-colored head in earnest conversation with an unkempt dog standing in the gutter, who seemed bewildered. In my daughter's small hands was a large bone. Part of the bone was still in the dog's mouth.

I swear I heard my grandfather's voice: *Don't scream.* I didn't run, either, but my friend said later I covered the pavement with the speed of light.

"Diry. No good." Her face was an inch from the dog's muzzle. "No good," she repeated firmly, and yanked the bone from between his teeth, stood up, and threw it as far into the street as she could. At the same instant, I picked her up, the dog gave an astonished yelp and dashed after his treasure, my daughter kicked me violently in the ribs, and gave a howl of frustration.

When I reached my friend, she said, "Don't faint. I can't get you home." Her own face was faintly green.

"Here comes the man on the horse," I managed to gasp, and luckily I was right.

All things considered, I suppose it wasn't surprising that the children never showed the slightest fear of animals. There would be other incidents, some of which I witnessed or heard about, but the only one I knew of that might have been serious was when Ann had a touch of sunstroke while riding in a ring, and that was the fault of adult misjudgment.

Impo was not much impressed by the arrival of our son. His *laissez faire* attitude was in sharp contrast to his intense interest in the first baby. "What, again?" he seemed to say. He did watch the bathing process which, as before, he obviously rated as bungling and inefficient, but he found it hard to make the leap over the crib bars which had been so easy for him two years ago. Impo was old.

If there is any scientific foundation for the old theory that one year in a cat's life is the equivalent of seven in a man's, I never heard it, but if true, Impo as a human would have been one hundred and forty years old—a record even for the yogurt eaters in the Albanian mountains. The force of his personality had, however, increased with the years.

Prohibition parties were sometimes messy, and one cocktail party we gave was rather worse than that. We wanted it to be on the formal side and had even sent written invitations, including "five to seven" and "R.S.V.P." More ringers than legitimate guests showed up, and we didn't like any of them. The objective had been to entertain several potential clients, and the guest list had been tailored to fit that purpose. It was small consolation that the stars were behaving like everybody else.

As the hour grew later, the uproar grew greater. A three-cornered argument boiled up into fisticuffs. A table holding a lamp was overturned, a woman screamed, well-meaning pacifists shouted instructions and imprecations at the combatants. . . .

At the height of the clamor, one large, black cat walked silently into the room. He picked out the center of the vortex and sat down. He curled his magnificent tail around his front paws and looked around. His green eyes were slits of cold scorn and I saw one woman shiver when they passed over her. When someone stumbled too close, he spit but did not move and the man drew back as if he had indeed been bitten. Little by little, people began to drift away, giving a wide berth to our Imp o' Darkness.

There were a few echoes. One guest of honor was reported to have said that he'd stick to his home-town architect; New York was even worse than he had expected. But a couple of the others were undeterred—a pretty fair average One of the invited guests called to thank me for a "terribly exciting afternoon" and to confide that she was through with the man she had brought along because he was actually afraid of our cat. "Imagine!" she caroled. "Scared of a *cat!*" I laughed, and told her he wasn't the first uninvited guest Impo had chased off the premises . . .

Our house was flanked by rooming houses. On the west, all was stiff, tidy, and disciplined. The owner kept herself to herself, and if I ever knew her name, I have long since forgotten it. On the east, our neighbors were the Barrys, slap-dash, warm-hearted, excitable, and timorous. In addition to these qualities, Mr. Barry was also morose, but this might be attributed to the effect gin has on certain temperaments.

Mrs. Barry and I became friends almost immediately. She was a bosomy, florid, excessively yellow-haired woman of uncertain age, whose garments were as hopelessly untidy as her house was spotlessly clean. She was irrepressibly kind, and her roomers were likely as not to be out of work or "ailing" or dead beats who had known better days. She had no children and five dogs of some nameless, and probably shameless, breed, very large, whitish, and short-haired, and accident-prone. One of them impaled herself on a spike in the fence separating our front yards. Somehow Mrs. Barry and I pulled her free and somehow she survived and even thrived. The dogs were stupid to the verge of insanity, but Lewis claimed they couldn't be all that stupid for no young were produced in all the years we lived there. "They know something we don't," Lewis insisted darkly. Curiosity made me pry a bit, but Mrs. Barry was so shocked by the idea of "interfering with Nature," that I never again tried to penetrate the mystery. Once she confided that she thought she was "just a tiny bit pregnant," but I heard nothing more about it and hesitated to pry into that, either.

It was a blockful of rampant individualists, whether old-timers or newcomers. By and large the newcomers shared a professional interest in The Arts, which made it easy to form new friendships and consolidate old ones. Being New Yorkers, native or by adoption, there was very little running in and out of each other's homes and even less fraternizing with the old-timers, most of whom wouldn't have welcomed it anyway.

Mrs. Barry, accident-prone like her dogs, was also crisis-prone. It sometimes seemed that if I were not binding up some wound on her ample figure, I was being called on to reduce some crisis to manageable proportions, if not to exorcise it altogether, or at the very least to listen while she recapitulated crises now over and done with, or predicted others she feared were imminent. The latter she always discussed in sibilant whispers, perhaps hoping that what the Fates couldn't hear they wouldn't think of.

So far she had been spared the ultimate horror—calling in the police.

My limited experience at the Hudson Guild had taught me the prevalence of this irrational fear even among those with no records and not even their names on a police blotter for some minor infringement of the law. Barry was too lazy to be pugnacious and preferred to do his drinking at home and usually alone. Mrs. Barry's reputation was as clean as the floors of her house. I had gone so far as to check with my friend the Sergeant at the local station house. (Even a hit-or-miss association with the Guild vastly increased one's circle of friends.) However, in one crisis, the Barrys had to submit.

Basically, their house was much like ours—the same number of rooms, the same ship's-ladder stairs, the same low-ceilinged top floor with the front windows set high under the eaves. In that top-floor front room lived an elderly man who seldom spoke but had a ready smile, and gave the impression that he may have known better days.

The children had gone off somewhere with the Scottish nurse-cum-housekeeper we had recently taken on and I was luxuriating in a quiet hour or so to listen to music when the doorbell rang several times. Mr. Barry stood outside. For a wonder he was entirely sober and asked rather breathlessly if I would mind coming next door? Something was going on they didn't understand. Mrs. Barry opened the basement door, looking pale and worried. I sniffed.

"What's that smell?" I asked.

Barry stammered, "We—we ain't sure. The Missus is in a taking."

I followed him to the top floor. The smell grew stronger. Gas.

Barry and I stood outside the door to the front room. He shook the doorknob.

"Locked," he said unnecessarily. "I can't get in. He don't answer."

I put a handkerchief over my nose and told him to get something, anything, to open the door, or break it down. And hurry.

For once, he hurried. He seemed glad to be given orders and I could hear Mrs. Barry wailing downstairs. I leaned over the banister and shouted to bring up wet towels.

Mrs. Barry stood in the hall below, moaning, "Oh, Jesus, Mary, and Joseph!" And, "He kept a chain on the door. I'd tell him, suppose there's a fire, God forbid . . ."

It took all Barry's strength, a crowbar, and a hammer before the door crashed in and the full wave of gas swept over us.

Gasping and coughing, the wet towel tight over my nose, I went in. The windows were closed and the cracks stuffed with rags. The old man, fully clothed, lay on the bed. I didn't need to look twice. Somehow I managed to turn off the gas cock, told Barry to get the windows open if he had to break the glass and fled home to telephone.

When I came back, Mrs. Barry gripped my arm. "Not the cops," she whispered. "Not the cops. An ambulance. Get him to a hospital . . ."

I was somewhat overwrought myself and I shook her off. "He's dead. Did he always stuff up the windows?"

She looked bewildered; she hadn't seen the room. "Kept 'em shut. I kept tellin' him . . . Just the hospital, dearie!"

Pulling myself together, I said as gently as I could, "I know this is terrible for you, but the man is dead. It might have been suicide. Believe me, the hospital would have called the police if I hadn't."

She groaned. "The disgrace. I'll never live it down if I live to be a hundred."

I lost patience. "Don't be a fool. There might have been an explosion. Your house might have caught fire . . ." I had no idea of what I was talking about, but it served its purpose. She steadied down a little. We could hear Barry retching in the bathroom and in a minute or so he came down the stairs, looking green.

"Got one window open," he mumbled. "Didn't want to break the glass. Costs money, those off-size panes."

The police arrived without noise, but it was bad enough. Three enormous men in blue piled out of the car, an ambulance clamored authoritatively in the distance, and windows across the street snapped open.

The Barrys gave the effect of clinging tightly to each other, though I don't think they were even touching, while I led the cops upstairs. The gas was still too strong to be healthy and on the way up I got one of the men to open windows in other rooms, which were badly stuck.

The ambulance men had a bad time getting down the narrow, sharp-cornered stairs and the small halls. It was pretty gruesome. Then the ambulance departed and the Barrys were questioned. The police were polite to them, but they looked like frightened rabbits, stammered, huddled together, and in the end knew nothing about the man except his last name; he had lived in that room for ten years. One of the men went to search the room for papers and came back with a mate's certificate twenty-five years old.

When I finally got back, the children were home, Impo met me and sniffed distastefully. Giving the nurse an expurgated version of what had happened, I stripped and spent about thirty minutes under the shower before I felt clean again. I had left Barry opening a new bottle, and Mrs. Barry with her head on the kitchen table, unable even to cry. As I had entered my own warm house and heard the children playing upstairs, it occurred to me that the Barrys were almost as alone in the world as that sad man with his old mate's license.

Even without the Barrys, the neighborhood demanded a good deal of stamina from its residents.

Almost directly across the street lived a woman whose family wouldn't hear of "putting her away in one of them institutions." They kept her locked up in the second-story front room where she could "see out and feel like she was alive." (I heard those remarks often enough to remember them exactly.) They undoubtedly meant to be kind, but it was a little trying for everyone else. In the summer she sat at the partly opened window and hurled curses at passers-by. One day, perhaps in a moment of lucidity, she managed to push the sash all the way up, and jumped.

If she had indeed been hoping to end her misery, the wish proved vain. She broke a leg, an ambulance doctor cut short her screams of agony with a hypodermic needle, she was carried away, and never returned. Her people were shamed and distressed; the City, or the State, had intervened and she was "put away" after all.

The waterfront was within easy walking distance, but we paid little attention to the realities of what went on there. Dock workers and stevedores struck for better pay and shorter work hours, but the unions were not yet strong enough to organize and finance a sustained walkout and the supply of scab labor seemed bottomless. A handful of old-timers had jobs of one sort or another with shipping companies or factors and if we happened to know who they were we might notice them around the neighborhood at odd times and think vaguely, "Oh, yes, that strike's still on," but that was about as close as newcomers ever came to the waterfront world. At daybreak in early winter I accidentally caught a quick, an almost illicit glimpse, into that unknown world.

I had a special job to finish that day which was so much on my mind that I actually woke up as dawn broke. Feeling virtuous, I even got up and slipped downstairs to make a cup of coffee, or two or three, with the idea of getting a lot done before the household round began. I stopped at the front door to see if the paper had come and shivered in the sunless dawn as I bent to pick it up. Still only half awake, I noticed a considerable number of men walking steadily and quietly on both sides of the street. Dock workers, I thought sleepily, probably come by here every morning; that strike must be over.

Then I stood riveted. Out of four black cars poured a crowd of men, two dozen perhaps, armed with clubs. In almost complete silence, the men with clubs methodically beat up the men on the sidewalks. The only sounds were the crack of the clubs and the thud of falling bodies. No one spoke, no one cried out, no one protested.

Then the men with the clubs got into the cars and drove away. The whole thing was over in half a minute. Prone bodies began to rise, some slowly, and the men walked again towards the waterfront.

There were a few who did not rise, however. Two men in the gutter across the street did not move. One had fallen against our fence but before I could get down the steps he had pulled himself up and followed his companions.

Shaking, only partly from cold, I called the police.

The man on the desk said, "Scabs." And sighed. "Silly fools. That's a quiet street. Why didn't they take Twenty-third with the trolley and more people? Look, if those men are still there, call me. Betcha they won't be, though."

They weren't. But a mystery remained. I thought I could understand the silence, even the lack of resistance. The last thing either side wanted was interference. But why *had* they chosen our street? And how did the strikers know they would be there? The beatings had been carried out with an almost military precision. Apparently none of the scabs had been seriously injured, and they had all continued on towards the docks. It was too bad we had no acquaintances among the strikers—or the scabs—who might have answered the questions.

The monkey came in the heat of summer.

Screening the windows of that house was a problem Lewis had never satisfactorily solved. We fell back on Flit—or whatever anti-bug spray was called then—put up screens where possible, and let it go at that. The floor-to-ceiling casement window in the front room on the first floor presented insuperable difficulties and had been blithely ignored from the first. With the decline in horse traffic, the city's fly population had also declined.

We were having a heat wave and I had been perspiring over the typewriter when visions of iced tea danced through my head, and I went down to the kitchen to make them come true. I found Impo sprawled full length on the kitchen floor (below street level and facing north, it was the coolest room in the house) looking far more comfortable than I felt. Cats' fur seems to serve as protection against heat as well as cold. He lifted his head, said hello, purred and went back to sleep. He was sleeping a great deal nowadays.

Coggie, nicknamed by John because he couldn't pronounce her Scottish name, had taken the children over to the River to watch the boats and perhaps catch a breeze. The house was blessedly silent and I leaned contentedly against the counter under the window, throwing an occasional word to Impo, who might or might not open a green eye out of politeness, and thought about the paper in my typewriter. Suddenly we both jumped. Directly above us crashed the most appalling racket. Someone was at the piano . . .

I flew up the stairs and skidded to a stop in the doorway of the front room, unable to believe what I saw. A sizable monkey was running up and down the keyboard.

He grinned at me briefly but didn't stop. I screamed over the hubbub, "Get out of here! Go away!" or something equally intelligent. He bared yellow teeth at me, not unamiably. He was having the time of his life. I advanced a step or two into the room, hoping to head him towards the wide-open casement. He paused for an instant and rose on his hind legs. He was undoubtedly male and, upright, he looked gigantic. From his vantage point on the piano, he towered over me.

The only monkeys I had ever seen were attached to a street organ or in a zoo. I had always thought them rather jolly; we might have evolved from worse. I was rapidly revising this opinion. The visitor had gone into his Josef Hoffman act again.

I left the room, closing the door carefully behind me. Impo was in the hall, his fur on end, his tail thrashing. But he showed no desire to tangle with the monster, for which I was devoutly thankful.

"You stick to humans," I advised. Impo retreated to the top of the basement stairs, a foot in both camps, as it were. The house rocked with simian creative ecstasy. When I picked up the telephone I wondered if I could hear what, if anything, the police had to say.

I heard my friend, the Sergeant, burst out laughing. But he said something about sending over a couple of the boys as soon as he could. Slamming the receiver back on the hook, I took a moment to wonder whether our second-hand piano would survive. But as long as music filled his soul, the monkey would not think about my almost new typewriter . . .

There was an ear-splitting crash, and then dead silence. I tore down the hall. The monkey was sitting on the floor by my desk, apparently deep in thought. His eyes glittered under beetling brows. He made a move in my direction and I stepped back fast, slamming the door. The beast mustn't be allowed to roam the house, tearing the place apart, chasing Impo . . . I thanked heaven the children were safely out of the way, and sat on the top step beside Impo who seemed pleased to have me there.

The silence was sinister. Or had the intruder decided to leave before the Force arrived? Somehow I doubted it and the detonations of falling objects confirmed my suspicion. Something else fell. What?

Then came a tinkle of breaking glass. Telling Impo to stay where he was (an order he never obeyed unless he wanted to) I tiptoed to the closed door.

Silence. Inch by inch, I pushed open the door. The room was empty. Roget's Thesaurus and a bottle of rubber cement lay on the floor; Roget's back was broken, but the bottle was intact. The lower windowpanes were broken. I guessed the

CATS AND OTHER PEOPLE

clumsy brute had made some miscalculation in leaving, or had maliciously broken the glass on purpose.

"Perhaps he cut himself and will bleed to death," I said aloud.

Impo stood in the door, and if a cat's nose can wrinkle, his did. A distinct smell of zoo lingered in the room.

When I opened the door to the two policemen, I said, "The monkey's gone. As usual, you're a little late."

They came in to look at the damage. They were enjoying themselves. I described the creature, trying not to exaggerate.

"Look," the older man said, "we know that monk. Wouldn't hurt a fly. Loves children. He belongs to some nutty dame on Twenty-thoid Street. She called just after you did to say he'd got out again . . ." He looked skeptically at me. "Mean to say you never heard about him before? All the time you've lived here."

Speechless, I shook my head.

He scratched his chin. "Lucky you ain't the hysterical type. Well, we'll get along. Hot, ain't it?"

As I let them out the door, I managed to say, "Why didn't the Sergeant tell me that when I called?" The injustice of the thing struck me, and I said angrily, "If I'd known, I'd have given him a banana. The Sergeant, I mean. Not the monkey . . ."

The other officer turned at the gate and said solicitously, "We'll find him all right. Don't you worry, ma'am."

I shut the door with a bang that threatened to shatter the old wood panels.

A threat of eye trouble that might become serious if he didn't get away from the drafting table set Lewis thinking about another jaunt to Europe. The first time we had skimped on London and Paris, to concentrate on Italy. Two months, including the leisurely boat trips should allow time to have a real taste of the two cities. Coggie, competent both as nurse and housekeeper, was devoted and sensible; our top floor had been turned into a flat for my mother, my free-lance work was unimportant, so why was I dragging my feet? What was there to stop us?

There was nothing, except an aged cat who was sleeping too much and eating too little. My mother pointed out that he might be expected to live until I came home; two months was not long. Coggie was a little miffed. If I were willing to trust the children to her, why not a cat? My husband did not say very much, but he was bewildered and hurt: I was putting loyalty to a cat above loyalty to him. He walked away, buried himself in a newspaper or made a telephone call, when I began to explain that Impo had been an integral part of my life for many years more than he, it was not a question of loyalty but of love . . . I would reach this point in the unvoiced argument and pull myself up short. Pleas for a mere delay in the sailing date fell on deaf ears; a friend would be traveling with us and must be considered. And, they said, what made me think I could time all this so neatly? Unless, of course, I were to take the sensible course, the merciful way out? Theoretically, I agreed—but not for Impo. I am not given to foreknowledge; the "second sight" my grandmother apparently possessed, had passed me by. I did not forecast a day or an hour, but I knew, and Impo knew that we had very little time left. I have never regretted for an instant that I was a neglectful mother, wife, and daughter during those final days and nights, before he opened his emerald eyes for the last time, and went into the dark.

We sailed on the appointed date.

There were many amusing and pleasant hours. Lewis was a good traveler, intelligent about architecture and the fine arts, friendly with strangers, good-humored when things went awry.

Our traveling companion, a gay, sweet-tempered woman, craved constant activity and as this was also his preference she made congenial company for him, making it easy for all of us to satisfy our own whims. We had been younger, on the first trip, unburdened by responsibilities or problems, and perhaps the differences between Italy and England also had some effect on each of us.

While the other two went sight-seeing and experimented with all the proper places to refresh themselves afterwards, I could spend hours wandering through London's streets, playing games with Dickens' people. The clothes were not the same, but their faces were, and so were their voices and even turns of speech. I frequently lost my way, refused to carry a map, but asked directions of any one I met who looked approachable and some who didn't, and in a short time picked up a little firsthand knowledge of a place and a people I had only known through the printed page.

London busses gained another devoté, and alighting at the end of the line, I sometimes found myself in regions unmentioned in respectable guidebooks. A horrified Bobby at one terminus hustled me back into the bus with strict instructions to the driver not to let me off until we reached Piccadilly. It was the closest I came on any of these expeditions to being "molested," and to be held in the calm, unyielding grip of a London Bobby was an experience I wouldn't have missed for all the tea cakes in the Savoy.

❁ SIX ❁

The luggage had hardly been unpacked and the gifts distributed when a familiar voice on the telephone asked in sepulchral tones—which were supposed to be mysterious—if I would be at home tomorrow about four? I said yes, I could be, but why?

"It's a surprise," he said, and rang off.

I sat looking speculatively at the telephone. He was a dear, a favorite friend, generous to excess, and sensitive up to a point, but he was incapable of realistically assessing other people's desires and temperaments. His mistakes in judgment made him so unhappy that everyone tried to conceal them from him.

When I opened the door at half-past four the next day he was beaming with self-satisfaction and anticipation. In one hand he held a sort of case in which something very much alive was wriggling and whining. When he opened it in the hall, a small white dog leaped out and made for me.

Irwin said happily, "See! She knows who she belongs to."

In order to say something, I murmured reprovingly, "My dear, your grammar!" and led the way into the living room, the puppy at my heels.

Settled down with a glass in his hand, he explained that he thought I would be lonely, coming home to find no Impo, and he knew I wouldn't want another cat, and so . . .

I leaned down to pat the puppy, hoping to hide my dismay. "Why is it quivering so?"

He explained airily that it was a characteristic of these wire-haired, highly bred terriers. "Doesn't mean a thing. You'll get used to it." He pulled out a long envelope and shoved it at me. Her pedigree. It was longer than she was from her nose to her chopped-off tail. I could show her if I wanted to. "Might be amusing," he said. And, when properly mated, we could make some real dough by selling the puppies. "But you needn't think about that for quite a while," he added hastily.

My intentions were good, but I suppose there was something wrong about my expression.

"Would you rather have had a white Persian kitten?" he asked anxiously. "I found a beauty, but I thought . . ."

I stood up, trying not to step on the puppy, and mixed myself a drink. What could I do? Not only his kindness defeated me, so did the little dog.

Instead of investigating the strange place, she sat at my feet, quivering, waiting for me to notice her. She didn't even glance around for possible dangers, she seemed to have no normal sense of self-preservation. It gave me an uncomfortable feeling of a responsibility for which I hadn't sought. Her liquid brown eyes said she adored me at first sight and, taking me for granted, she would adore me forever, whether or not her love was requited and no matter what kind of monster I turned out to be on closer acquaintance. I hated that, but I couldn't hate her. I picked her up and cuddled her.

"Her name is Grazie," I said.

He looked pleased but puzzled. "Because she's graceful?" he asked doubtfully.

"It's Italian for thank you."

When the rest of the family drifted in, Grazie was greeted with amazed delight. My mother said she understood wirehaired terriers were very fashionable, and the donor looked smug. The children scrambled around finding toys for her and John said, "Why does she shake like that?" I repeated my lesson: it was natural, we would get used to it. My mother cooed love-talk, to which Grazie listened with pleasure. Lewis said rather wistfully that this was the first dog he had ever had, and patted her affectionately. When she came back to me and looked up imploringly and nervously, I told the children to take her down to the back yard. The Barry dogs had never barked at Impo, but Grazie sent them into fits.

As time went on, we did get used to her perpetual tremors, or at least learned to ignore them. When anyone took her out on a leash, she created something of a sensation. Boardman Robinson scratched his spectacular red beard and remarked, "Well, I never expected to see *you* with an effete little creature like that on the end of a string." Mrs. Barry was hurt because I wouldn't let her play with the Barry dogs. I said she was still too small, but maybe later . . . My mother was upset because Grazie paid more attention to me than to her and was not appeased when I said nothing would make me happier than to have the positions reversed.

Her slavish dependence continued to plague me. I tried to recall little Pudge who had been dependent because he was tiny and helpless but had never, I thought, been subservient. On the contrary, he had been distinctly bossy. Macgregor had been my guardian and then my friend. It was ludicrous to imagine Macgregor playing slave to anyone, even Karl. Those were the only dogs I had known well, but I had always been suspicious of the gruesomely sentimental stories about the loyal canine and the brutal master. Grazie might have played the star role in one of these dramas . . . she was, apparently, that kind of idiot. Nevertheless, it was impossible not to love her.

Her intelligence was keen enough, but narrow. She never lost her temper; I doubt if she had a temper to lose. In a group of people who were talking and paying no attention to her, she had a way of sitting quietly, her eyes bright, her red tongue hanging out, her nose quivering while she looked from one person to another, shivering with excitement and joy when someone noticed her. She had an absurd habit of lying on her back with her feet straight up until a desire for activity suddenly hit her and she would go flying around in circles until she dropped flat, exhausted and panting. Like all puppies she loved to chew on anything that was tough and yielding. House slippers and gloves were not safe, but when scolded, she became so abjectly apologetic that we spoiled everything by petting her back to happiness.

The only real problem Grazie created involved the Barry dogs. They were becoming a neighborhood noise nuisance and Mrs. Barry blamed the complaints on Grazie or, to be accurate, on me because I steadfastly refused to let Grazie play with them. Why she thought this would automatically lower the decibels, I don't know, but we nearly had a falling out over it. Moreover, some of their fleas jumped the fence to get at Grazie's dainty white meat. They had never bothered with Impo and, except for the Italian fleas that had tormented Lewis but left me severely alone, this was my introduction to the pests. I hoped the acquaintanceship would stop right there.

Mrs. Barry and I made up, and she wept bitterly when I told her we would be spending the summer in the country and the bone of contention would be out of the way until autumn.

Lewis had bought a house and some property in Connecticut. Commuting was feasible, the place had woods, fields, a muddy stream, complete privacy on a little-traveled back road, and no neighbors within sight or hearing; it would be a pleasant change from the Chelsea block. Lilac trees—they were too tall and big to rate as anything less—overshadowed one end of the pre-Revolutionary building, and in the spring we discovered that they were white and the most magnificent specimens I have ever seen anywhere. The house itself had to be equipped with plumbing and a kitchen, but there was a huge central chimney giving vent to three fireplaces, one of which spanned almost the full length of what had once been the big kitchen and would be our living room. There was a good well, and a cellar which a light rain turned into a swimming pool. It was entirely enchanting.

Coggie would not come with us. The country held no charms for her and a nurse-housekeeper of her capabilities could be—and was—offered half a dozen jobs better than ours before you could say Tam o' Shanter. I wasn't too sorry. It seemed to me our American children had had all they needed of the British Nannie treatment and were old enough to take the rough with the smooth, find their limitations for themselves, and begin to learn their strengths and purposes. Nevertheless, it was a sad leave-taking, and when Coggie turned to wave before stepping into the waiting cab, it seemed as if the rosy red of her cheeks had concentrated in her eyes.

Grazie, the pampered thoroughbred, found the brook while we were still unloading the Model-T Ford, and came bounding back with her tongue hanging out and her glossy coat a murky brown stuck with bits of mud and thorns, yelping vociferously that This Is the Life.

We had been a little worried about passing cars and delivery trucks, but although she chased them, she had sense enough to keep at a safe distance. After an abortive attempt to keep her groomed, I thankfully gave up. Often burrs got stuck in her thick wiry hair and she would come trotting to me for help. The process of removing them was sometimes painful, and when I hurt her she had a way of turning to look at me with reproachful eyes, but when I hurried to say I was sorry she would wriggle and lick my hand and stand still again—quivering, of course—until the torture was over.

Several neighborhood dogs, well-cared-for and well-behaved, came calling but apparently she never returned the compliment; perhaps she felt herself too fine a lady for reciprocity.

We were not very far from the Sound, and once in a while I allowed myself to be argued into walking instead of driving to the beach. Houses were few and far between, cars preferred the main roads which we could conveniently circumvent, but occasionally we met some riders jogging along and these sent Grazie out of her mind with excitement—until what I had fully expected, did happen. One of the horses, tired of the small yelping creature at its heels, kicked out. Grazie escaped unhurt, but subdued, and only needed a reminder to behave like a lady thereafter.

Very often, I thought despairingly that she spent most of her time mucking about in the muddy brook, but the gay little waves that lapped the beach seemed to terrify her. While we paddled around at the edge of the water, she sat with her ears cocked, watching us intently. But the moment anyone got beyond paddling depth, Grazie became hysterical. She ran madly up and down the beach, small stones airborne under her scurrying paws, barking until it made your throat ache to hear her, breaking into little moaning cries, and sometimes going so far as to get her own feet wet. We could never make up our minds whether it was the waves or the salt water that bothered her. The shallow, sun-warmed water could not have chilled even her sensitive feet, and thinking of Macgregor swimming like a seal in the ice water of Penobscot Bay, I dubbed her "Sissy." Then I apologized. It wasn't her fault that strong, useful terrier virtues had been bred out of her by humans who saw a chance to set a style and cash in on the novelty.

The owners of the kennel had told Irwin positively that she

would not be coming into heat before winter. The event, although not the exact date, is burned into my memory. The fires of this particular hell took a couple of days to get going full blast. We thought she might have eaten something spoiled on one of her forays into the back fields. I knew nothing about a bitch in heat and Lewis—never having been allowed to have a dog because it might "dirty up the house"—was equally at a loss. The "stomach-ache" lingered and I called the kennels. After I described the symptoms, the woman at the other end seemed surprised and even incredulous. Then she told me what was probably the matter and added cheerfully, "Well, my dear, you'll just have to ride out the storm. But don't—*don't* under any circumstances allow her to run. She's valuable and her pups will be worth a lot of money, but *only* if she mates in her own class." A pause. "She's too young, really. Better let her get past this, and I'll put you in touch with some people in that area . . . Oh, you'll be back in the city? Well, if you'll give me the address, I'll send you a list of breeders. And a vet. Just in case." She laughed pleasantly and hung up.

Those were the halcyon days before everybody knew about atomic explosions. We had a preview. Even for experts, I understand keeping these explosions confined is a complicated operation. We weren't experts. The leash was resurrected for functional visits to the out-of-doors, and I suppose I should have known this was a mistake. Every dog for miles around got wind of what was going on. Have you ever been beleaguered by barking, howling, quarrelsome, four-legged demons? The experience defies description. Daylight hours were bad enough, for Grazie's well-vocalized misery, her squirming and wriggling, reduced the children to tears. They fled the house; half the time I didn't know where they were. Getting in or out of a door required the agility of the double-jointed man in a side show. Staying in the same house with her would have finished off the patience of Job. And with the dusk came her suitors.

It happened that Lewis was working on a big, important project and, before disaster struck, had brought home all his notes, sketch plans, exterior sketches, specifications, and so on, in order to work quietly at home instead of in the turbulence of an office. Everything had been set up in a little-used room off the living room where he could work without interruption. He was badly cramped for time.

There was no peace and very little sleep. The kennel Grazie had come from was too far to carry her in the flivver, and the only one nearby was so dirty we ruled it out after one visit. Anyway, we said, this wouldn't go on very long. Any nightmare seems endless, and I have no clear recollection of how long this one continued before we broke. I know it was a Saturday night, because half a working weekend had been ruined, when Lewis said, "How long did they think this would last?"

"They were pretty vague," I said wearily. "But it simply can't go on much longer."

"Well, I can't go on *any* longer," he said. "I'm putting her in the barn right now. The weather's warm. She'll be all right."

I stared at him. The barn! It was as full of holes as a sieve. It leaned tipsily on its foundations. I was the one who drove the Ford and I knew, as he did not, the gaping holes around the so-called garage space. A Shetland pony could maneuver its way through several of them. And suddenly I felt almost gleeful. Who wanted puppies with nothing but blue blood in their veins?

He was down at the barn for some time, and I heard a good deal of sawing and hammering. He came back looking pleased with himself. He had, he said, fixed up a good, warm, safe place. She couldn't get out and nothing could get in. He snapped on the leash and carried her down the dark lawn. He returned panting and a bit wild-eyed but reported Grazie was safe. The dogs were fighting among themselves and he had to run for it. I thought he seemed a little less certain of his security measures.

In the morning Grazie was at the kitchen door. She was disheveled, tired, and happy.

So much for our dreams of avarice. I picked her up, we kissed each other fondly and I assured her it didn't matter a damn what her little bastards turned out to be, she was the one we loved.

The course of Grazie's pregnancy was noteworthy only because she was the exemplar of what a pregnant female should be. She was not nervous, she did not burst into inexplicable tears, if she was apprehensive, she certainly kept it to herself. The kennels had given us the name of a reputable veterinarian in the city who was particularly interested in wire-haired terriers. He said she was carrying several fetuses and the birth might be difficult; she had better be hospitalized where he could keep an eye on her.

She gave birth a week before her scheduled performance and no one was in attendance except me—and that was accidental.

I had been working late on a free-lance assignment and went down for a cup of coffee to keep me going for another half hour. When I turned on the kitchen light, Grazie blinked at me; I saw the first baby on her sleeping blanket.

I rushed for sheets and towels, thought of calling the vet, dug out a hot-watter bottle, and tore back to Grazie. She seemed glad to see me, it is always nice to have even a small audience for your star performance.

It was just that. There was nothing for me to do, except to keep the place warm and give her an encouraging line of patter. Bagheera's kittens had been born while I was at school,

I'd had two children—but at the last minute I'd been doped (which I hadn't objected to at all), and I found the calm with which she endured the pains and her unruffled assurance about what to do after the birth, wonderful beyond belief. I had tried to sterilize a pair of sharp scissors; she bit the umbilical cord herself. One. Two. Three. Four.

After the fourth, she seemed tired. I began to worry. Was there another which wouldn't come down? What about the afterbirth? Was something going to go wrong *now*? She opened her eyes and looked at me as if she knew what I was thinking. Then the afterbirth appeared and Grazie sighed contentedly. She completely relaxed for a few moments—or perhaps it only seemed that long—and then picked up her maternal duties, sniffing and licking, showing the newborn where to find their sustenance.

I staggered upstairs to wake Lewis.

He said, "You must have been dreaming," and followed me down to the kitchen. Bending over to see the pups in the dim light, he exclaimed so loudly that Grazie jerked out of a doze and opened her eyes.

"Hey! They look like wire-haireds . . . No, they can't be . . ."

But they were. The one thoroughbred wire-haired terrier in the vicinity had won out over the hoi polloi. There might have been a sociological thesis there, but I had witnessed a miracle, and it would take a while to come down from the mountaintop.

The puppies were enchanting, but as their size and their capabilities increased so did their nuisance value. There were times when the four seemed like forty. They were greatly admired by all and sundry, and one of the sundries overreacted. That winter we were relying on "dailies" who were uncertain, coy, and hard to please. One of them was caught trying to smuggle out a puppy. The plot was actually foiled by Grazie who saw the kidnapping and flew at the woman with such ferocity that she almost scared me, entering the scene a second later, and frightened the would-be thief out of her limited supply of wits.

The devastation wrought by four growing puppies is less spectacular than the destruction of Sodom and Gomorrah, but there were moments when I felt Lot's wife had the best of the bargain. Nothing within their reach was safe. We had two decent Oriental rugs in the dining room which were rescued just before they became a pile of old rags. If one of the children left a sock or a shoe or a piece of underwear on a kitchen chair in the hope that it might catch Mummy's attention, it could as well have been thrown in the trash first as last. I loathed lisle or cotton stockings but learned fast that only Mrs. J. Pierpont Morgan could afford silk stockings *and* four puppies.

Our only break was their inability to climb the ship-ladder stairs. Perhaps, we said hopefully, the stairs would continue to defeat them until their passion for the wrecking business had cooled. The basement was roomy and pleasant, they had plenty of light, space, and air, but they were trying to conquer those stairs with a persistence that rivaled Hannibal's when he crossed the Alps.

Preparing a meal became an exercise in acrobatics. Lewis said, "I've never been able to dance but, by God, I'm learning," as he sidestepped two puppies attacking the toes of his slippers as two others nipped at his heels. They had a ludicrous and disconcerting way of suddenly lying down and dropping off to sleep wherever they happened to be, catching their breath perhaps after a game the children called "You chase me and I'll catch you." En masse, they were signposts to a loony bin. Separately, they were adorable.

My mother was naturally ecstatic about them, but when I caught her trying to teach them to climb the stairs, I protested violently.

"But I want them to come up to see *me*."

"We wish thee joy," I said sourly, but that Saturday night when we came home from a party or something, she was carrying one of the puppies down to the basement. She said defensively that she had been lonely and had taken one upstairs for company. The stairs to the top floor were as steep and straight though not as long as those in the Brooklyn house where I had fallen and killed little Pudge.

The next morning, I went up to her flat and asked her please not to bring the pups up there any more. "When they can climb by themselves, we won't be able to do anything about it, but if one of them fell . . ."

She was offended. "Well, of course, they're *your* puppies."

I said, "It's not that. Maybe I'm being silly, but doesn't thee remember that I killed Pudge by falling downstairs?"

She stared at me blankly. I thought later, why should she remember it? Pudge had died because I kept hold of him. If these four toughies fell downstairs, they might be a little dazed, if that. I had spoiled her fun by committing an emotional stupidity, and I was sorry. Somehow, I must make it up to her, but the first real opportunity did not come immediately.

The vet said admiringly that Grazie couldn't have done better: two males and two females. We called them Him and Her, He and She, but they were so much alike no one was sure which was what or who. Placing them had been easy. Two amiable families on Long Island estates would take two as soon as they were officially of age. The others would be together, but we were to keep them until their prospective people returned from a protracted round-the-world cruise.

Soon after that was settled, the vet called to say he wanted to come down and "get the little fellers in proper shape."

I gasped, "Down here?"

"Oh, sure. Nothing to it. Don't worry."

I had wrung one concession from my husband about the clipping operation: It was to be done at the hospital and damn the expense. But the vet said firmly it was better for the puppies to be at home, they might be frightened at the hospital. I remarked feebly that I doubted if a mere hospital would bother them in the least.

He said, briskly, "Fine. All we need are a few clean towels and a flat surface."

By common consent we had not mentioned the necessary transformation from natural terriers into "show dogs" in the children's hearing, and I had no trouble extracting a promise from their father that he would keep them away from home even if it meant playing hookey from the office. He didn't want to be around either, as I well knew.

The vet fixed up a neat operating table on the laundry tubs, assured me that within a couple of hours at the outside they wouldn't know anything had happened, and he would leave some ointment that would hasten healing.

"Healthy little chaps," he said, picking up the nearest pup. "Now if you'll just hold him . . ."

He had suggested that Grazie might be better off in the back yard and added that we were lucky to have such a fine playground for the dogs. Pretty soon they could get rid of some of their surplus energy out there. He chatted away casually, and it was all over in a very few minutes. By the time the children came home, the pups were almost back to normal.

To the children's horrified outcries I explained as prosaically as I could that the same thing had been done to Grazie and that for this kind of dog short tail and clipped ears were as necessary as wearing clothes in public is for humans. They looked thoughtful and wanted to know *why* clothes were necessary? I told them to ask their father and left the room to prepare food for anyone who could eat it, remarking over my shoulder that I wanted a drink, a *strong* drink, before dinner.

By early spring two of the puppies had gone to their new homes. Grazie sniffed around in a rather negligent search, but their departure relieved rather than worried her. She had done her job well, and knew it. She took no impudence from the remaining two but shed responsibility for their well-being and behavior with obvious satisfaction and became, it seemed, even happier and more ingratiating than before. Again she followed me everywhere, upstairs, downstairs, from room to room. When I left the house without her she hurried to the front window where she could see me walk to the gate, her stub tail drooping, her eyes mournful. When I returned, she met me at the door, with ecstatic barks and leaps and wild dashes up and down the hall.

When I thought about it, I was shocked to realize that I had not only grown accustomed to this blatantly expressed devotion, I had become dependent on it. But I didn't think about it often.

A major change was blowing up, like a destructive wind through our little section of Chelsea where individuals owned their houses but leased the land from the Moore Estate. The landowner had the option not to renew the leases and to buy up the houses at a "fair price." When a building changed ownership, the sale included whatever period remained of the original lease (which had been, I think, ninety or one hundred years), and ours, for instance, had had ten years to run. Lewis had bought with his eyes open, like most of the newcomers. Many of the old-timers went into a state of shock; a twenty-, thirty- or forty-year lease had become, in their minds, a fact of life no man could change.

To people like the Barrys, it was shipwreck, as sudden and inexplicable as the sinking of the *Titanic*. Having lived for the twenty years of their lease in a state of wishful ignorance, their incredulity and despair were pitiable. They had borrowed so heavily against the house that little would be left to go on with. I suggested buying a small place in New Jersey, perhaps, where they could keep the dogs and, I nearly added, where the state's crop of bootleggers was still ample. Mr. Barry listened and even jotted down some figures, but Mrs. Barry wailed that the country scared her, she only knew the city, the dogs might run away . . . People in the country poisoned dogs . . . The best I could do was tell the right people at the Hudson Guild that the Barrys might need help in relocating and warn that I didn't envy whoever took over the Barry case.

The Connecticut place would be remodeled for year-round living. Lewis had been raised in a small town and that—or something approximating it—was what he wanted for his children. We took the children for a long weekend in Connecticut, staying at a local hotel, while Lewis made final arrangements with the contractors. Plans and specifications had been completed and approved, only some loose ends needed attention, and John tagged after his father in a state of high excitement and budding ambition for his own future career. At the house, Ann and I sloshed around in the spring mud, making grandiose plans for lawns and gardens and a terrace and God knows what else.

Grazie and the two puppies had been left in my mother's care. It was the opportunity I had wanted to soothe my own conscience for the neurotic prohibition against carrying the pups up and down stairs. She was delighted, but there was a tiny barb concealed in her last whispered remark to me, "Thank thee, darling, for trusting them with me." While she was at her office, the door to the back yard could be left open for them, and by now of course the entire house was theirs. Our "boarders" could come to no harm and with luck the damage to furniture would not be extensive during her absences. She waved us good-by early Friday morning, looking blissfully happy, while Grazie crouched dejectedly at her feet watching us go.

We were met on Wednesday by a woman I scarcely recognized. She collapsed into my arms and wept as I had never seen her weep before. The story was soon told. Given the freedom of the back yard, one or both of the puppies had occupied the time digging a hole under the fence, which had gone unnoticed. It was just big enough for the small dogs to squeeze through into the Barrys' yard. They were dirty, but so was our back yard and she had brushed and combed and laughed at them and thought nothing more of it, until she met Mrs. Barry by accident, who said how glad she was about the puppies' visits and now the ice had been broken, so to speak, why shouldn't Grazie be allowed to have some fun too? My mother had put her off with a vague reply but she was worried, she didn't quite know why.

For some time, Lewis and I had been aware that the fence was developing new cracks and gaps between the old boards, large enough to allow inquisitive noses to poke through from the next yard. Lewis, who was responsible for many well-built, handsome houses, had neither taste nor ability for making minor repairs around his own home, nor had I. The family tool chest was unloved and neglected, there were no handy boards lying around that could be used for patchwork and, anyway, by then the Chelsea house, like an outworn car on its way to the city dump, had lost its importance. Grazie and our puppy boarders had had the run of the yard in good weather for weeks. It was a relief to get them out from underfoot while preparations for evacuating the place absorbed our attention. We had, indeed, mentioned once or twice that the freedom and exercise seemed to have a calming influence on the riotous little dogs, and all three harried adults noticed that Grazie and even the puppies seemed very conscious of the general upheaval around them and were depressed by it . . . "Instinct," my mother and I remarked in our infinite wisdom. "Remember how Macgregor changed when he knew he was leaving Richmond Hill?"

Alone with her charges after seeing Mrs. Barry, these small facts returned with hideous clarity to my mother's mind. Had she, or had she not seen some slight catarrhal discharge? Had she been overfeeding them, or did food left in their dishes mean loss of appetite? Panic-stricken, she called the vet. (All this, of course, was before the days of routine distemper shots.)

He confirmed her fears, looked over the fence at the Barry horde, set the Health Department on the trail, and then took all three dogs to his hospital. He had held out little hope for the two pups, but said Grazie might still be saved. Half an hour before we opened the door, he had called . . .

Whatever regrets there may have been about leaving the Chelsea house were swept away in the flood of this disaster. We couldn't get away fast enough. My mother blamed herself, of course, and nothing we could say was of any help. She fled into the apartment she had taken near Greenwich Village before it was ready for her. She said, with a shaky laugh, that the paint smell might explain her reddened eyes.

We were all sorry for each other, but no one thought any better of me for the pity I expended on Mrs. Barry. Her wretched, beloved dogs, with their presumably self-induced, self-sustaining immunization factor had been forcibly removed by agents of the Department of Health, who allotted me a liberal share of the blame. Why hadn't I reported the dogs years ago? "You're educated," one man said. "What's the matter with you?"

With the exception of a very few incidents, memory flatly refuses to co-operate in recreating that summer. Nothing has stuck in my mind about moving. I think Mary, who would take over—in her own fashion—where Coggie had left off, came to us quite soon. There was a black-and-white cat who was unmercifully bullied by catbirds. There was a small boy about my son's age. He wore thick spectacles which were forever being broken or lost; he was completely delightful.

As established members of the community, no longer mere summer residents, our social life expanded, and I disliked all the people I was expected to like, and vice versa. It's hard for me to understand why someone—my husband, for instance—didn't hold my head under the muddy waters of the brook until I drowned.

One trouble with that summer was the morbid smog of guilt in which I lived. The bulk of responsibility for the deaths of Grazie and the puppies was mine to carry. I had known more about Mrs. Barry's dogs than anyone else. She had had sense enough to keep them in the basement—inhabited only by the Barrys and visited only by myself and a very few other choice spirits. I was taken into her confidence when the two oldest ones died—of old age, she told me, and I believed her. How and where had the bodies been disposed of? Were they buried in the back yard? I had not thought about it before and the implications were extremely unpleasant.

Too much reminded me of Grazie, but the details are blurred except for one enchanting and, to the children and me, mysterious sight. We were walking down to the beach. It was a clear hot day and the dust swirled around our feet. At a turn in the road we saw a parade of young grouse, with a single hen marching behind them. In the sun's glare and the dust they seemed to number in the dozens—small, bustling, crowding together.

We stopped. If the hen had heard us, she paid no attention. She was keeping her charges under close surveillance, flapping her wings when someone got out of the group, keeping them in the middle of the narrow road. We were all thinking the same thing: Oh, please, no car! Please, no horses! Perhaps the intensity of our wishing reached the hen, for she turned her head towards us, hesitated, apparently decided we weren't worth bothering about, and continued to keep the procession on its course.

At a break in the roadside hedge, some sort of signal was given. Right face . . . Slithering and scrabbling, the young birds climbed over the rough ground and one by one and in little groups, they disappeared into the field. The empty road lay before us.

John sighed. "If only Grazie'd been around! She'd have chased them."

And, having run them into the wayside grass, she would have trotted back to me, her tongue lolling, her eyes bright and proud. "See? I got rid of them, didn't I? Quick work, too!"

"She might have hurt them," Ann speculated. "Not meaning to."

"We would have had to rescue her from the hen," I said, and the children giggled.

We wondered why they were on the road, with the safe fields all around, and why there were so many chicks and only one hen. There were grouse in the untilled field opposite our house, but we didn't interfere with their lives and knew nothing of their habits. Grazie had once gone after a whirring bird but came home almost immediately, looking crestfallen.

"If either or both of your parents hunted," I told the children, "we'd know all about grouse. Maybe we should look them up in the encyclopedia."

"It's more fun just to look at *them*," John said firmly.

Our part of the world was living in a fantasy. Few people could be found who dared say in public that the illusion had no more substance than such stuff as dreams are made of. Even level-headed citizens like my husband could not resist an occasional flutter in the market. Knowing nothing about finance and economics, I found it possible to ignore this antic dance most of the time; to an uninterested outsider it appeared more ridiculous than alarming. That viewpoint changed radically when I started on my first full-time editorial job.

My office roommate was a woman of great intelligence and perspicacity, who was playing the stock market with every penny she had saved or could lay her hands on . . . Apparently the entire staff was similarly afflicted, from the highest echelon down. They didn't call it "gambling." If they thought of it in those terms at all, it was "betting on a sure thing."

Gambling or betting, all that had vanished from my ken when my father died and there was no money to play with. Intelligent people, I had been led to believe, didn't lay bets they couldn't cover, primarily because that was dishonest and also because it spoiled the fun. The few hard-bitten gamblers I had run into at the Hudson Guild were not exactly intelligent, nor fun-loving for that matter, so my childish assumption remained intact until demolished by my clever, high-powered, respectable colleagues in that summer of 1929. I learned to interpret a special glitter in the eyes, a tension around the mouth, heightened color or a sickly pallor: something had gone up, something had gone down. Certain nervous habits signaled uncertainties: was that broker on the level? So-and-So says buy Such-and-Such. Should I? And so on and on.

Much as I liked most of the people, I hurried down to my one-room apartment in Greenwich Village every week night, and shut myself into solitude. There was a great deal in the work I would have enjoyed talking about, but none of the rest seemed to feel as I did. They had been touched by the wand of a wicked fairy.

On October 29 I stayed at the flat, by special dispensation, to edit a translation that had turned out badly. I had no radio, no one telephoned, no extrasensory perception warned me anything was wrong. It was a lovely day. I read about the Crash in the subway the morning after.

The entire staff looked as if they had been on an all-night drunk. No one attempted to do any work. My office mate, of whom I had grown very fond, looked ghastly and I kept an eye on her as inconspicuously as I could. I tried to think of some casual way to suggest that we spend the evening together, which we had never done. Reports of disaster kept coming in and she had several low-voiced telephone conversations. At lunch time she said she didn't think she'd eat anything right then and I brought her a paper cup of hot tea.

Her desk phone rang. After she hung up, she sat very still for several moments, looking straight ahead at nothing. Then she opened the drawer where she kept her handbag, and I saw her take out a small package. She seemed to have forgotten that I was in the room. Paper rustled, and I knocked a box of white tablets to the floor and stepped on them, and then held her close while she cursed me. Was I right? I don't know.

That afternoon I took the train out to Connecticut, and Lewis and I talked until the living-room windows lightened with a gray dawn. Perhaps we should have done so long ago. Would it have made any difference? I don't know that, either.

❂ SEVEN ❂

In most theater productions, even today, major changes in casts and settings are made behind drawn curtains or on a darkened stage. The convention has its merits and will be followed here.

I left my husband and married another man. We had loved each other for years and continued to do so. For potent reasons, which need not be detailed, the children were in the legal custody of their father, and I hope his character and our relationship have been made sufficiently clear for it to be no surprise that frictions and incompatibilities stopped short of the children. It would be false to pretend that their situation was ideal; given the circumstances and the personalities involved, it was as good as love could make it.

The Depression, like an implacable and irresistible avalanche, after a period of rumbling and grumbling, now fell. Industries, businesses, homes, property, jobs were swept away. Arthur and I were left with only his work as publicity director of one of the city's museums, and before many months, drastic cuts in the municipal budget reduced this to part-time, part-pay. Our free-lance writing took up some of the slack. The children were safe, and their particular oasis was, almost miraculously, undamaged.

We gave up our midtown apartment and moved to a small city in Westchester County, an easy train ride to New York. We liked it, cramped as it was. Most of the people we knew were in the same boat, yet gaiety, if not joy, reigned unconfined. Perhaps it was hysteria. We saw nothing hysterical, however, about our desire to share our hardship with a cat.

We borrowed two. They were very young, very gray, very much alive. But just why Teste and Clytie were lent to us is lost in the mists of that extraordinary time when so many people were doing so many unlikely things.

Neither of us had ever lived in close quarters with a pair of kittens, and we had a great deal to learn. The moment after they bounced out of the mutilated carton in which they had been confined for a short train ride, they took over our small flat with glad cries of, "Hey! This is just the right size for us!"

We had a few treasured pieces of sculpture, a Dresden shepherd and shepherdess, a Meissen bowl, a few pieces of rococo Venetian blown glass (which we didn't care much for but might still bring a few dollars if we had to sell them). We had two typewriters, and Arthur had a collection of catalogues and some rather valuable art books, kept in the bottom of the bookshelves. It wasn't much to boast about, but Teste and Clytie made it clear we wouldn't have even that very long if it remained within reach. We stowed the things away on a top shelf, hopeful but not entirely convinced. The kittens were into everything.

They opened closet doors, cupboard doors, bureau drawers, desk drawers, the cleverest modern garbage pail, uprooted typewriter covers if left unlocked. Sometimes we saw them in action, but we couldn't be around all the time, and we never did figure out several of their tricks.

It was impossible to be angry with them. Clytie sat in Arthur's lap, Teste in mine, purring and affectionately digging their claws into the handiest portions of our anatomies. On their first night in a strange place, we had encouraged them to sleep on our bed. Later we tried to shut them out of the bedroom. The howls, the cries, the scratching at the closed door, were the greater of two evils. And it did seem that their exile had taught them something for, having won, they were relatively quiet afterwards.

Physically, they were exquisite. Their gray-and-white markings were almost alike, but Teste was bigger, stronger, with a fine width between his ears and a masculine swagger, while Clytie was delicately made and feminine from her white nose to her fluffy tail. Her staying powers exceeded Teste's, her wits were quicker, and half their mischief was cooked up in her active little brain.

Among the assorted artists with whom we foregathered was a successful illustrator of books about animals. The kittens entranced him and the first time he came with his sketching pad, his eyes were alight with anticipation. At the end of the evening, he threw his piece of charcoal on the floor and shouted, "I'm going to stick to fish!"

He returned, with grim determination. "I can draw tigers, lions, panthers, cougars," he said furiously. "They're *cats*. Damned if I let a couple of miserable little kittens lick me."

"Spend a whole day with them," Arthur suggested. "That ought to do it."

He shook his head. "I'm frustrated enough as it is," he said, squinting at Clytie who had taken a leap onto Teste's back, a signal for him to spin like a top across the living room. A few years later, I noticed a book he had illustrated—about cats. The drawings were superbly cat.

When the time came for Clytie and Teste to return to their own people, we were able to be philosophic about losing them. With a self-restraint for which we gave ourselves considerable credit, we had held a little aloof. The posture had not been easy to maintain, especially when they began to mature.

"The sooner, the better," Arthur muttered as Clytie, standing on his knees stretched upright to put her front paws on his shoulders and soak his face with kisses. He didn't have to explain what he meant. As kittens they had been fascinating, enchanting, entertaining. Now they had developed personalities, and the sooner the tightening bonds between us were cut, the better for everybody.

The wrench of parting was made easier by an unexpected piece of luck. Arthur came into some money. It was no great amount, but to us it glittered like all the gold of Dives. We decided to spend several months in France on a tour of the wine country. Prohibition was nearing its unlamented end, Arthur was interested in wine and had already written a handbook on American wines for salesmen; we dreamed grand dreams about columns, articles, all sorts of activities that just a little more experience would bring within our reach. I don't know how much of all this we believed. After you have been trapped in a dark cellar, you don't complain about the quality of the light when the door opens.

Spring, the wanderlust season, had come when Arthur burst into the flat, shouting, "Get ready! We're sailing in two weeks. Everything's set."

"Two weeks! You're mad!"

He waltzed me around the living room. "If you're not ready, I'll go without you."

It was a long trip without a dull moment. We wound up for a rest on Majorca with Jo and Reg. They had a small house in a suburb of Palma, where Reg was working on the cartoons for a big mural commission. We had left the rented car in Marseilles—I think—and would drive back to Paris by way of the Riviera where we had friends who were resentfully adjusting to the necessity of returning to the gross, materialistic country they had fled; now that their native land had gone off the gold standard and the last of the money was running out. In a way, we sympathized. But not very much; they had escaped the most depressing aspects of the Depression. Jo, a magnificently sane woman, warned us in advance.

"The professional expatriate attitude will annoy you," she said, "but just remember they've been living high on the hog —or the franc. We're lucky. I'm past the age when I need a lot of Things, and Reg keeps his eyes on his paint pots."

Reg was also keeping an eye on a recently acquired dog. I don't remember his Majorquin name, but Arthur and I called him Scratch. He was a Basenji, a breed originally from Africa and, I believe, fairly common on the Islands which are only a hop, skip, and jump from the Dark Continent. Scratch was thin, eager to please, and lived in perpetual expectation of a beating. Reg had wanted him as a model for a scene in the mural, but Scratch was working his way into their hearts, as dogs will, and if he had been as safe from fleas as he was from a beating, his life would have been idyllic.

Reg, a gentle soul, had theories about dog training, about the proper way a man's dog should behave, about the activities a proper dog should enjoy. What no one, including his wife, could get into his head was that a Basenji is bred and trained for a purpose—to hunt, and to bring the catch back to his master without loitering along the way and, definitely, without taking a single nibble.

The weather was cold. The expatriates who claimed they wanted nothing better than to be natives, said it was "unseasonable." The Mediterranean was a grisly gray and its temperature ran a close second to the waters of Penobscot Bay. Well back from the sea, we could bask in the sun contentedly, but it worried Jo and Reg that we weren't getting the full Mediterranean treatment.

One day several people reported happily that the sea was at least blue, and we all piled into the Renault, complete with dog. The water was indeed blue and sparkling, but a large iceberg was apparently submerged not far away. Jo and I soon decided that the better part of valor was to sun ourselves on the beach. Reg, better padded by Nature than the rest of us, jeered, and Arthur, I suppose out of masculine loyalty, decided to stick a while longer.

When my back was pleasantly cooked, I rolled over to see that Jo was watching Reg with unmistakable nervousness. Just then Arthur, who I now realized had also chickened out, stood up and strolled down to the water's edge.

Jo and I heard him shout, "Hey, Reg, we've got ice water at home, and other things. How about it?"

Reg said something I couldn't hear. He had Scratch by the collar and was dragging him farther out. A brisk wind had risen. So had the waves.

Arthur turned and came back. "He won't stop, Jo," he said. "It's getting rough out there. Something ought to be done. That dog's never been in the water before."

"I know," Jo said, and got to her feet. She was unusually tall for a woman and with her gray curls tossed by the wind and her superb carriage, she looked regal, even in her bathing suit. We couldn't hear what she said and wouldn't have listened anyway; this was between Jo and Reg.

In a dead silence we went to the car. Arthur and I took the shaking dog in back with us and wrapped him in blankets. Not a word was spoken until we reached the house, when Jo said, "Drinks, lots," and Reg said, "Splendid idea."

The episode was never mentioned again, at least not in our hearing, but I'm sure it didn't fester; they weren't that kind of people. Because of a family emergency, they left Majorca soon after we did. We never heard what happened to Scratch.

Arthur and I were not exactly babes-in-the-woods and were not too surprised when the ostensible reason for the trip turned out to have been no more than an excuse for doing what we wanted to do. We had been away for nearly five months and at least a dozen authorities, well-known or not, had been signed up for columns and articles. When we rolled down the gangplank, fat as pigs from too much good food and wine and ready to lick our weight in wildcats, we didn't have a place to live, or a cat, much less a wildcat.

The first lack was filled at breakneck speed. In our half-stupefied, half-exalted frame of mind, we rented a house without much thought and no professional advice. We bought a second-hand car; it was a good car, but we had lived in the house for less than a month when we decided it had been built out of cartons that wouldn't have held Teste and Clytie for five minutes, with a facing of third-rate bricks. What continued to appeal to us was its location.

It stood on a hill, and there was not another house in sight. Trees and fields surrounded it, and New York was readily available. For the time being we didn't care that the hot-water heater was psychotic; the furnace was no worse than temperamental. The windows leaked. The doors shook under the slightest draft. The plumbing was subject to fits of hysteria, the kitchen equipment was fraudulent. There was a concrete slab the real estate agent assured us was a terrace.

But there were three bedrooms and a big bathroom on the second floor, a "powder room" on the first, the living room was spacious and a pleasing shape. Dining and living rooms were lined with false wood panels which were quite pretty until they began to warp. There was an honest-to-god fireplace. We were the first tenants.

Almost immediately, we were adopted by a cat.

It was one of those autumn days in which this part of the world excels—warm, the sky a clear light blue with exactly the right number of clean white clouds forming lazy patterns. The air itself was golden and the trees were beginning to try on their red and gold costumes. We were on the terrace—already beginning to crumble at the edges—when we saw him strolling towards us through the next field.

There were several cats and dogs in the not-too-nearby houses, but this one was new to us. He was full grown and quite large and from a distance he looked black, but as he came closer we could see the white vest and forelegs. He moved with a kind of youthful swagger, but not with the lissomeness and flexibility of a very young cat.

We had been making up limericks and laughing ourselves silly at our own wit. Apparently our ribaldry pleased him for he quickened his pace as he came nearer. Very much aware of him, we pretended not to notice until he was within some fifteen feet.

Arthur said, "There was an old man of senility, Who refused to allow his gentility . . ."

"If that doesn't scare him off," I interrupted, "nothing will."

The cat moved a little nearer.

"See," Arthur said. "I knew that was a good start. This is a person of discrimination."

The stranger sat down and tried to brush off his black coat. The white markings were immaculate, but the black reminded me of elderly waiters in a memorable but unpretentious restaurant—a little shabby, a little rusty.

I said in a conversational tone, "Hello, there. Nice of you to come." His yellow eyes opened at me. "Could we interest you in something to eat?" I emphasized the last word and repeated it. He got it. I stood up slowly. "Stay here with Arthur, while I get you something to eat . . ."

There was some chicken casserole in the refrigerator and I separated the meat from the bones—which are *not* good for cats—warmed it a little and carried it out in a shallow bowl. Arthur would have told me if he had gone. He hadn't moved. Arthur was mumbling along lazily while the cat listened.

He was polite, and he was hungry. Where had he come from? Arthur shrugged.

"God knows. I think he's had a rough time. Let's hope he doesn't have an itching foot. I like him. Don't you?"

He lapped up the last drop of gravy, and licked the plate. I'd forgotten milk. Angry with myself, I moved more quickly than I intended and he jumped.

"Sorry," I told him. "You wait right here. There's *milk*. Do you like milk?"

He was washing his face when I put down the bowl of milk, on the terrace this time, and waited. Would he take the dare?

He must have been trained within an inch of his life, for he looked all around before going slowly to the bowl, not as if he expected punishment but as if violating a code of behavior. It was interesting. Neither of us had ever seen just that reaction in a hungry animal. He wanted it, too. Perhaps the salt in the casserole had increased his thirst.

We named him Russia. He reminded us of a Russian *émigré* we had run across in a sidewalk café in Paris. The place was crowded but there were three chairs at our table. He sat down after asking permission and we invited him to have a glass of the Chablis we were drinking. He accepted eagerly and Arthur called for another glass. His English was difficult but better than our French. He said he was Prince Something-or-Other and gave Arthur his card. In Paris at that time you almost had to be a prince if you were Russian, but he was charming anyway. His white shirt was clean, so were his white socks as I noticed when, relaxed, he crossed one leg over the other. His black suit wasn't dirty but had that uneven look serge gets when it has been cleaned too often and too cheaply. The black cat brought that ephemeral occasion back to us and Arthur tried to find the card, but it had gone wherever unwanted cards go.

Russia stayed. In a little while, the resemblance to the down-at-heels prince vanished completely. The black fur became thick and sleek and in certain lights looked burnished.

We found out where he was from. There had been a disreputable bar in the village where, it was rumored, you could play the ponies and other less innocent games. However, the couple who ran the joint weren't even normally bright; it wasn't a community uprising against immorality that cooked their goose but the neighbors' desire to enjoy their own pleasures in at least comparative quiet. The boys and girls in the back rooms got out of hand several times too often and, we were told, every law enforcement agency on the books cooperated in closing the place. We were still too new to be up on local gossip, but we heard this had taken place a week or ten days before Russia showed up in our field.

He had been the Senora's pet and a favorite with the habitués. A neighbor who made us swear not to tell his wife he had ever been inside the bar, said the cat—he couldn't remember its name—would make the rounds of the customers and when there was a fight would get under a table, safe from flying missiles, and peer out at the proceedings until things quieted down.

Aside from the accidental gift of Russia, the village gave us a postal address and that was about all. The people we knew best lived a little farther north and in more affluent areas. They complained bitterly about the steps that led up the hill from the road and were the only means of entrance or exit to our house.

"Get those damned steps fixed or somebody'll break a leg and don't expect me to help pay the bills," was a more or less typical comment.

An architect spent most of an evening working out, on one of Arthur's sketching pads, an elaborately graded staircase with resting places at strategic points. We heard that someone said, "Oh, we're going slumming. Dinner with Arthur and Tay," followed by the ritual response, "Well, don't fall down those steps."

Arthur worked on them, and we did our best to torment the owner into action. The gibes of our American friends did not perturb us unduly, but when General Brutinel wrote that he would like to spend a few days with us if we could find it convenient, we almost fell into a panic.

The General owned a famous vineyard in the Bordeaux district. He was also a noted engineer, a financier, and heaven knows what else. A friend of his had listed the lot for us before we met him, but afterwards we forgot the trimmings. He had entertained us royally at his palatial home outside Biarritz, in Paris, and at the Canadian Club in New York. It goes without saying that he was a connoisseur of wine and food, but we knew him well enough not to let that worry us. All we asked was that our erratic, crazy house would behave while he was in it and that the steps wouldn't collapse.

The General—no one seemed to call him anything else—had been in Canada when the war broke out and had organized and equipped a tank company (the first, I think, in the Canadian Army), had been made an honorary Canadian citizen, and dining with him at the Canadian Club was like eating with royalty, only much more fun and far noisier for we all argued up hill and down dale. He had begun to suffer from arthritis in his back—a real and poignant reason for regretting that the steps closely resembled a rickety ladder insecurely set against the side of a barn.

The General arrived. He ascended the steps with the agility of a mountain goat. He fitted into our casual establishment as if he had never had seventeen house servants, and household equipment that our ingenious country wouldn't know about until after the next war.

We knew he didn't actively dislike cats, for we had seen several wandering around the gardens and porches and terraces and patios and the swimming pool (there was only one) at the Biarritz place, but we hadn't counted on Russia. We loved the General; Russia worshipped him. When forced by nature to leave the house he came streaking back, and if his Divinity had moved he searched until the god was found again. The General made no special overtures. However, on the second morning of his stay, I heard him talking in some language I couldn't guess at and went to investigate.

The General looked at me quite seriously. "I am trying him on Hungarian," he said. "He doesn't seem to know Spanish, in spite of what you told me about his former life. A dialect I don't know, probably. Italian doesn't excite him either, so I thought I'd go a bit farther East." He laughed. "I'm showing off to your cat. I'll say it before you do. This cat, he flatters me."

Later, the General, in a big apron, was helping me get lunch and scolding me roundly for being careless about something or other when he accidentally pushed Russia with his foot. He looked down. "Did I hurt you, *mon cher?*" Russia made ecstatic sounds in his throat and rolled over.

"You know, darling," I said, "it's not really you he loves, it's your shoes."

He looked at me severely. "You, my dear girl, are nothing but a jealous bitch, which I have long suspected."

It was on the tip of my tongue to say that I was indeed jealous of his shoes, but I knew he would worm out of Arthur the size I wear and soon after his return to France I would receive a pair of "ladies' walking shoes" with no card enclosed. We had quickly learned to be discreet about things like that.

He had come equipped for a rugged weekend, and when Arthur complimented him on his foresight, he said, "But, my dear boy, I'm used to English country houses. This is the Ritz compared to them. I love and admire the English, but I despair of understanding them."

We discovered that he preferred cats to dogs. "Dogs are necessary and sometimes I find them agreeable. But cats are, to me, more sympathetic. They are independent . . ."

Russia raised his head from the General's foot, startled by our laughter, in which the General, after a moment, joined. "Yes," he said, giving Russia's ear a gentle tweak, "even this one. We have a rapport, God knows why, but when I leave he will not cower in a corner and sicken because I am no longer with him." He paused a moment. "I had a dog. I was a small boy. I went away to school. The dog died. They told me she had died for love of me. I believed it. I have never freed myself from the—the horror that made in me—that is not good English, is it? No, I don't know how else to say it. You will find it incredible, but I was a sensitive child, and it is not good for a nine-year-old to be burdened with the death of what he loves."

I said slowly, "How would you feel if you knew that the dog really fell ill because she thought you were gone forever—and it was the illness, not your absence, that was directly responsible?"

He moved impatiently, and held out his glass to Arthur.

"May I? It is good scotch." He looked back at me. "I don't suffer fools gladly. I was a fool to believe it. Animals don't die so easily." He scowled at me. "You are getting me mixed up. What do you mean?"

"I think it's conceivable that your dog became depressed and unhappy because of your absence which she couldn't understand, and that she died because unhappiness—loneliness, bewilderment—lowered her physical resistance until she couldn't throw off some germ or whatever it was that attacked her. I can believe that. I saw it—in a cat—and only a wise man pulled him back to life. It would have been easy to believe he died of unhappiness, but not literally true."

We sat in silence for a few moments. The General took a good swallow of scotch and set his glass down carefully on a table. He looked down at Russia. "Yes," he said. "Yes, I see. It is an idea that helps take some of the itch out of that old wound."

On Saturday we gave a small dinner party. Arthur had gone to a lot of trouble to supplement our modest cellar with white and red wine from the General's vineyards—a good though not spectacular year. He would have thought that ostentatious.

A French bakeshop in the next town was owned by a woman from Lorraine who would, under certain conditions, cook a meal in your own kitchen, serve it and clean up. She liked us because we knew a little about her country, for which she was homesick. When I explained the identity of our guest she turned pale with excitement, planned the entire menu, ordered all supplies, and arrived in the middle of the morning on the busiest shopping day of the week. So the General had two worshippers, and we ragged him unmercifully in order, we said, to keep his ego from exploding.

The lowering weather had blown away overnight and we

took him for a long walk through the fields and nearby woods. Russia, slightly torn between the almost irresistible smells from Marie's cooking and the General, came along, showing off by dashing ahead to a hidden path and telling us to follow *him* because he knew the best places. We worried a little about the General's arthritis, but he laughed at us.

Dinner began with Quiche Lorraine, one of Marie's *spécialités*, and that night she surpassed herself. I caught the General sneaking bites to Russia. He winked at me.

"This is a cat of judgment. He is French. I shall take him home with me, where he belongs."

We had chosen our guests with three criteria in mind: Did we like them? Would the General like them? Would they like the General? Since we could be sure of the answer to the first question only, that was the one we relied on. It worked. One of the wives liked to pose as, among other things, a Francophobe, but we thought we could count on the General to take care of that, if no one else did. She whispered to me as they left, "My dear, I'd crawl up those steps six times just to see the General."

When I went out to say good night to Marie, tears were rolling down her cheeks. She said, "The General—he kissed me. Right here." She touched her cheek. "And then . . . and then, *he kissed my hand!*"

I was pretty sure that more than a kiss had pressed her hand, but I knew that wouldn't reduce Marie to tears. Bless the man, I thought as I went back to the living room, she'd follow him home to France if he said the word.

(P.S. We saw the General for the last time in the spring of 1939. He met us as we walked into the Canadian Club, and for a moment we were shocked into stammering like a couple of kids. We knew that the arthritis had been growing steadily more severe, but until that night he had put up a good front. He could no longer hold himself erect and his face was ravaged. He welcomed us with all the old warmth, but over dinner, the familiar arguments became acerbic. He was far more worried about Russia than about Hitler.

(He asked, as he always did, about "our Russia." We had told him before about Russia's end, but we told him again. After a moment, he said, "Ah, yes. You told me. I forget, these days." He looked with some of his old mischievousness at Arthur. "Did you know that once this woman of yours asked me how I knew so much about cats? Now I tell you." He sipped his brandy. "I will tell you that if you understand women you will have no trouble with cats."

(I interrupted. "Even male cats?"

("Be quiet. I am talking to your husband. Yes, even male cats. Woman nature and cat nature are much alike. Neither is quite human." He burst into a roar of laughter. "But without them the rats of the world would overrun us." A spasm of pain contorted his face. I began to gather my things together. He said, "Yes, go, my dear ones. I . . . I can't sit up any longer. It would delight me to think I have persuaded you to recognize our worst enemy, but I know you too well. Only promise me one thing." He got painfully to his feet. "Promise me you will not name another cat Russia."

(We promised solemnly, and the evening ended on a light note. But we were very silent on the way home.)

The winter we spent in the house on the hill began well as far as weather was concerned. Arthur was able to do some patching on the steps, and I could drive over to see the children without worrying about chains. Russia roamed the neighborhood on his own affairs which we safely assumed were many. He wasn't a youngster, however, and on cold nights usually stayed with us by the open fire. His only hang-up—from his former environment—was a tendency to crawl under furniture when arguments became heated and one voice topped another.

Our taste in people was catholic, ranging from artists, architects, stockbrokers, and writers to local politicians and—you might know—the chief of police and some of the men from the State Police headquarters not far away. We learned a little more about Russia's previous life from the police, and the more I heard the more thankful I was that Arthur had persuaded me out of an effort to locate the Senora and put her mind at ease about her cat. The police may have been prejudiced but they were certainly specific. Even if half of what they told was true, how had he come through that shambles of violence and brutality with his sweetness of nature intact, his manners unspoiled, his intelligence unmarred?

With the onset of cold weather the deficiencies of the house became tiresomely apparent. We didn't exactly regret our rash behavior—after all, it had brought us Russia—but two open winters in succession would be agin Nature, and what would life be like during a normal Westchester County winter?

Near mid-March we drove into the city for dinner with a writer and his wife whom we had last seen on the Riviera. They were living in luxury in an apartment hotel on Fifth Avenue. He had a play on Broadway and Hollywood was on its knees. Their Scottie had been left in Cannes until they could settle down, when he could be shipped home to them.

"We could run over and pick him up," Hope said largely, in his new role of successful playwright.

"Yes, Mr. Micawber," Dodo murmured.

"But you'll never desert me, will you?" Hope retorted.

Dodo said he'd better not count on it, and Arthur looked at his watch. It was one o'clock.

"The furnace will be out," he said resignedly. "And the pipes are frozen."

We didn't bother to peer between the heavy draperies that covered the windows.

The doorman said cheerfully, "Hope you can find your car. It's an honest-to-god blizzard."

For a moment we hesitated. Stay in town somewhere, or take a chance? We thought of the furnace and a hungry cat who could, of course, get in or out, but visions of broken waterpipes settled the question. We found the car without difficulty and as we brushed off the snow, Arthur muttered, "That guy's just an alarmist. There's more wind with a blizzard, at least where I grew up." We would find a filling station and have the chains put on, just in case Westchester was getting the same storm. The station we finally found was just putting out its lights, but the attendant, obviously of the opinion that mad people should be humored, helped with the chains. And as we turned north, the wind hit us.

"What velocity does the wind reach in a Midwest blizzard?" I asked conversationally.

Arthur growled, "Shut up and tell me where we are."

I rolled down my window and managed to see a sign. The wipers worked valiantly, but by the time we reached the Parkway the weight of the snow slowed them to a standstill. With head and neck out the window, I shouted directions against the screaming wind. It was a lonely world, where everyone was sane except us.

A snowplow had gone through and our heater—which we had given each other for Christmas—was doing its best. "We'll make it," we said jubilantly. I think it was then that a police car stopped us.

"Can't go no farther," the driver shouted. "Snowplows ain't been through."

Arthur said, "Ask him what we do. We're about half way. I think," he added under his breath.

After a prolonged shouting match, I reported that we were a little better than half way, that if we got stuck, nobody's gonna pull us out . . . If we go ahead, it's our funeral.

"I don't like that guy," Arthur muttered. "What do you say?"

I said, "Lay on, MacDuff," and we drove on.

All memory of that crazy ride is as vague as the swirling snow that surrounded us. I know we laughed a lot. The chains of course broke miles before we reached the turnoff to our road. The hill, we saw, was an Alp. And at that moment, the car went into an uncontrollable skid and dove headforemost into the ditch.

We climbed out somehow and made for the steps, or where we figured they should be. I had read about mountain climbers lying down in the snow to die, and I wanted nothing so much as to follow suit.

The front door, facing north, was blocked solid. "Back door," Arthur gasped. "Can you make it?" We beat our way around the building and as we turned the corner, we heard a cry. We called. Something struggled out of a drift not far from the cellar window that was always left open on a crack for Russia. I nearly fell headfirst trying to pick up a half-frozen cat. Caked in hard snow, he felt stiff in my arms.

I shouted, "Have you got the key? I think I left my bag in the car. Or dropped it."

The back door was comparatively protected, but the wind seemed to come from all directions and it was an eternity before the door opened. We fell inside. We were not sure that we had any feet.

Russia was so quiet, I thought he was dead.

The house was warm.

Arthur whispered, "My God," and it was a prayer of thanks. I put Russia down on the sofa. He wasn't dead, but I wondered why not. We, after all, had been protected by the car.

Arthur built up a roaring fire and went down to make love to the furnace. I unearthed half a bottle of cognac, heated milk for Russia, uncertain what to feed a cat half done for from exposure, then warmed up more milk and added a dollop of cognac. He promptly deserted the unadulterated nourishment.

What had happened to him? We guessed he had been on the prowl and on returning had found his window already blocked. He would stay near instinctively . . . but for how long? Arthur said naturally he wouldn't want to talk about an experience like that, but we did. Drinking hot toddies and sitting almost inside the fireplace, we managed to lift even the climb up the steps to the apex of hilarity.

Nevertheless, we were aware of somber undertones. This time the furnace had done its stuff. And this time we had hauled ourselves up steps invisible under deep snow and ice. The telephone line was down. One misstep and a broken limb, or a heart attack, and we would have been in bad trouble. As a general rule, might-have-beens are better left unspoken, but having aired this one, we looked at each other soberly, drank a special toast to making a move, and went to bed.

Russia was not in the habit of sleeping with us, but he came upstairs with alacrity, snuggled down at our feet, and began to purr. Each cat I have known has had an individual song. Russia's was deep and positive with a sustained organ note breaking into the regular cadence at unexpected intervals. It was a restful sound.

Arthur reached down to pull a corner of the quilt over him. The yellow eyes blinked in the gray light of a snowy day and the purr rose to a crescendo.

"A very fine cat," Arthur muttered sleepily. "Thank God we didn't turn back when those cops told us to."

I yawned. "They couldn't have dreamed up a surer way to keep us going, bless their hearts . . ."

❀ EIGHT ❀

The caretaker for a large estate near Pleasantville had built a house where he and his wife could live in solid comfort when he retired from his undemanding job. We rented it for a year. The place had many pleasant features but had been designed for Mrs. Swanson, and we never felt at home. When she decided there was no good reason to wait for retirement, we were bored and annoyed but not sorry. Mr. Swanson was more upset than we were and hesitantly suggested the estate owner might be persuaded to rent us the caretaker's cottage. We rather liked the idea; we seemed doomed to a nomadic life and if we could take it on a month-to-month basis, why not? Except for the Swansons and the remaining livestock, no one had lived there for years, and the owner, vastly amused at the idea of renting the cottage, gave Arthur permission to do anything we wanted with the house, except burn it down, Ha Ha.

There were bonuses we hadn't reckoned on. Water was piped from a private reservoir; there was a sizable pond where we could swim; a long, shallow pond visible from the house became a local skating rink in winter and a haven for migrating birds in spring. A level space in back, as big as a suburban lot, bordered by trees and fields, would be a cool refuge in summer; when we first moved in, Mrs. Swanson's chicken house occupied one corner and inadvertently set the tone for the coming summer.

One of the pullets found a way to escape from the coop. She was, without doubt, the most unattractive chicken imaginable. She had grown a few feathers here and there on her ungainly frame, she wobbled dangerously when she ran, her cackle was high and ear-splitting. Her presence among Mrs. Swanson's sturdy Rhode Island Reds was a mystery. She showed up the second day we lived there, eager and friendly as a puppy. Russia gave her one look, spit in her face, and ignored her from then on. Dopey's personality overcame her disabilities. It was impossible not to be fond of the little horror, and we encouraged her by giving her bits of cheese and crackers which she gobbled up and demanded more. We suspected the rest of the flock gave her a bad time, for she would eat anything in sight. She even nipped off the lighted end of a cigarette, considerably to our alarm, but before I could go for some vaseline, she had closed her beak, the ludicrous expression of surprise had vanished, and she was asking for more tidbits.

The next afternoon we saw Mr. Swanson feeding the chickens and asked him about Dopey. He looked embarrassed.

"Something went wrong in the egg," he muttered. "The Missis was after me to get rid of her, but by damn, the little thing was quicker and busier than the rest of the hatch. Made me sorta laugh. I kep' puttin' the Missis off." He gazed speculatively at Dopey who was trying to climb up Arthur's leg. "She bother you folks?"

We said no, not really. We couldn't help liking her, she was so spunky. Mr. Swanson brightened. "That's it," he said. "Spunky." His voice dropped conspiratorily. "Truth is, I don't think as much of chickens as the Missis does. Stupid, mostly. But this one . . . She's sick, though. 'Taint right." He added that the new coop would be ready maybe day after tomorrow and then he'd see . . .

During the next two days Dopey tried madly to get in the house, and then began running in circles and knocking herself against chairs and table legs and the side of the house. The evening was too cool to sit outdoors, but we caught Mr. Swanson and told him the latest developments.

"Well, that's it," he said, and stood hesitating by the back porch. "You folks've sure been kind to the pore thing. I'll take her now and . . . and thanks."

Mr. Swanson was a good farmer and a merciful man. We were sure Dopey didn't live to the end of our roadway. We rather missed her, and the next morning Mr. Swanson came with the truck and carted the rest of the chickens to their new home. Then he tore down the chicken house and discovered the hole Dopey had dug, as her secret escape route, in a dark corner. Arthur had gone to the city, and Mr. Swanson showed it to me with a sort of pride. He'd looked for it before, he said, but it was well hidden. "Pretty cute," he said admiringly. I liked him for that so much I helped him with the smelly job of cleaning up the chicken yard.

Without the Swansons' rooster to wake us, we might have slept late in the mornings, but the migrating ducks and geese dropping off at the shallow pond outside our windows took care of that. They were enchanting to watch on the water, exciting and beautiful when in flight, and sometimes we lazily wished we knew more about them, but soon they were gone and the pond was left to the blue herons who nested on the opposite shore where the trees came down to the water.

All the boundaries of the estate were lined with boldly lettered warnings prohibiting hunting and fishing, but the bog that edged the pond was its best protection. Frozen, the mud was no deterrent, but when the spring thaws set in, the wildlife of the pond and the bog was safe from intrusion. We watched from a distance, and almost immediately fell captive to a muskrat.

Even on cool mornings we drank our coffee with our feet hanging over the edge of the back porch where we had an uninterrupted view of the pond before the trees and bushes came into full leaf. Most conspicuous were the long-legged herons standing on one foot waiting for unwary fish and while admiring their beauty and laughing at their ungainly, high-stepping walk, we saw the wake of something small start from the shore near the herons, coming to our side and leaving a wash as straight as if it had been drawn with a T-square.

We were lucky enough to catch it going back a while later, and after that we watched the regular passage every day.

We named him Daniel Morgan, Washington's general who had the reputation of always reaching his objective. Our Daniel's objective was one patch of marsh grass on our shore, and on his way home he made a wider, three-cornered wake, and sometimes a few pieces of stiff grass would rise straight over his head, like the mast of a ship. I suppose we should have named him for a Naval hero, but Daniel Morgan pleased us better.

Sometimes we castigated ourselves for lack of initiative. Here we were in the midst of unspoiled natural surroundings, yet made no attempt to study, to learn, to investigate the lives of our wild neighbors. It was shocking. At the very least, there was the Britannica on our bookshelves, and an excellent library in Pleasantville.

"It would be more fun to write Cousin Nick, he'd know," I said, without thinking.

Cousin Nicholas, who had introduced me to sleeping bats and inspired me with a temporary ambition to be a geologist when I grew up, and who longed to know what the Something is that persists after our dust returns to dust— Cousin Nick had died years ago. When he was over ninety, perhaps by three years, he had gone to the West Coast because he wanted to see the Redwoods which he had, somehow, missed before. He had seen them, and a great deal more, and slept his life away, his active body and his restless mind ready at last to be still.

And instead of bothering with the Encyclopaedia or the library, I told Arthur about Cousin Nicholas and much about my grandfather he hadn't heard, and it was far more interesting, although it was all information neither one of us would make use of, and of no educational value whatever.

A few days later, Arthur had gone to the city, grumbling about the evils of work, for it was a lovely warmish day, and I was sitting under the greening trees, driving out of burning Moscow with the Rostovs. Natasha had just learned that André was dying of his wounds in a carriage behind her, when I came back to realize that I had been hearing extraordinary sounds—from the pond, or more likely, the bog.

Curiosity about Daniel Morgan's choice of building materials had led us once into an exploration trip, but all the mosquitoes and assorted bugs in Westchester County were holding a convention there, the mud tried to suck our sneakers off our feet, we floundered into unexpected little estuaries, and on the same day we were warned that among its other delights the bog boasted some areas of quicksand.

The possibility that a dog might be caught in the treacherous stuff leaped to my mind. Mr. Swanson had turned off the barn lane for the village, a few minutes before. There was no time to get help, if my guess was right, and I started down the steep bank leading to the pond. It was thick with wild blackberry bushes, tall weeds, old stumps, and fallen trees. The closer I came to the sounds the more they sounded like somebody struggling to free itself from—something. As I pushed my way through the mess of underbrush, horrible reasons why the dog didn't bark or—if a child—why it didn't cry, occurred to me and sent me slipping and sliding faster than before.

My foot slipped on a slimy hillock and I almost pitched headfirst on top of the biggest turtles I ever saw outside the Bronx Zoo. They were apparently fighting to the death, the muddy water roiled by their battle splashed over my feet and legs.

It's impossible now to say why I was so scared. If the creatures had been aware of me, they might have been more frightened than I, but that possibility did not cross my mind. Ignominiously I began to crawl up the boggy rise on my hands and knees until I reached dry ground. All my training had taught me that blind panic is shameful, reason told me that if I *had* fallen, the experience would have been unpleasant but not fatal—and I was shaking from head to foot. I smelled of something primitive and alien.

Safe in our yard, I called myself names. That helped, and I went upstairs and showered, and wasted a lot of the General's most recent present of Guerlain perfume.

When Arthur came home, he sniffed pleasurably. "Wow!" he remarked. "Where's the party?"

I had been of two minds about telling him what a fool I had made of myself, but of course I did. He called me all the names I had thought of and a few I had missed. Then he took me out to dinner at a roadhouse we had been avoiding because it was too expensive.

There was a curious lack of the more charming rodents on that property. Perhaps nut-bearing trees didn't thrive there, and of course by this time the chestnuts were dead. A pair of chipmunks chattered at us and sometimes would come close enough to nibble a cracker. A red squirrel decided to live in the small attic, but apparently he was a bachelor. Energetic guests who liked to tramp over fields and through woods said they saw snakes occasionally, but no one seemed to know what they were. I have seldom seen any sound excuse for walking and had reached an age where I wasn't ashamed to say so. The distance up to the swimming pond and back was enough for me, and Arthur could walk or leave it alone. Most of the five hundred acres were left to the deer, the pheasant, the grouse, the rabbits, and the birds.

The birds, plenty of them, came to us, anyway. Neither Russia nor the barn cats disturbed their conviction that the entire place was a bird sanctuary. Someone, out of pity, gave us a bird book, but by the time some exquisite creature had winged away into the woods, any reason for finding out its name seemed to vanish with it. I did learn to recognize a few; it was unavoidable, and given sufficient time, I might even have learned to accept their passion for telling the world *they* are Up and Awake at the crack of dawn; that malignant practice is their own business and why can't they keep quiet about it?

Robins were the only birds we ever knew Russia to catch, and those, of course, were babies. Robins are careless about their young which, it seemed to us, were forever falling out of the nests. Even Russia got bored with them early in the season and then Arthur, at the risk of breaking his neck, would pull out the tree ladder and try to get the infant back where it belonged, while the mother did her best to thwart him. He scratched himself bloody when one small robin got itself caught in a barbed wire fence, and it was too late anyway.

Old Tom took to ambling down from the barn. He was shy of us but, as Arthur said, he liked our grub. We had seen him sometimes on our way to the swimming pond, a battle-scarred veteran, a Maltese who must have been handsome in his youth. Most of the time, he and Russia seemed to get along amicably enough and we would see them now and then going out in the fields together, presumably on hunting trips. However, when Russia overstepped some sort of boundary line Old Tom was quite capable of sending our larger, black-and-white male staggering down the path for first aid, but when he realized that we actually lived on the place, the Maltese slowly began to make overtures. We were flattered and Russia's expression of superiority when Old Tom discovered the taste of beef liver was worth the price of admission. None of the females came to see us, and a half-grown kitten who started down the path was chased home immediately.

We never went inside the barns without Mr. Swanson's permission, but felt free to talk to his cows when they were in the pasture. They were a motley lot. There was a big-boned brindle; three nondescript browns; a little brindle who was bullied by her mama; a pretty "Jersey" whose mother had been careless; and a stocky, pushy character with the proper Holstein black-and-white markings but much undersized for that breed. It seemed to me the owner, even though absentee, might have put together a more distinguished herd, but Mr. Swanson said they were all good milch cows, which was what counted. In the late afternoon light, the pasture might have been painted by Constable or Millais, with its sun-dappled grass, spreading trees, and a brook running down to the pond.

When Hope and Dodo came for a weekend, we took them along the lane to admire the picture. Lights and shadows were exactly right and, led by the big brindle, all the girls came galumphing to the fence to whiffle in our faces and ask what we had brought them. In the field back of the house some special sort of grass grew which they dearly loved and I had picked an armful for them.

Dodo said, "Oh, what darlings! I think I'd like to be a milkmaid. I'm so tired of our rackety life."

"Milkmaids must be buxom," Hope remarked decisively. "It's an unbreakable convention, probably started by the big butter-and-milk boys. I'm afraid there's no opening right now. Just leave your name and address, dearie, and I'll be in touch if something opens up."

On Monday the weather turned hot, and the two men went off to the city, cursing their hard luck. Dodo had announced she was going to stay, at least until the next day, or maybe she'd *never* leave.

"Good," said Arthur, giving her a hearty kiss and a smack on the fanny. "I've always wanted a harem. Life with just one woman gets monotonous. Nothing ever happens."

Having washed the dishes and made the beds, Dodo and I were relaxing in deck chairs and planning lunch.

"A sandwich and iced tea," Dodo suggested. "Or maybe, gin and tonic. We didn't drink up all the gin, did we?"

I replied loftily that there was plenty of gin. "We always spend our last penny on liquor when you and Hope come out. No sacrifice is . . ." I sat up suddenly. "What's *that?*"

The lane that led beyond the pasture fence into the back fields and upper woods narrowed to a footpath down a gentle slope to our vegetable garden. The trampling and crashing sounded like a herd of . . .

"Cows!" I exclaimed, and ran.

There they all were, led by the big brindle, making straight for the succulent corn, the juicy tomatoes, the lettuce, the herbs, the leafy cantaloupe plants.

"Towels," I shouted at Dodo. "Anything I can wave at them. They've got to be headed off somehow."

How did you head off seven cows who had grown three times the size of the gentle pets in the pasture? What would Granddad have suggested? My mind was a blank, except for the determination that if they got into Arthur's garden, it would be over my dead body.

I had succeeded in giving them pause for thought, anyway. The troops were milling around behind their brindled leader who was regarding me with bovine surprise but a set look in her eye that boded no good. Dodo ran up with her hands full of bath towels. Good girl, she had brought one for herself.

Dodo's appearance had confused the brindle a little, and I think they might have turned aside, but the pseudo-Holstein pushed her way forward, her head lowered. Stepping forwards, I snapped the towel in her face, the brindle took the lead again and swung to her right, towards the grass, the flower garden, and Mrs. Swanson's rhubarb bed. I breathed again—but the vegetable garden was equally vulnerable from the lawn.

For the moment they were pretending to be Ferdinand among the flowers, which wouldn't entertain them long. I gave a despairing thought to the asparagus bed, but you can't cover all fronts at once. Dodo and I conferred briefly on strategy, and I saw that damned would-be Holstein looking in our direction. We advanced deliberately. If we could head them uphill along the path to the barns, Dodo could leave me and telephone the Swansons.

Unexpectedly, they all began to walk towards us. They weren't hurrying, they were just coming at us with the inexorability of a freight train. We yelled. We flapped our towels. I wanted a stone, but in the hope of making a lawn, Arthur had carefully picked up odd stones and put them in a pile—beyond the corn and tomato plants.

They advanced, but it seemed to me under divided leadership. Gasping to Dodo to take care of the brindle, I went for the pygmy Holstein. I was hating that animal with every fiber of my being, and throwing caution to the winds, I ran straight at her, too enraged even to scream.

She flung up her head, and turned. No one, except possibly the big brindle, was more surprised than I. Then she galloped ungracefully around the side of the house. I shouted at Dodo to stand guard in case they turned back, and ran to the narrow pass between the garage and the fence, which led in a beeline to the garden. I would hold them there, I thought wildly, like the Spartans at Thermopylae . . .

And then I heard a car coming up our road.

Mr. Swanson, on his way home from the village, had caught sight of his precious cows bursting around the side of the house into the front field. Within a few seconds, he had the situation under control. With soothing noises and unmistakable authority, he got them up the hill and into the barn, wasting no time on two crazy women whose antics had undoubtedly ruined the day's milk supply.

He took the short cut from the barn to the pasture and was looking embarrassed when he reached us. Part of the pasture fence was down. He couldn't understand it . . .

From the depths of a deck chair, I said, "Watch out for that smarty-pants Holstein, she's capable of anything."

He drank the beer Dodo, unasked, had brought him. "Maybe you're right," he said slowly. "I'm sure sorry you ladies had such a fright."

"Oh, we weren't frightened," Dodo assured him brightly. "It was nothing, really. We were just keeping them out of the vegetable garden. Otherwise, the dear girls could have had the run of the place," and she winked at him. I had never heard Mr. Swanson laugh so hard.

After he had gone, apologizing again but still chuckling, we went for a swim. The two elderly horses, whom we called Darby and Joan, swam out from their shady cove to join us.

As Dodo fed them sugar tablets, she said, "Remind me to whip up some cyanide for that black-and-white monster. In fact, while I'm about it, I'll make enough for the whole bunch. I've changed my mind about living the good life."

After Labor Day, we took an early train on weekdays and seldom got home before dark. Russia was alone, but we didn't think about that at first. He was free to come and go, he had a full life of his own, he wasn't dependent on us for entertainment or interests or even food for the barn cats were well fed and Mr. Swanson seemed fond of him. Even when we found him waiting at home, night after night, we didn't worry: the house was more comfortable than out-of-doors. Towards the end of December we changed our tune.

He had taken one of the living room chairs for his own and we noticed that the cushion looked as if he had slept on it for hours. He had always been glad to see us come in; now his welcome seemed tinged with surprise: "Well, hurray! So you got here after all. I was beginning to wonder . . ." After he had eaten, he went back to his chair. Without talking about it, we began to refuse parties in the city, even dinner; we made an effort to catch the first train we could, and drove a little faster from the station.

We remembered his devil-may-care swing as he crossed the field to the house on the hill. When had he lost it? He was so much part of our lives, we had paid little attention to changes, as one may say of a son, "Why, he's a middle-aged man! How did he get that way?" Or of oneself: "I'm old. When did it happen?"

We asked our acquaintance, the local veterinarian, to take a look at him. Come out and have a drink, we said, we'd rather not scare him by taking him to a strange place. He laughed, but he came. He felt Russia's body, his legs, looked into his eyes, his mouth, but as if he were just making friends.

"He's well along in years," he said. "You don't know? Well, it's not premature senility. He's just slowing down. He's not sick. He's not unhappy. What more do you want?"

He was happy when we were at home. He was far too happy when we came back to him after a day's absence. The money we were earning was important. Economic conditions in general were easier, but we had a talent for being out of step, and we saw no way out of our dilemma except to give up our fun-evenings in the city, which wasn't difficult. We were getting older, too.

The winter passed. Arthur worked in the garden on weekends. Russia lay in the sun and blinked at us comfortably, but he had lost the spring in his back legs. Baby robins, field mice, moles, small snakes were unmolested. When the weather turned nasty, which it did very soon, he went back to his chair. When it wasn't raining, it drizzled; the best crop that year would be mildew.

Standing on one foot scraping mud off his shoes, Arthur said, "Thank God Ruth and James are coming over for the Fourth. The weekend will be wet—but more fun than this."

Russia stepped disdainfully around the house, picking his way through wet grass. He stopped, washed one foot, and looked at Arthur who had turned his attention to the other shoe. I burst out laughing. Their expressions of disgust and offended dignity were identical. Russia thought I was laughing at him, and announced that he wanted to go in the back door and I could jolly well open it for him, he wasn't going to wade through any more mud to reach the cellar.

He walked into the house, switching his tail, his head high. Amazingly, he had grown more beautiful with age. There was a fine-drawn quality about him now that can be seen in some old people who have made good use of their years and waste no time on regret for the present or fear of the future. Since his carnal interests had waned, his sleek black coat was polished and his well-shaped ears were unmarred. How splendid if we could all grow in beauty as we grow in age . . .

Ruth and James were disgruntled by the weather and worried by civil war in a country they loved. We gathered in the living room with the proper refreshments while rain beat against the windows. An afternoon shower, Arthur called it.

"You wait," James said gloomily, "this business in Spain is just a match in a powder keg, and the next war I'm going to sit out. I'm going to be an Isolationist. I'll go AWOL before the Army catches me."

Ruth said soothingly, "Darling, if the Army saw you in your present revolting condition, the whole lot would go over the hill before you could wobble up to the nearest recruiting station."

"Oh, he's not all *that* bad," Arthur said judiciously. "A few months, say a year, of good clean living and they'd give him his sergeant's stripes in a flash."

"Hell," roared James, "*I* was an officer and a gentleman, you little squirt. *You* were the sergeant."

"Master sergeant," Arthur pointed out. "And non-coms are the backbone of the Army. Kipling said that—I think—and he ought to know."

It was a red rag to a bull. Probably out of sheer contrariness, James claimed to detest Kipling and all his works. Elaborate insults ricocheted off the walls. Russia, ears pricked, eyes bright, got under a table.

"If they get it out of their systems early," Ruth said comfortably, "we might have a little intelligent conversation."

"Like what?"

"Oh," she replied vaguely. "Politics. Art. Have you seen any good plays recently? Books . . . that kind of thing."

"We haven't seen you for so long, you've forgotten what they're like when they get together."

She grinned. "I haven't, really. Let's leave the old buddies alone before they get mad at each other. I hate that."

So did I, but it never lasted long. Walking boldly between the firing lines, I knelt down to tell Russia he'd be welcome in the kitchen with Ruth and me. "They won't come to blows," I assured him. "At least, they never have." I stroked him and got a quick lick on my hand. He looked rejuvenated.

When Arthur came out to get more ice, James followed him, with Russia at his heels; there was a lull on the Westchester Front but Russia seemed hopeful that hostilities would break out again at any moment. He had the instincts of a war correspondent.

For a wonder, Arthur's "afternoon shower" had stopped and when we ambled up to the pond to see Darby and Joan, Russia came along running ahead almost in his old form. Hoping that his *joie de vivre* would not involve him in competition with the younger generation, several of whom were his own progeny, I warned him to expect neither sympathy nor first aid. He twitched his tail and went into the barnyard.

Old Sol pulled up his socks and prepared to go down in a burst of glory, so we dragged the deck chairs out of hiding and sat on the front porch. Traffic on our quiet back road was unusually heavy; across the field we caught glimpses of all the jaloppies in the neighborhood and a number of high-powered sports cars we hadn't seen before. Russia watched the passing cars from a dry patch under one of the thick pines, where he also had an unobstructed view of James and Arthur. Ruth said lazily she never wanted to move, and that reminded me of something. Reluctantly, I broke the news that we had agreed to have dinner at the Country Club and watch the fireworks from the terrace.

"We're not members," Arthur explained, "because we're snobs, you understand, but we know all the Right People. We warned them about you, James, but they insisted . . ."

"We'll go," James said. "Our presence might persuade them to offer you a free membership."

By the time dark came—and a light patter of rain—we had stored up enough energy to think rather well of the idea. Ruth said it would save her from having to get dinner for us all; Arthur mumbled something about veterans showing the flag, to which James retorted that he knew one uppity non-com who was so short-sighted he couldn't tell the difference between the Kraut flag and the Glorious Stars and Stripes Forever . . . and we all went upstairs to dress.

Russia looked disappointed when he saw us leaving and Ruth wanted to take him along. I promised him we'd be back early and there would be tomorrow for more of the kind of fireworks he liked.

After the first flares exploded against the black sky, I lay back in my luxurious lounge chair and thought about our fine life and had some ideas about the manuscript I was editing, which looked terrible in the cold post-holiday light, and we left as soon as we decently could. The weather had cleared, temporarily at least, and a moon we had almost forgotten about rode high in a star-spangled sky. Russia was nowhere to be seen. We decided he was either paying us back for leaving him or, more likely, had been overexcited by his earlier visit to the barn.

I woke late, to hear voices and activities in the kitchen, thought, "Ruth's taking care of the boys," and dropped back to sleep.

When I wandered downstairs, the house was empty. The sun was shining and I sat on the edge of the back porch with a cup of coffee and felt warm and dry for the first time that summer.

Ruth came around the side of the house. She sat down beside me.

"It's Russia," she said, without preamble. "He was run down last night. He couldn't have felt anything. The boys have just buried him. Under the big pine out front."

After a minute or two, I said, "Who found him?"

She said, "Arthur." She didn't know why he had gone down to the road. They had noticed Russia's continued absence but had decided to let me sleep; he would show up in his own good time.

I dropped from the porch to the ground and went to meet Arthur.

He said, "It's all right. You didn't want to see him, did you?" He was pale and calm. We looked at each other for a moment.

James said, "Struck on the head. Merciful. Hope somebody does it to me."

Ruth had put a fresh cup of coffee on the porch and I picked it up. The sun was hot on my face and arms. I said, "He had a glorious time with you two idiots. Happy ending . . . Do you think it's warm enough for a swim?"

Word got around fast. Friends called to commiserate, and we wished they wouldn't. The holiday visitors with their fast cars had left a trail of minor disasters behind them. One woman complained that nothing was safe any more, and I said Russia was old, his reactions were slow, and hung up rather abruptly. The telephone rang before I could get out of the room.

A clear English voice said, "Look, there's only one thing that makes sense. I know. Start fresh. Immediately, if you can. I'll be right over."

I was alone. Arthur had gone to the city, but I had the day off, a bit of holiday generosity I could, right then, have done without. What on earth did Elsie have up her sleeve? She looked as fragile as a piece of Venetian glass but there was nothing breakable about her will power. She made me nervous, and I attacked the weeds in the flower garden with unaccustomed vigor; the sun was out but the ground was still wet and a fair half of the garden looked almost professionally neat when a car skidded to a stop behind the garage, plowing a rut into part of Arthur's "lawn."

Elsie called through a cautiously opened window, "Sorry, but I didn't dare let the zoo out by myself and I guessed you'd be back here."

Fastened by leashes in the back seat were two black cats. They were full-grown, but young. They had yellow eyes and modest white vests. One was blazing with fury, the other seemed placidly interested in its unusual situation.

Elsie said briskly, "I looked for something to carry them in but there didn't seem to be anything big enough to hold them." She unwound their leashes from the blanket rope, and added, "Leave those damned collars and the leads on for a while. Slow them down a bit, you know."

They were twins, altered males and in need of a home because their people were moving to England and, Elsie said, "My native land is stuffy about immigrants." She didn't have to explain why she didn't keep them, she had four, two of them females who would have been charter members of Women's Lib if it had been thought of then. This wasn't a temporary arrangement—if we liked them, that is. Did I want to wait until Arthur came home before deciding?

The angry one was trying his best to bite his leash off. The other was trying to wash it away and I snapped it loose. Elsie looked embarrassed. "They're really nice people," she said. "They just don't know much about cats." Between us, we managed to get hold of Angry long enough to get the leash off, whereupon he vanished into the back field.

"Names?" I asked, as I removed Placid's collar.

"I hate to tell you. Lancelot and Guinevere. But don't worry, mostly they were called pet names. I don't think they've heard the others often enough to recognize them."

Elsie left rather hurriedly. (She admitted later she was terrified that I would refuse to take them.) And I caught Arthur at the Museum just as he was leaving for the train. His reaction had been a stunned silence, and I waited for him with mounting trepidation. It was useless, though I tried, to blame my spinelessness on that mysterious British quality which has thrown strong nations off base.

While I waited, the cats decided they were hungry and I fed them in the kitchen. They looked around, smelled Russia, went upstairs, came down . . . Recklessly, I showed them the cellar with its merry brook, and how to get in and out. The quiet one curled up in my lap while I sat on a kitchen chair and tried to figure out what I had done—and why.

By the time I heard the car come up our lane, I was half sick. I had cried for Russia, while the cat on my lap purred and rubbed against my arm. He had an even, gentle purr, unlike Russia's basso profundo. The other cat stood by the door and said he wanted to go out. I said, no, he had to wait for Arthur. He gave me an indignant look, thought for a minute, and made for the cellar. He's bright enough, I thought, and almost against my will stroked the black fur on my lap.

The other had been momentarily baffled by the swinging door to the cellar, and when he heard the front door open he went down the hall like a shot and I heard Arthur say, "Hey, let's have a look . . ." and the door slam shut. Arthur came into the kitchen with the cat squirming in his arms.

"Didn't you say two?" he asked.

We named them Talleyho and Talleyrand, for no reason that I can remember. Perhaps Elsie's theory was right. Certainly, the two cats were distracting, and it was better to come home to them than to an empty house. Old Tom never came near us again.

The new cats were beautiful and intelligent, and within a week Talleyrand had run away. He returned after a couple of days, and seemed quite pleased to see us, but soon he left for a longer stay. He was a wanderer and a hunter, and his life would, we assumed, be short. Freedom suited him. He grew leaner and bigger and more muscular; his coat might be untidy but his eyes were bright with, we imagined, the same sort of faraway look we knew from the eyes of a friend who could no more live long away from the wild places of the earth than Talleyrand could stay within the confines of a house, a lawn, a garden, a field; he didn't want a home any more than Bud Holdridge did. What Matto Grosso was to Bud, the untouched woods and fields around us were to Talleyrand. He reminded me of those urban mavericks of my childhood, Flotsam and Jetsam, who had come and gone as the whim took them.

But Talleyrand was a loner.

Talleyho was glad to see him but not bothered by his absence. Talleyho wasn't bothered by much of anything. He had a happy, loving, generous personality. He was so sensitive to our moods that when we were depressed or worried we tried to conceal it from Talleyho, but he knew anyway, so we stopped that nonsense and made him one with us. We had plenty to trouble us in the months that followed.

The estate was to be cut up into building lots. Superior lots, to be sure, of two, three, or four acres each. The caretaker's cottage was to be remodeled; we were, as I remember it, given first option to buy the place, but the idea was so ridiculous that my memory may be at fault. A great deal of ourselves had gone into that house and the land around it. We felt lost.

One evening Arthur said abruptly, "Remember that night we drove home in the blizzard? Climbing those damned steps? You said you just wanted to lie down in the snow and never mind what happened? Well, I feel like that now."

Talleyho had been sitting on a table by an open window, looking out at something invisible to us in the dark, but as Arthur spoke the cat turned his head, jumped down, and went to him. Arthur made room in his chair and the cat settled down with his chin on Arthur's knee. It was the kind of thing Talleyho did which made him special.

In the end we took the easiest way out. Our friend, the real estate agent, found a "darling house" in the next community north where most of our friends lived. I guess it was "darling," but it and we had nothing to say to each other.

Not long after we moved, Elsie brought us a kitten. We didn't want a kitten, but this one was so funny, so pretty, so crazy that we found her irresistible. Elsie said of course we wouldn't mind having a female because she could be spayed, and Talley would have company while we were away. The kitten had an absurd way of twisting her rear end and we named her Funny Fanny.

Talley seemed to find her an endless source of entertainment. So did most of our friends of whom we now saw a great deal, since the darling house was, so to speak, cheek by jowl with the homes of the majority of people we knew in the area. I was the first to walk out on a Funny Fanny show.

She was a tireless performer, she never heard an exit line. She was a scene stealer. No praise was too gross, no applause too prolonged. Much was forgiven her for she was a beauty and a comedian. When she bent herself into a U-shape and wriggled, with a comical look over her shoulder—Am *I* doing that?—it was as funny as any vaudeville act I ever saw. Her high jumps were spectacular even at that age, and as graceful as a ballerina's. If we had been hunting for social acceptance, she would have been a real asset. She could always command an audience, even if it were only Talley, who watched her antics with such sincere admiration and delight that it made the applause of her human audiences seem affected. Her repertoire was quite extensive, all things considered, but it had its limits and the only member of the family who didn't tire of it was Talley. Funny Fanny wasn't very bright and there was a quality about her—something I couldn't put my finger on—that occasionally gave me a twinge of discomfort.

When we drove her to the veterinarian's hospital, I cuddled her tenderly for she was terrified of the car, and I was sorry for her and a little anxious; it was a tricky operation and after the anesthetic wore off she would hurt. Arthur was looking rather grim, and if we hadn't reached the vet's at that moment I think we would have called the whole thing off and taken our chances on Funny Fanny in the role of Mother.

I put her in the hands of a pleasant-faced attendant at the door, and went slowly back to the car. As we started off, we heard a shout behind us. The attendant was standing on the path still holding the kitten in his hands.

"Hey!" he called. "Lady, this here's . . . it ain't a female. It's a male. Want to pick him up tomorrow?"

We laughed so hard, Arthur finally pulled up at the side of the road. "I can't see," he gasped, wiping his glasses. "What do we do now?"

"Have ourselves a good lunch somewhere. Think of all the money we've saved. And call Elsie."

At the restaurant we crowded into a telephone booth. Elsie said nothing for a couple of breaths. Then, "Dear me, you do have all the luck, don't you?"

We told her she had put us through great suffering and the least she could do was to give us a proper name for the changeling.

"Francis, of course," she said promptly. "Whatever else?"

The steps that led from the road to the darling house were as long and steep as those to the house on the hill, though in better condition. The back of the property was almost entirely occupied by an enormous rock garden, there was no level space even for a small vegetable garden. Its complete privacy had been one of the points that sold us, but it was the privacy of a prison cell. We were within walking distance of people we liked and knew very well, but we saw too much of them. We weren't in the country; we were in a suburb that didn't have the honesty to face the facts about itself.

Arthur persuaded the owner that he could rent the house more easily in the summer than later on, the lease was canceled, and we moved back to the city in the middle of a heat spell.

We had escaped the good life, and none too soon.

❂ NINE ❂

We should have learned to expect the unexpected from the cats in our life, but we entirely miscalculated the reactions of the present incumbents to city living. Talley had spent his time out of doors when we weren't around. He didn't mind cold or even snow; he hunted. Francis preferred the warm house, we never saw any evidence that he hunted, we had to keep a pan for him even after he grew out of kittenhood, snow sent him into a panic.

But what happened when we dumped them into a city flat? Talley adjusted immediately. Francis acted as if we had maliciously deprived him of everything he held dear. He sulked, he cried, he scratched at the door, street traffic frightened him, he even balked at using his pan.

We were still unpacking cartons when a fire broke out in a building across the street—a wastebasket, the superintendent of our place reported—and fire-fighting equipment of every variety roared and screamed outside our first-floor front window. Francis bolted under the sofa in the dining room at the other end of the railroad-type apartment and stayed there for two hours after peace had been restored.

Quivering with excitement, Talley stationed himself at the floor-to-ceiling living-room window, where he had a front-row seat and didn't miss a thing. When the last siren died away, he couldn't believe the show was over but stayed at his post peering hopefully at the flow of ordinary traffic. That was his introduction to the delights of traffic-watching; it never palled.

The long, narrow apartment had disadvantages but happened to suit our needs at the time, and we liked it. The kitchen, at the rear, was large, square, and sunny. We used the dining room as a sitting room, and fixed up the big front room as a more formal place for entertainment, business, and otherwise. Off the front room was a room we turned into an office, for Arthur was setting up his own business, in which I would be an active partner after the new year. While Francis acted like a spoiled child, Talley shared our excitement and hopeful expectations. He tried to pull Francis out of the doldrums but the younger cat was playing a tragic role—something out of Ibsen, perhaps, or one of the gloomier Russians. He annoyed us and we left the thankless task of coaxing him back to normal (whatever that was) to Talley.

The change came suddenly. An unusually high, ornate mantelpiece soared above a small and unusable fireplace, lending a surprising accent of elegance and grace to the long room. We had arranged several decorative objects along it, and were admiring our artistry when Francis slunk out from under something and, to our astonishment, joined us. We pretended we didn't notice and he looked up at the mantelpiece. Then he jumped. That's wrong: he floated. It was beautiful, neat, exact. Not a piece of bric-a-brac so much as trembled. It deserved applause and got it. Talley sat still and gazed up at him adoringly.

After that he became, as Arthur said, "normally abnormal."

Was "togetherness" a popular word then? Whether it was or not, that was what we had. Even in the "darling" house, the four of us were not cooped up unless we wanted it that way. Now either Arthur or I or both were likely to be working in our office, the cats had plenty of space but within four walls. Francis could always make his moods felt. We thought, rather naïvely, that it might help if we could figure out what made him tick.

After the revelation that Funny Fanny was not what she

appeared to be, we had idly speculated about her-his psychology. Krafft-Ebing was old stuff but the general subject was riding high. Homosexuality was weightily discussed, even though most of us had been more or less aware of it since puberty. If Francis was normally abnormal, Arthur was abnormally normal and, moreover, had been lucky or unusually selective in his choice of friends. I had not, and had dipped into more books on psychopathology than he had, so I could talk rings around him and, I am ashamed to say, did. He liked or disliked the homosexuals we knew, men or women, for other and better reasons than their physical or emotional bias, which he regarded as "none of our damned business." But Francis was underfoot and our responsibility because we had chosen to make him so.

Looked at objectively, this point of view seems absurd. He was a neuter—thanks to a small incision—he was only a cat, and a cat's life, at best, is short. Who cared? Why did we? Perhaps our pride was touched. Neither of us had lived with an unhappy cat or dog; unhappy, that is, within itself not because of external situations or events. Francis was unhappy. Francis was "insecure." Why? Had Funny Fanny been unhappy? Not as long as she received the praise she craved. Physiologically, Funny Fanny had been as male as Francis; the error was human. (About then, I think we wandered off into the still-green field of artificial sex changes in humans.) In general, we agreed that Funny Fanny had been happy and "secure." Should we, I tentatively suggested, try to build up his ego?

Arthur exploded. "Ego! His ego outranks Mussolini's," and we fell into a game of naming historic egos against which to pit our cat's.

These discussions, more weighted with verve than erudition, took place intermittently until their inconclusiveness bored us, and Francis, hearing his name, would listen with apparent attention while Talley, the psychologically untroubled, dozed contentedly. And all the while there was a simple answer: He needed our love. It was a weird little twist of the tragic component that lies at the root of comedy. But if we had understood, what would that have availed Francis? Each of us knew from experience that mere affection, good intentions, effort, pretense, pity, yield only artificial fruit without a core.

In the office we had two desks, at which we faced each other, typewriters, a duplicating machine, filing cabinets, and bookshelves. Arthur had designed the shelves but had no time to build and set them up, and the carpenter he hired spent more time playing with Francis than working. When Arthur protested, the man said, "Look, mister, me old woman has the asthma so we can't have no cats. I won't charge you regular, we'll work it out." We badly needed the shelves, but the attention and activity seemed to help Francis adjust to the apartment and that was worth some inconvenience.

Talley was becoming something of a neighborhood showpiece, as Impo had been on Amity Street. A woman who lived upstairs stopped me in the hall one day to say, "I watch for your black cat in the window. I never liked cats much, they're sneaky, but that one, why, she just seems to smile right at me! Like she knew me."

I didn't fluster her by asking her to come in and meet the paragon, but I did bring in a strange man who had tipped his hat and said, "Excuse me, but isn't that cat in the window yours? I think I've seen you talking to it." He looked shy. "Not prying, honestly, but my wife died not long ago and she loved cats and used to talk to them."

On impulse, I said, "Want to come in and meet him?"

He was startled, but followed me. Talley came to him immediately, as if in recognition, and for a moment I thought the stranger was going to cry. Francis, of course, made an entrance, but got rather short shrift. Arthur came home while he and Talley were still expressing mutual approval. I've forgotten his name, but he came back quite often. He was a draftsman in the office of an architect we happened to know slightly, but Arthur promised he'd beat me black and blue if I invited any other strange men in, on any excuse. I advised him not to make promises he couldn't keep, but I didn't push my luck.

Then we acquired a "daily help." I had forgotten how dirty New York could be, but we couldn't afford to look grimy—the living room was used for interviews as well as entertaining, the ceilings were high, the cornices old-fashioned, and beyond my reach in any case. I spoke to the Scandinavian superintendent whom we liked. He looked thoughtful and said he'd look around.

That Sunday morning we were in the dining-sitting room surrounded by Sunday papers when the back doorbell rang. The super stood at the door with a taller man behind him. He jerked his thumb.

"This here's Jek," he said. "Friend of mine. He needs work. British sailor. Knows how to scrub down the decks . . ."

Arthur said, "Come on in. Have some coffee."

Both men were clean and neat and, I thought, looked rather morning-afterish. Jack's eyes were blue, but the whites were red-streaked. He was carefully shaved but had cut his chin. He had been in the British Navy and insisted on showing us his "papers" as proof. It was a grimy, brief document. He was, or had been, Able Seaman, his name was signed in copperplate script that made our scrawls seem illiterate. He said he had gone to a Council School in London. Yes, he had served in the War. On his uppers now, he said. Couldn't do any "regular" work, "had a bad ticker," the doc told him.

"Regular work," of course, meant loading and unloading on the docks, or ditch digging. I had known similar traps snap shut on men in Chelsea, and I asked if he was married.

He grinned sheepishly. "Never got up me nerve, Lady," he said, "but I can keep yer 'ouse neat as a new pin, Lady. Honest."

"How do you feel about cats?" I asked.

He looked over at the chair in the sunny window where the two cats were curled up together, watching the company. With a glance at me for permission, he stood up and moved slowly towards them. Talley rose and sniffed the gnarled hand held out to him. Francis rolled over voluptuously. When he came back to the table, he was grinning a little. "Me mum," he began. Then, "Know what a Maltese is, Lady, Sir? Well, she had one when I was a little tyke. Me da, he brought it from Malta, the island, y'know. Never forgot that cat."

I took him through the apartment and showed him what I wanted done. I said we both would be out sometimes and he would be alone with the cats. His face lighted up. "They'd be safe with me, Lady."

I guessed he was a wino. The signs aren't hard to recognize. He would at times drink heavily of the cheapest, most horribly adulterated stuff usually miscalled wine, but would probably leave our liquor supply alone. His beverage seems to kill all taste for anything better, rots the gut, and softens the brain.

"No drinking on the job, Jack," I said.

He looked shocked. "No, Lady," he said and crossed his heart.

"Where do you live?"

"The Bo'sun—that's what he was when I knowed him first on North Sea duty—he'll doss me down. Got a cot I can use. His missis, mebbe you know, she took the long voyage a while back."

I thought I'd leave the Bo'sun out of the business end, and we settled on terms before going back to the others.

When they left, the super whispered to me, "Lissen, he's honest. Stake me life on it. You won't regret it, missus."

But I said to Arthur, "We're going to regret this. I've got a feeling in my bones."

"Well, why did you do it then?" he asked reasonably.

"Partly because I like him and partly because I didn't have the feeling until too late."

We did regret it, but not for any cause we could have imagined then.

Jack made an admirable audience for Francis, but it was Talley who had his heart. He soon caught on to our way of talking to the cats and sometimes I would hear Jack talking to Talley in the kitchen: "When me da died, me mum she was up against it proper . . ." or, "Me da was a sailor, too. Only merchant, y'unnerstand . . ." Talley knew more about Jack than we did.

His accent was a conglomerate of Cockney and dockside New York, and I can't reproduce it. His grammar was amazingly good, and the occasional written messages he would leave were, visually, almost works of art. He would have taken over all the housework, including cooking, if I had let him. Arthur said the place was so clean it made his eyes hurt. Jack stayed off his ghastly tipple for a long time, then fell with a thud. I told him to get out and not come near us until I could see the whites of his eyes.

He sobered up very quickly and I was convinced Talley was responsible. When he showed up, shame-faced, Talley met him, waving his tail happily, purring, and rubbing against his legs, and Jack cried.

Francis was jealous, but Francis was something of a snob. He liked Jack's admiration, but never went in the kitchen without some good reason. It seemed to me Jack was aware of this discrimination, but I also thought he didn't care because Talley made up for any snubs from Francis. If the black cat weren't waiting for him in the morning—which seldom happened—we would hear him call softly so as not to disturb us: "Talley, luv, Talley, luv . . ." But when Francis' big moment came, he wanted Jack's huzzahs added to ours.

Between the dining room and the kitchen was a narrow hall, with closets along one side and the bathroom on the other. The apartment ceilings were ten feet high, but these closets had been a later addition, of shoddy construction, thin wood, and none too steady on their hinges. We used them because we had to, and Arthur cursed them roundly every time.

For once we had an evening with no work hanging over our heads, and were settled comfortably in the dining-sitting room, reading for pleasure not profit, glad that Jack had finished in the kitchen and was no longer singing sea chanteys or less innocent ditties in his surprisingly tuneful voice. Talley was taking up all the room on the sofa between us and Francis was prowling in and out of the hall.

"What's the prima donna so restless about?" Arthur asked.

"He wants to get in the closet. He's fallen in love with your galoshes."

Groaning, Arthur got up and opened the nearest closet door. "Open Sesame," he told Francis and went back to his book.

A slight unidentifiable sound startled us. The sleazy door was swinging gently. From its top a tiger cat looked down at us, yellow eyes gleaming with triumph.

Arthur's whisper was awestruck. "That's plywood. It can't be more than an inch wide. It's impossible." He walked over to the door and said, "Where's the mirror? Going in for prestidigitation?" Francis beamed down at his five-feet-ten. Standing beside him, Talley cried. Arthur said quickly, "Don't jump against the door. He'll fall." Francis moved slightly and the door wobbled.

"How will he get down?" I was standing with the other two. "He's no lightweight. He'll hurt his feet if he jumps." I looked up at our gorgeous cat and said, "Now you've topped yourself. What are you going to do next?"

We gave Francis his meed of praise, sorry Jack wasn't around to add his voice. Should we get the super's ladder for The Descent? Arthur was doubtful. "It might be a case of Humpty Dumpty falling off a wall, only there'd be two of us. I don't believe I could manage it."

Finally we left Talley to watch by himself.

"ASPCA?" I asked. "Fire Department?"

"Not the Police?" Arthur teased. "Fifteenth Precinct isn't far. You could run down there and get acquainted. Unless, of course, that front is already covered."

The telephone rang in the office. It was for Arthur, and in the few minutes we were out of the room, Francis had solved his own problem and, like a champion, was getting a rubdown from Talley. Apparently, he wasn't proud of that part of the act, or he would have waited. He was wrong there. The door was still swinging slightly, a few faint scratches could be seen. When we first accidentally caught him on the way down, it took our breath away. Head first, he *ran* down . . .

Being Francis, he couldn't leave well enough alone. He had to show the world. Jack never did get over the wonder of it all, but for Arthur and me, and even loyal Talley, repetition took the edge off. Now that he knew he could do it—probably he hadn't been quite sure the first time—the act became a matter of course. It was never commonplace for the leap itself was superbly beautiful, but the element of surprise had gone. Arthur measured the door: nine feet exactly, but he had underestimated the width of the wood, one inch and a half.

One of our friends remarked, "That isn't a leap or a jump or anything material. It's an act of levitation. He could make a fortune at spiritualist seances." He was one of the young breed of Protestant ministers, and added, "I can get you some introductions. I meet a few of the lads and lassies in my line of business."

"Them, or their clients?" Arthur wanted to know.

"Oh, both. We try to get the gulls off the hook." He sighed. "But usually they've swallowed hook, line, and sinker. Francis might do some good. *He's* healthy, anyway."

We were running our business on a shoestring which seemed to be attached to a good substantial shoe, and we kept our overhead down by doing everything ourselves, and that meant long hours and occasional periods of exhausting pressure.

We were plunged into one of these high-pressure areas early that spring when our three most important galleries decided to have Big Openings during one week, two important artists set the same week for visiting the city—each of them expecting us to place New York in a subservient position at their feet—the Museum was like a popper of corn over hot coals, the woman who had agreed to help us over the jumps went to the hospital for an emergency operation, and the people upstairs complained that the noise of our typewriters kept them awake all night. The last item was the only one we could bring under control. We asked them down for a drink, sobbed on their shoulders, gave our word of honor it would all be over in a week and—if it weren't, we invited them to our funerals. They were a nice, elderly couple whose eyes bulged when Francis, by our special permission, floated up to the door top, they thought we were "witty" and "interesting," and went away sorrier for us than for themselves. As the door closed behind them, we went to our desks.

For the next I don't know how many days and nights we lived on black coffee, milk, and something Jack made for us, called Mulligatawney. God knows what was in it, but it seemed to be nourishing and Jack was so excited about cooking for us that his feet never touched the floor. We shut the cats in the back part of the flat, apologizing abjectly but remaining adamant. Francis cried at the closed door as if cruel parents had flung him out into a blizzard, "with an illegitimate baby, I suppose," Arthur suggested absently.

When we dropped into bed, or rushed to the bathroom, we tried to reassure them, but the tension we were under made our words sound false in our own ears, nor did we dare relax long enough to give them the sort of leisurely attention they were used to. Once I said, after a foray into the back regions, that Talley seemed to be taking it hard, but the telephone rang before I finished the sentence.

The hour came—at about two in the morning—when we saw a glimmer of light at the end of the tunnel. I was sticking stamps on the batch of releases to be mailed in the morning when I remembered that the deadline for a monthly magazine column had been two days earlier.

"And I haven't an idea in my head," I moaned. "Have you?"

"Yes," Arthur said savagely. "I have the idea that if we don't get some sleep right now, we'll never wake up . . ." He pushed some papers across my desk. "We can proofread these tomorrow." He took off his glasses and peered closely at me. "You look like the Wreck of the Hesperus," he commented.

"Well, you look the boy on the burning deck whence all but he had fled, and nobody could blame them."

We laughed, tied up a couple of loose ends, and fell into bed. I remember Arthur muttering something about a funny noise somewhere. But he was asleep before he reached the end of the sentence, and so was I.

Somebody . . . something . . . was crying. Not outside. Close by. Kitchen . . .

I fumbled into my slippers and bathrobe. It was chilly. The sound didn't come again and I decided to let Arthur sleep. Overtired, imagination, not enough sleep, probably nothing . . .

Talley was on the kitchen floor, in convulsions. I tried to call Arthur, but the cry stuck in my throat. I looked up and he was there.

We warmed blankets in the gas oven. A medicine dropper of brandy hit against his clenched teeth. It was four o'clock in the morning.

"He's going," Arthur said quietly.

We wrapped the body in a sheet and left it on the laundry tubs where he had liked to sit, at a height near ours, and watch us fuss around with cooking and listen to Jack talk about London and the Navy and mum's Maltese cat, and now he was dead.

We couldn't go to bed again. We went back to the office, mixed drinks, and worked out an idea for the overdue column.

Suddenly we remembered Francis. We found him in the front room, but how and when had he got in there? When the office door was shut there was no way through. Arthur had gone to get our sweaters around midnight when the steam heat went off. He had had his mind on other things and Francis could have slipped through then. We stood and looked at him for a moment or two. He blinked up at us and then curled around with his head almost out of sight.

"I wonder . . ." I said, as we turned away.

"Yes," Arthur said, "so do I. Do we want to know?"

Two hours later, Jack showed up, earlier than usual. At first he held himself together rather well. He said he had been worried about Talley. He noticed he was "under the weather."

But we were working so hard, and he didn't like to interrupt and the telephone was always ringing . . . And he knew cats had nine lives anyway and the care we took of Talley—he had eight left anyway . . .

And then he put his grizzled head down on the kitchen table and sobbed.

When we took the body to a place where we knew it would be decently cremated, we were told Talley had probably died of uremic poisoning. The early symptoms are general lethargy, difficulty in breathing, loss of appetite. Urination stops. Professional help, if obtained early enough, might be effective, but at any stage cystitis was dangerous.

How could poor Jack have known? No matter how sincerely we tried to make him understand that the blame fell on us, he hardly seemed to hear. He went through the motions of doing his work and when he left at night his eyes were so swollen he could hardly see. We didn't hear from him for a week. Then the super said he was on a drunk. He felt so bad about the cat he didn't care what happened to him.

We went through the gala openings, palavered with the Press, entertained the visiting artists, and were sorry when the hullabaloo was over.

"It's our way of going on a drunk," Arthur said.

"There are too many hours when I'm cold sober," I complained. "The worst of our kind of business is that you can't come down with a handy sore throat and stay home from the office."

"Just try it," Arthur threatened, "and I'll dissolve the partnership and chuck you into the alcoholic ward at Bellevue."

We were going home grandly in a taxi from the next to last Big Event and we were a little frightened of the emptiness we would have to face—and the guilt.

A few days later, the super said Jack was in the alcoholic ward in Bellevue and would I please go to see him. I have a deep admiration for Bellevue Hospital and asked the super how he got there. It seemed Jack had turned in one too many false alarms, one of his favorite games when he was "under the influence." The police had picked him up, decided he was too sick for a cell, and turned him over to Bellevue. "A home away from home," I muttered, but the super said severely that Bellevue was a hellhole and he hoped I would get Jack out quick.

The ward was packed with beds as tight as a new pack of cards. A pretty nurse told me where Jack was, waving vaguely in the direction of a double row of cots down the middle of the long room. He saw me coming and stood up. He looked well and so happy to see me I was almost ashamed to give him the small packages I had picked up on my way down. We sat on the side of his bed and I thought how jealous Francis would be of the interested audience listening avidly to every word.

Jack said, "How . . . how's Francis?"

"He'll be glad to have you back," and I told him about the tiger cat's latest gambit. Typewriters are almost irresistible to cats and Francis had recently discovered a particularly irritating trick. The instant my back was turned or I was on the telephone, a swift paw would pull the ribbon out—and out, and out. Then he would vanish.

While I was feeding Jack this fascinating tidbit, our audience had swelled and I found myself telling a group of scarecrows about Francis, with Jack chiming in, proud as Punch; his Lady was making a hit. Talley's name was not spoken, and when I looked at my watch and stood up to go, I said, "We'll see you soon, won't we?"

He stammered, "D-d-didn't know if you'd want me back. After what happened."

"Any time you're well enough," I said briskly. "I'll have a word with your pretty nurse on my way out."

His face lighted up. "She's right pretty, ain't she? And just as nice, too."

"Nicer," snapped one of the bystanders, and I left them arguing.

He was nervous when he did come, looking out the corners of his eyes like a skittish horse, and hesitating over the hand Arthur held out. He had on his "best" clothes and we guessed the others had gone down the Bellevue incinerator, a guess the super confirmed. We were matter-of-fact and gave him crisp orders. We had maneuvered him into the kitchen and stood around for a few minutes, leaning casually against the laundry tubs. Arthur kidded him about the pretty nurse and I told him she had said as I left, "Oh, Jack! He's a sweetie pie," at which he turned purple with delight.

Francis had made one of the company from the first and I saw Jack reach timidly to touch him and then jerk his hand away as if Francis were a hot stove. As we went out to the office, Arthur murmured, "Hope he makes that hurdle without a tumble."

If we had known anyone who would take Jack on, we would have encouraged a change of venue. We threw out a few tentative lines without getting a single nibble. Jack was a bum, and who, except a couple of mavericks, would have him around the house? The shock of Talley's death and his part in it—which he felt even though he didn't understand it—went deeper than we could estimate. We were perhaps the worst people for him to be with but the only ones who would provide him with money and food. The super did the rest, and we knew Jack paid him for the corner where he had his cot. Francis was not much help and was, in fact, a constant reminder. Jack went on another binge, not very long or disastrous, but a pattern was forming.

Francis without Talley was becoming a nuisance. A cute kitten jumping at you from behind a door is one thing; a full-grown, athletic cat is quite another. Damaging my typewriter ribbon was just a start. I came home one day to find all the keys clustered in a small bunch, two of the bars so badly bent a repairman had to be called. Francis seemed to take special delight in teasing Jack. When Jack brought his socks, underwear, and so on upstairs to wash—a long-established custom—Francis dug them out of the water and left them strewn on the floor. This, not unnaturally, would drive Jack up the wall. Francis got hold of his pipe and tossed it around the flat like a catnip mouse. Jack hinted at his conviction that Francis was taking revenge for Talley's death. It was not a pleasant thought. Something Had To Be Done.

The turning point came when I was bandaging a nasty gash on Jack's arm, the result of a playful buffet from Francis.

"Y'know, Lady," Jack said, "Francis don't mean to be bad. Talley, he was so quiet you might not notice, but he was the Cap'n. He kept Francis under control, like. The way a Cap'n keeps his crew. Francis *needs* a Cap'n."

When I reported this to Arthur he said, "You know, I'll bet he's right. I don't suppose Jack has any ideas about where we find a Cap'n?"

There's an unwritten rule in New York that the nearer you live to people you particularly like, the less you see of them. There's no use trying to explain this: it just *is*. Not two blocks away, lived some friends with two children and a gray female cat whose personality was impressive and likable. Her kittens were always in demand and probably we were too late to take advantage of her most recent litter. And, anyway, how could a young kitten be a Cap'n? Arthur said the fame of the British

Navy rested on its youthful officers. Francis would wallop the tar out of a full-grown stranger. What counted was personality. The argument went round and round and ended in a telephone call to our neighbors.

Yes, we were told, one kitten was still available; the people to whom it was promised had lost their nerve at the last moment. Camilla added that he was about three months old, and a male. And why not come over right now? There were nibbles, but they'd like us to have him. "He's quite something," she said.

The kitten was gray, like his mother. His head was wide, his stance was self-assured and jaunty. He carried a rather skimpy tail proudly. He was friendly, examined us both carefully, sniffed Francis on our clothes, and lay on my foot. When we left it was arranged that daughter Wendy would bring him to us the next afternoon, a Saturday. They didn't want to give him away without Wendy's knowledge and she was asleep. We walked home, feeling rather dazed and suffering from second thoughts. The kitten was spunky, but so little . . .

A few people were coming for cocktails about the time Wendy would bring the kitten, which we had forgotten, but decided to let it ride. Wendy was late, and our guests arrived promptly: a couple of painters, the public relations manager for a famous entrepreneur, and the editor of the magazine for which we wrote a column. They were all strangers to each other, but talked the same language, and soon the living room was awash with shop talk and hilarity. Francis was in his element, did his mantelpiece trick to the usual accompaniment of startled applause, paraded from one guest to another, looking beautiful and well aware of it, lying in his most seductive pose in front of the mantelpiece. We had almost forgotten about the kitten, when the doorbell rang.

We had, of course, told Jack what we were up to. He was bewildered and scared, and as I went to the door I saw him standing in the office. There were plenty of men around, I thought, to take care of any contingency.

Wendy, a serious, stocky child of twelve, was clutching a paper bag which seemed to have a life of its own. She said breathlessly, "I didn't know if I'd make it or not. I *told* Mummy . . ." and walked quickly into the room.

The paper bag split open and the kitten fell on the floor. Oh, Lord, I thought, that's done it!

The kitten got to his feet, looked around him, then turned on the paper bag and beat it to pulp. He was furious and methodical. I don't think anyone drew a decent breath until he gave it a final wop with one paw and left it. He sat down and washed his face.

Wendy said, "Well, I guess I'll be going. Mummy said to let us know if you have any trouble," and marched out, closing the door firmly behind her.

For a moment the room was perfectly silent. One small gray cat, washing away the ignominy of that paper bag, was the only thing that moved. Then I looked at Francis. When Destiny rang the bell, he had been lying on his side, his long slim body relaxed. When the door opened he must have risen, on the alert for any newcomer to charm. He was on all fours, legs stiff, glaring at the kitten. He looked enormous. His eyes glittered. He took one step toward the kitten, slow motion, sinister. It was like the parody of a gangster movie.

I stepped towards him. Attracted by my movement, the kitten looked at Francis, one paw held ready to continue his bath. The two felines regarded each other steadily. Then the kitten gave himself a final lick, stood up unhurriedly and walked over to the sofa where the black-haired man from Hollywood was sitting, climbed the sofa arm, got up on the back, biffed the man firmly on the ear, raised his back but not his fur, pranced sidewise along the wide cushion, and waited for his new pal to make the next move.

The man said, "Hey, Butch!" and tried to grab him. The kitten eluded him neatly, scampered on, found Arthur who was, I think, paralyzed, sniffed, apparently remembered something recently met, and went on to the next. He made the rounds. I stayed close to Francis, wondering if I was really seeing what I thought I was.

Then Francis moved. He made a long leap that brought him within a foot of the kitten. He crouched, a jungle beast ready for its prey. His mouth was open in a snarl. I thought, Dear God, what have we done? Francis' hindquarters wriggled, his tail slashed once, and I got my hands on him just before Jack reached him.

The tense room broke into movement, but I gasped, "Please, I've got him," and began to talk into his ear. I wouldn't be able to hold him indefinitely but a shift from one grip to another might be fatal. Jack, good man, was hovering; the British Navy ready for action.

The kitten . . . The kitten was the only relaxed person in the room. He was sitting on the floor, looking at Francis. He wasn't frightened, he was curious.

The whole thing could not have lasted a half-moment, but it seemed like an eternity. I felt Francis deflate under my hands as if the wind had been knocked out of him. The black-haired man, who was nearest, reached out a long arm and picked up the kitten. I released my hold on Francis (my hands ached from tension) and he rose from the crouch, looked at his new housemate, and with immense dignity and all his customary grace, walked off stage, and out of the room. Arthur said Jack followed him, but I didn't notice; I felt as you do when just coming out from under an anesthetic.

The black-haired man, obeying the kitten's command, set him down on the floor, saying under his breath, "Hey . . . Butch," as if it were a prayer.

I pulled myself together and got to my feet. "Butch, nothing," I said. "This is a brave gentleman, the bravest of all King Henry's men, and the most reckless." I couldn't stop talking. "This is Percy, Duke of Northumberland, commonly called Percy Hotspur."

"We could all do with a drink," Arthur said and got up a little stiffly. No one protested.

The kitten had gone to explore the rest of the apartment and I let him alone, hoping Jack would do the same. Little Percy wouldn't stand a chance in a physical encounter, but I doubted if it would come to that. Not now. Francis had revealed himself as a coward; I was ashamed for him. Poor Francis . . .

When I happened to meet the black-haired public relations man again, he asked if we always put on a show like that? I told him, emphatically, no, and added that the tiger and the kitten were the best of friends.

It was close to the truth. Percy continued to keep the upper hand, but we began to realize that he never made a point of it, he allowed the other cat plenty of rope, he let Francis feel superior until some boundary line, which we could never define, was overstepped. Percy and Francis knew the limits, but *how* they knew or by what means Percy exerted his authority, lay beyond our understanding. Thanks to Jack's instinct, Francis again had a Cap'n and was the happier for it.

❀ TEN ❀

The war James and Arthur had half-kidded about on that Fourth of July weekend, had begun. The British called it the Phony War, the French Army sat smugly in its Maginot Line, Americans were divided and nervous.

Jack's behavior became, if possible, more erratic, his services more chancy. There could be no doubt that he stood in awe of Percy; Arthur was sure he saluted when we weren't looking. When the super retired to live with a daughter in some Jersey town, Jack lost a friend and his living quarters. A man and wife of ambiguous background and uncertain intelligence took charge of the building and, of course, threw Jack out. He told us he had found "sumpin'" near by, and insisted that we take care of his precious "papers." We protested but he was so insistent Arthur finally had the grimy sheet photographed and tried to return the original. Jack wouldn't take it. The copy, then? He didn't believe in it; it wasn't real, but he stuck it indifferently in his pocket.

He never told us where the "sumpin'" was located, and kept his meager wardrobe in one of our closets. In despair, and with considerable reluctance, we said he could have a fold-away cot in the kitchen, but he stared at us with a horrified expression and made a lengthy, unintelligible speech in which the word "'aunted" recurred. I am ashamed to say we were relieved. There wasn't much more we could do, and it never occurred to us to fire him.

Conditions in our apartment building went from bad to worse, and when Percy proudly laid a young rat at our feet one morning, I first reported it to the Department of Health, and then called the owner to tell him he could either cancel our lease without fuss or talk to our lawyer, naming one of the most eminent members of the Bar who was an old friend and nearly laughed himself into an attack of apoplexy when we told him.

We moved our home five blocks south, still on Murray Hill, to smaller but more felicitous surroundings. As a minor concession to common sense, we sold the car.

Arthur insisted I had selected the new place because it was two doors away from the battered and historic Fifteenth Precinct station house which had been the scene of dramatic action during the Civil War Draft riots, but that was a canard. Francis expressed his disapproval of the change by sulking and slinking, while Percy showed immediate appreciation of the sun that poured in through big south and west windows, of the elevator right outside our door, and the general atmosphere of coziness, cleanliness, and comfort. I think he brought Francis around by ignoring his bad temper and turning a deaf ear to his whining.

Percy would never be a beautiful animal, like Impo, Russia, Talley, and Francis. His gray kitten-coat had taken on a great deal of white in haphazard markings as if someone had flipped a brush of white paint at him. His fur was neither thick nor thin, his tail remained skimpy. His figure was also nondescript, neither thick nor thin, big or small. He never showed off. He gave his friendship after due consideration (there were a few exceptions to this rule), and then the bond was permanent and unshakable. Dislike was expressed by a devastating withdrawal of attention, if physical absence wasn't feasible.

One could be deprecatory of his coat, his figure, his tail, but never of his head. What most people first noticed were the unusually large, beautifully shaped, wide-set ears. The jaw line was strong—not belligerent but positive, self-confident. It was a fine head, but the eyes were amazing. I'm sorry for people who think cats' eyes are all alike, with perhaps slight variations in color. They have never really looked, and I have even heard a few admit they are afraid to look straight into a cat's eyes—it makes them "uncomfortable." Percy's eyes were a rather strange combination of shades of gray and blue with specks of topaz visible when the pupil was contracted. I never saw any others quite like them. They were beautiful, and best of all, they were alight and glowing with intelligent awareness.

As Percy matured, and as we came to know him well, we wondered why we had been surprised that Francis had surrendered so quickly. It was simply another proof that mind is superior to matter.

Jack helped us pack and went away when the van arrived, muttering that he'd see us at the new place. We told the elevator man to expect him, but he walked upstairs. He had been drinking but we were too busy to bother with him then. Perhaps an hour later, he came to me and said he was going now. Preoccupied, I said casually, "We'll see you tomorrow, Jack. Be good."

I heard the door shut. For some reason I ran after him and heard him clattering down the stairs. I called, but he didn't answer. After three days, I paid my first visit to the Fifteenth Precinct, a barn of a place with a deceptively narrow entrance off the street. Walls and floors were scrubbed old wood, clean and smelling of disinfectant and nameless odors, and stretching back a long distance to the cells. A wide staircase curved upwards, and later when I had occasions to climb them the steps shook under my weight. A huge Sergeant (the old Fifteenth harbored New York's "Finest") looked down at me from the high desk. He said, "Oh, yeah? Jack? Well, we'll keep an eye out for him. Sure. We know him. Likes to play with the fire alarm boxes." He peered closer at me and rubbed his chin. "How come you got mixed up with him?"

I explained as briefly as I could (the whole thing sounded phony even to me) and then asked if he knew So-and-so in Chelsea. It seemed a good idea to clarify the situation and my reputation. As I was leaving I added that the Sergeant in Chelsea wouldn't know me by the name I had now and gave my previous one. "He'll know that," I said confidently, and went home thinking that modern life can be very confusing at times.

We never saw or heard of Jack again.

Francis found another door before we had lived very long on Thirty-fifth Street. Here also we had closets in a narrow hall but these were noble affairs and we revelled in their size. Francis was clearly pleased with his discovery, but we wondered if we only imagined that he didn't levitate with his former spectral ease. Once we noticed that his balance wavered but the door's solidity and its slightly greater width might have thrown off his calculations. There was no doubt that he was quieting down, yet he was still quite a young cat. Jack had been his butt—perhaps he missed him. Perhaps Percy's inconspicuous discipline was responsible.

The two cats played together wildly and happily. There was less space in which to run but much more sunshine and better air. Sometimes there was a spat, when Francis played too hard with the smaller cat, but generally they got along well. They slept together on the sofa, curled up in one big, multicolored ball, or stretched out back to back, or facing each other with their legs intertwined—and proximity sometimes meant trouble. Every once in a while, horrible, piercing screams of anguish would rend the quiet of the night, and at first we both rushed madly to the rescue of one or the other or both. Percy was the noise maker, Francis the aggressor. Seeing us, the racket stopped and they would settle themselves at opposite ends of the sofa. Percy looked at us as if we had been responsible for the disturbance, and we thought Francis looked surprised. It made us feel foolish, and eventually we pulled the pillows over our heads and waited for silence to descend. The most meticulous examination never revealed the slightest wound or scratch or even a missing clump of fur. What was it all about? Who began it? Francis seemed to do all the biting and snarling while Percy did the screaming. So far as we knew—we weren't there all day—the impulse to battle was strictly nocturnal.

Our most favored theory was, perhaps, a touch esoteric. Percy was the undisputed boss. Could he really be wise enough to understand that the pent-up resentment of the underling should be given some outlet which is, however, still in the control of the boss? Only a fool sits on a powder keg until the fuse burns down to the end . . .

"Or," Arthur suggested, "it's like one of those office picnics— I remember a couple when I was in Wall Street—when the Boss gives you a chance to strike him out in the baseball game, and comes in a poor last in the swimming contest. That sort of stuff. Gee whiz, Old Sourpuss is really a good guy when you get to know him, huh? It works, too," he said thoughtfully. "I got fooled once. I hadn't been in the Army then. The next day, I asked for a raise." He grinned.

"What happened?"

"Nothing."

It was as good an answer as any: a shrewd way to take some of the heat out of Francis' itch for supremacy. The idea made me laugh. "I wouldn't put it past him. I wonder what it's like to be a cat with a mind like that? That is," I added hastily, "if it *is* like that."

We glanced at our two felines. Percy was looking smug while Francis licked him affectionately; one handsome gray ear twitched.

"He finds it satisfactory," Arthur stated positively.

Percy and Francis were unaffected by Pearl Harbor. We hoped they could stay that way; their indifference was restful. All the old boys I knew, Arthur and James in particular, were trying to get into the act again. James thought he almost made it; he had been a first lieutenant. Of course, neither of them did. Ruth and I shed crocodile tears where they could see us. Ruth had no children and said she was thankful for the first time. Mine were both in up to the neck. Arthur ended up as sergeant major in a State Guard regiment and commuted between Murray Hill and upper Madison Avenue. His lively little business became moribund and then died. By a stroke of dumb good luck, I got a job I liked with people I respected, only to learn quite soon that respect was inadequate, after which I gave them what they deserved—a deep and abiding affection.

We joined Civilian Defense, as a matter of course. When I join anything, even voluntarily, I immediately begin to kick against the pricks. Civilian Defense was no exception. Arthur was patient and popular; if a bomb could have dropped on me alone, our sector would have given three cheers. Everybody was living on their nerves. The English had had the threat of destruction from the sea and from the air hanging over them for so long they had, we were told, learned to live with it. For the first time in a century and a half, America was uncertain of its physical safety. People were affected in odd ways, and we would come home from meetings, and tests, and exercises, and lectures, overstimulated and overtired.

On the way home from a lecture with moving pictures,

which explained in graphic, close-up detail what an atomic bomb could do to you and what *you* could do about *it*, I missed the curb and sprained my ankle. I stayed home with the cats for the next drill, a terribly important affair. Ours was a well-disciplined street, all lights were out (not even a candle flicker to be seen—there had been complaints about that), nothing moved. I leaned out our bedroom window and blessed the dark curbstone. It was impressive, looking on.

Suddenly, the eerie stillness was broken by the sharp yelps of a small dog in the apartment house directly opposite.

One of the wardens, complete with helmet, armband, flashlight (unlighted), bounced out from her doorway shelter.

"QUIET," she yelled at the top of her voice. "Quiet! *Stop that dog barking at once!*"

I nearly fell out of the window from an excess of delight. For the moment all my irritation with the fumbling and stumbling fell away; this vaudeville act made up for everything.

I could hardly wait to tell a couple of English friends who were here on a government mission. They were already quietly amused by New York's preparedness for all-out bombing. When they stopped laughing, Joan said, "Well, that's funny, of course. But let's tell you some of the nonsense that happened in London. You'll learn, chums."

Something was going on in our own home that we didn't understand. Francis was reverting to his kittenhood carelessness about toilet habits. This was bad enough. His increasing sluggishness bothered us even more. For days at a time, he wouldn't let Percy out of his sight. Then he would disappear, hide in a closet, under the bed, a chair, the sofa. Percy was concerned. But Francis hadn't lost his appetite, his physical functions, if not his habits, were in order, his coat was sleek, his eyes clear.

The war had a way of losing people in its unwieldy shuffle,

and we could think of no one to whom we could turn for advice about a veterinarian. We made much of Francis, and he loved it. Almost without noticing it ourselves, we dropped into calling him Funny Fanny. When he was Funny Fanny, the little clown, he, or she, had enjoyed a degree of fame, however limited. He had been happy when he was Funny Fanny. And who expects an acrobat to be a great brain? His ears twitched when we slipped into the old name; I don't think that was our imagination. We were trying, too late as attempts to redeem old faults so often are, to give Francis what we had withheld; our love.

We heard of a vet who sounded trustworthy and I made the first date possible. On the way through the living room that morning, I saw with surprise that both cats were still on the sofa. Percy lifted his head to look at me, and if he had said the word, "Help!" his meaning could not have been plainer. He was huddled in front of Francis who was lying on his side, a normal position but it didn't look normal now. He was motionless, his legs unnaturally straight. I thought he was gone, but he was breathing. Just.

I called Arthur, we covered him with a blanket and put him in the carrier. Arthur was due on duty at the Armory and couldn't go with me, but called the vet while I went down for a taxi.

It was early but the waiting room was nearly full. When I gave my name to the attendant, I was taken immediately into the doctor's office. He looked at Francis, felt him, shook his head.

"Heart failure," he said. "I'm sorry. It's too late. I was afraid of this from what your husband told me. I'll take care of him." He carried Francis into the operating room, and I followed. "You don't want to wait, do you." It was more of an order than a question.

I said, "Yes. Don't worry about me." If there were the remotest chance that a tiny thread of awareness still remained, I had to be with him. I stroked his head between his ears, a gesture that always made him open and shut his eyes ecstatically. Was there a ghost of a flicker?

The doctor shrugged and filled a hypodermic needle. Bending down, I said clearly, "Dear Funny Fanny. Dear Francis."

The vet stood by the table. "It won't hurt him. He won't feel anything."

I nodded.

"Merciful," James had said of Russia. "Hope somebody does it to me."

My mother missed Francis more than any of us. She had recently taken a small apartment on the sixth floor of our building, an arrangement we found both convenient and troublesome. The affinity between her and the beautiful, dramatic, and dissatisfied cat was painfully obvious to anyone who knew them both intimately.

When I went down to tell her that evening, she wept and then sobbed, "You never cared two pins about him. You didn't understand him. You didn't try to . . ."

I looked at her helplessly. Just change the pronoun to "me" and we'd have the gist of it. "We tried," I muttered. She made a wide gesture with both hands, sweeping away my feeble protest. I stood up and kissed her. "He didn't have such a bad life. He wasn't easy to understand." A wave of exhaustion swept over me. "Remember what Nana used to say? 'Do thy best. Angels can do no more.'" And I went out, closing the door softly behind me.

The other person who sincerely mourned Francis was Harriet Hedrick. Mrs. Hedrick lived on our floor, a dozen short steps from us. Arthur said he knew about the steps, he'd counted them. When we moved there, Harriet was in her latter seventies, she had been one of the early group of brilliant women who crashed through the male barricades into the financial world, she had made herself wealthy, lived frugally without penny-pinching, and was terrified of electricity and electrical appliances. That was where we came in. Somehow she found out that Arthur could change a light bulb, mend a broken wire, replace a fuse, mend her small electric stove.

At first she tolerated me because I belonged to him, and when, after a considerable time, she admitted I might just possibly be worthy of him, I felt as if I'd been awarded the Legion of Honor. She was a craggy-faced woman, with fluffy white hair, keen dark eyes, a wide and mobile mouth, and a warm, affectionate nature. She had a remarkably acid tongue. She was handsome in a highly individual way, loved off-color jokes—good, bad, or indifferent—and for twenty years was to interest, amuse, and aggravate us. She had known my mother casually some forty years before we moved in and recognized her laugh. They picked up the acquaintanceship and became friends; or, in plain words, they saw a good deal of each other and each got a lot of pleasure out of complaining to me about the other.

Inevitably, Harriet became one of Francis' admirers. He went out of his way to be charming, playing up to her shockingly. She adored cats—and had the world's worst luck with them. I had a theory that they ran away, or sickened, because she never spoke to them except in baby talk, unless, of course, she screamed at them for doing something she didn't like. Soon after Francis died, some misguided or misinformed friend gave her a young female. I've forgotten her name but she was a pretty little thing with more intelligence than Harriet allowed her to show. Over weekends, when I could, I brought her in to visit Percy, or took him to Harriet's. That didn't often happen for he hated her mode of conversation and the way she rushed at him with cries of welcome. When I could persuade him to go down the hall, and inside her door, he would sit motionless, as unresponsive as a piece of granite. She kept comparing him unfavorably to Francis.

One afternoon, I came home to find Harriet standing at her door, waiting for me. The cat had run away. The boy with the groceries had let her out, she had bolted down the stairs and had not returned. Moaning and wringing her hands, Harriet demanded that I go all through the building, looking for her. Someone must have taken her—"stolen her," Harriet said.

With weary reluctance, I went from one door to another. There were only four flats on each of the nine floors, and these were soon covered. Eddie, the elevator man, said, "Look, it ain't no use. Mrs. Hedrick just can't *keep* a cat, don't ask me why." I reported everything but Eddie's comment and Harriet burst into tears. I said she might report it to the police. She looked scared, and I almost laughed out loud: Chelsea and Murray Hill were sisters under their skins . . . Hastily, I said that I'd take care of it.

"Well, darling," she coaxed, "go and talk to them, then. Don't do it over the telephone. *You* can make them listen, you're so wonderful with people."

Properly buttered up, I finally agreed, and she held out the carrot of a drink when I came back. Civilian Defense had kept us both in close touch with the precinct, and since the Sergeant Major vouched for me, the reputation which my association with Jack had undermined was now firmly established.

I leaned against the railing while a DOA case was got out of the way and ruminated on the variety of a policeman's lot— a missing cat on the heels of a probable suicide . . . What would come up next? The Sergeant listened and told me to go out back and see So-and-So who knew all about Mrs. Hedrick and her cats. I was met by groans and guffaws, but I gave the description, and added that if they'd had their laugh out, I was going back to enjoy the drink Mrs. Hedrick had promised me, and if they found the cat, I'd persuade her to give them a whiff.

The cat, we learned from the police, had found a home next door with a family who were "crazy about her," and indignant at the idea that they should give her up. I heartily agreed and Arthur finally managed to make Harriet leave well enough alone. However, she got in some nasty digs at me before I was returned to full favor.

We held out against the people, led by my mother and Harriet, who insisted that Percy needed companionship. He was alone all day, the two ladies cried, we went gadding around at night, either one of them would welcome him. Percy liked the rather spectacular array of plants in my mother's big south window, but after a delicate investigation between the pots, he would sit more or less patiently beside the door. We had to carry him to Harriet's. As for another cat, that was in the lap of the gods, and we hoped that lap was empty. We thought we understood Percy pretty well, we believed he was happy and contented with the way things were, and for once we were right.

The war dragged—and then exploded—to a halt. My daughter came home first. From Hollandia, the Air Force had sent her company to Manila, recently liberated. Then after some time, by boat to the Pacific Coast, then by troop train east. She came in one Sunday morning, without warning. She was travel-worn, her uniform was a mess, her skin atabrine-yellow, her honey-colored hair drab. I thought she was the most beautiful young woman in the world.

Later my son arrived. He had had a rough war in Germany

and had found Occupation Duty rough too, though in a different way. He laughed off the medal he had won. Neither of them had made better than sergeant, but I had been pleasantly surprised that John, at least, had not spent most of his time confined to barracks, or worse; he had an inborn skepticism about the wisdom of Authority, or of any Establishment, and an almost irresistible impulse to express it. He came by both honestly enough, but I swear I had never tried to encourage either.

Romances now went up like skyrockets, usually exploded in mid-air, and fell to earth. A lively group of wounded at Halloran Hospital had formed an organization they called Recon which met regularly at our place after they were able to leave the hospital during evenings, and these boys, the WACs, the nurses, and various friends of theirs who were interested in learning how to write, raised the temperature of our middle-aged lives to fever pitch. Percy enjoyed, almost as much as we did, the excitement of those weekly meetings when every object that was sittable was sat on, including the floor, but he was the only one who regretted the lessening supply of casts and crutches: he had played leapfrog over them, liked the smell of ether and antiseptics, and when he tired of that, went in the bedroom where he wallowed among the caps and coats piled on the bed. No new William Faulkners or Ernest Hemingways were uncovered, but neither our time nor the generous help the kids received from established writers, editors, and agents were wasted efforts.

Arthur, long out of uniform, found that war had changed the art world almost beyond recognition. The niche he had made for himself, which had seemed so secure, was being engulfed by more raucous approaches to publicity, and by an expanding dependence on use of space advertising even by the more conservative dealers. Several of the galleries that had been his stand-bys had been war casualties, others were making rather wild and often unsuccessful attempts to keep pace with changing methods. Paradoxically, art was booming, prices were beginning to soar, but all that had come too late for a man whose bump of competitiveness was rudimentary and whose abilities were more solid than splashy. Quietly, without useless complaints, he fixed up an ingeniously designed working space in a corner of the apartment and, to Percy's complete satisfaction, made home his headquarters.

Cats are creatures of habit—any of which they may break without warning—and we had often mentioned casually, with approving amusement, Percy's custom of always being at the door to meet us whenever we came home. Arthur began to pay attention, and what he saw bewildered him.

The room-length bookcase had been designed with bottom shelves high and deep enough to hold large art books, atlases, reference books, and so on, which provided a ledge about ten inches wide. Bookcase and ledge ended exactly to our entrance door, and when we—but not other people—entered, there would be Percy's nose at the crack. We took it for granted that he heard the elevator open and made a dash for the ledge.

"But he doesn't 'dash'," Arthur said plaintively. He hated not to understand things like that. "When I've been waiting for you—and who the hell were you out with today?—I've begun to notice something odd. We aren't the only pebbles on the elevator. It comes up here for the Scholems, the penthouse people, Miss MacDonald, Harriet's pals—Percy doesn't twitch an ear. But *before* the car starts from the ground floor—and I've checked—that lunatic is *on the ledge* with his nose at the door." He leaned back and looked at me triumphantly. I couldn't think of any answer, and he went on, "Tomorrow I'll be late." He leered. "I'm taking a dame to the Plaza for cocktails and I don't know when I'll be back."

I murmured, "Maybe never. Toss me away like a squeezed lemon."

"Not yet, anyway. I'm curious. You get home first, just this once, and watch what happens. I want to know what you see or else I'll think I'm going nuts."

Percy stood in front of me, reminding me of his dinner. On my way to the kitchen, I said, "I want to be nosy. Who are you taking to the Plaza of all places?"

He grinned, and named a former client who was almost as rich as Hetty Green, pushing ninety, and didn't know there was any other place to have cocktails except the Plaza. She would pick up the check, she always did. A nice woman. I told him for heaven's sake not to haggle over paying the bill and urged Percy to explain *his* door act, which seemed to make a lot more sense than levitating to the top of it, but he only complained again about the service.

Arthur's observations had been accurate. But before embarking on the project which was to occupy our spare time for a month, we tried to cover all the probabilities. The elevator was new, self-service, we couldn't hear that it made a sound. But a cat has sharper hearing. Voices in the car? Possible, of course. The entrance door from the street—did it bang or squeak? Arthur had checked; it was in perfect order. Moreover, this being summertime, it was left open until the air cooled off. (Those were days of innocence.) Someone ringing from the ground floor for the elevator? Possible again. Someone getting off at a lower floor? But the doors still opened and closed without a whisper. Accidental? We rejected that; it happened too regularly.

So Arthur drew up two charts. Average time between street door and elevator. Average time between ringing elevator bell and arrival of car. That was a tricky one since the car might have been left at any floor. Time from the first floor to the ninth. Other passengers. Delays. I think there were other items, but never mind. The second chart was for the person already in the flat and was simpler. The minute Percy went to door. Interval between that and arrival of newcomer. Notes on variations.

Arthur's devotion to charts was not shared by his wife, but this investigation interested me and I was pretty good about keeping my end up. After a month, Arthur carefully coordinated and compared the two charts. We hadn't been able to resist peeking, naturally, but the final result left us rather wild-eyed. There was no logical, factual, sensible answer. Arthur threw down his pencil and swore.

"Either we missed one essential time span, or we goofed on our records—or we're harboring a spook."

Percy, bored, jumped on the table where the charts and papers were spread out. He walked all over them, flicked a loose sheet with a paw, and lay down in the middle of the pile. He blinked at us, and yawned.

"ESP." I interpreted: "Extra Sensory Perception."

"I know what ESP means," he snarled. "You and Jane did nothing but talk about it a few years ago. Nuts." He yanked a piece of paper out from under Percy, who stood up indignantly. Arthur scowled at the paper. I was catching the yawns from Percy. It was one o'clock.

"Darling," I said. "Let's just settle for C A T. We're keeping our little mystery-monger awake. Okay?"

He rubbed Percy under the chin. "Okay. But I wish we'd found a—a rational answer." He began to tidy up the papers Percy wasn't sitting on. "I don't like the idea of sitting here, night after night, wondering where you are, when *he* knows all the time."

I laughed and pointed out that if we had found a matter-of-fact solution, we wouldn't be able to boast about our cat with a sixth sense and X-ray eyes. But I don't believe we ever mentioned it to anyone. Arthur was inclined to be embarrassed by the unexplainable, and it had been his game, after all.

Time slipped by like a white cloud over mountain peaks, darkened only by an occasional thunder shower. A few changes were taking place in the rest of our building but the ninth floor occupants remained stable: Harriet, Miss MacDonald (almost a recluse), our landlord, Fred Scholem and his handsome wife, Evelyn, ourselves. My mother was still a few floors below, determinedly active in spite of a broken hip. (Harriet, not to be outdone, broke both hips in as many years.) Percy was older, but so were we all.

My children were getting married. We had a hilarious wedding party for Ann, which threatened to be endless until I finally said to the principals, "Will you please get out of here? You'll miss your boat tomorrow—today, I mean." As a clincher, I added, "And we're running out of whiskey." The champagne had gone long since, although there had been a tubful in the bathroom to begin with. John and his girl had had the good sense to go away for a weekend and tell us about it afterwards. Each of the in-laws was a mother-in-law's dream, but I couldn't get inside the role and consistently underplayed the part.

Some time along there, I re-read *Henry IV* and realized that I had made a mistake. Henry's, or Shakespeare's, Hotspur wasn't one half as bright as ours. But it was too late to regret the impulse and, of course, it's conceivable though unlikely that Northumberland might have matured. Our Percy did. I was told on good authority that a friend had refused a dinner invitation by saying, "Oh, I'm sorry. We're having dinner with Percy and Arthur and Tay, that night."

She may have been among the four guests, I don't remember, and the date is lost too, but too much of the rest is clear, even to sitting slightly detached after the dishes had been cleared away, congratulating myself smugly on how smoothly everything had proceeded and wondering mildly why Arthur was taking so long in the bathroom. Then I heard him call and something in his voice shot me out of my chair and down the hall.

The bathroom looked like the scene of the bloodiest of bloody pogroms. Arthur was standing, swaying, holding on to the basin, his color a deathly gray. He whispered, "Explosions. Both ends. Disgusting. Sorry."

Why didn't I ask one of the men for help? Because no one else existed. In all the world there was no one but my love. Somehow I got him into the bedroom and on the bed. It was a hot night, there were no coats and paraphernalia to throw on the floor. While I dug out a winter blanket, I thought of Evelyn, next door. She was a doctor. The Scholems were gadabouts, they might not be home. Our own doctor was on vacation. What was the name of his locum tenens? Something warned me there wasn't much time.

I raced through the living room, flung open the door and threw over my shoulder, "Please go. Right away . . ." as I pressed my finger on the Scholems' bell and banged on their door.

Bless good hospital training. Evelyn had been in bed, asleep or reading, and she was with me in seconds. Probably I said, "Arthur . . ." for she strode ahead with not a glance at the stunned faces of our guests. She gave a look into the bathroom and at the hall, touched Arthur's hand, and left—not running but moving with the efficiency of a perfectly tuned racing motor. When she came back with her bag, she said, "I phoned. The specialist will get here as fast as he can. I want a little cool water—from the kitchen." She didn't, of course, but it got me out of her way. I vaguely noticed that the living room was empty, except for Percy, at the alert in the center of the room.

The doctor arrived very quickly. He was young, conversational, and competent. When they had done all they could for the time being, he and Evelyn sat in the living room and regaled each other with professional gossip until the ambulance came.

At Doctors' Hospital, I was shunted into a closet-like space with a chair and a table. They said I could smoke if I wanted, but would I please just stay put. The door was left open. I could hear voices over the loud speaker system: "Doctor So-and-So. Emergency. Room such-and-such." It was Arthur's room.

After endless hours, a nurse told me I could go home, everything was under control. She patted me on the back. "Get some rest, dearie."

The gray morning light dazzled my eyes, but a taxi pulled up, it was a long drive and the traffic was getting heavier. At our house, the driver said, "Got your keys okay?" I said yes. He said I had given him too much and handed back a five dollar bill.

Upstairs, Percy was waiting on the ledge. I caught him up in my arms and he kissed me.

All the windows were open, but the stench was thick. I had hardly noticed it before. There was only one thing to do, so I got down to it. Percy stayed beside me, following me from bathroom to kitchen and back; the water in the pipes wasn't very hot and I put kettles, pans, pots, anything that would hold water, on the stove. We had sometimes imagined that Percy's sense of smell was unusually keen, even for a cat. Whether we were right or not, those hours shut up there alone must have been hell.

When the bathroom was scrubbed, I tackled the hall where the evidences of disaster were less. Perhaps it was eight o'clock, perhaps nine; I didn't care. I was aware of Percy, always right there. Sometimes he moved slightly to avoid sloshing water, but not always. Sometimes I think I talked to him, and if he had told me, in so many words, that he wanted to help, I wouldn't have turned a hair.

I pulled down the blinds and fell on the bed. Evelyn had put something over it—how kind of her. Then I began to think. I am hopelessly stupid about illness, but I had overheard enough to know that without her there would never be a homecoming for him. Or for me.

"Get some rest, dearie." I supposed I was resting now. But where was sleep? Oblivion? Perhaps if I washed the dinner dishes? But I had done that first of all, there had been no room to heat water. I could dry them and put them where they belonged. I could clean up the living room. It wasn't too early to run the vacuum cleaner, or was it? People might still be asleep. What time was it? My watch had stopped.

Something landed lightly on the bed. Percy. At least he would be there when I woke from the sleep that must, must, must come. Suddenly I realized he was not in his usual place at the foot of the bed, and I groped for him in a panic.

It was all right. He hadn't gone away. He was settling himself solidly against my shoulder. A cold nose pushed with gentle firmness under my chin. He pushed even closer, I could feel his heart beat, and his breath on my face. I put my arm more firmly around him and he began to purr. The sound and the vibrations under my hand were like hearing and touching music. The music said, "He'll . . . be . . . all . . . right . . . he'll . . . be . . . all . . . right. . . ."

I fell asleep.

❁ ELEVEN ❁

A nurse told me Arthur was a good patient, and another added whimsically, "And he *is* so patient!" I said skeptically, "He is? Tell me about that sometime." But it was true. He wasn't subdued, it would take more than a ruptured ulcer to do that, but he accepted the hospital routine, did what he was told, gave factual answers to direct questions but asked none, never—to my knowledge—had a moment's doubt that he would get well, and regained health and strength at a speed that left even our own doctor out of breath, he said, trying to keep up.

When Doctor Zeman returned from his vacation and took over the case, I demanded to know how—and even more, why?—the sickness could have progressed to the danger point without his saying a word about it. "He must have been in pain, bleeding . . . I don't know what."

"Well," Fred replied, "I asked, of course. He said he didn't want to worry you. Oh, all right, I know what you're going to say. Don't bother. He's crazy. So are you. I rather like it that way. Makes a pleasant change."

The day before he was to be discharged, Arthur began to fuss again about Percy. He wouldn't remember. "You'll have to introduce me. Polish up your social graces."

Under a barrage of protests, I was carrying his bag, but he put his own key in the lock with a flourish. Percy was waiting on the ledge, his head about at Arthur's waist level. There was a tiny mewing sound, then the cat jumped to Arthur's shoulder, and nuzzled his ear. It was a kitten trick, he hadn't played it for years.

"Hotspur, indeed," Arthur said after a moment. "You should have been named Honeybunch."

Life picked up speed again. There was a granddaughter who had managed to combine the best features of John and his delectable red-headed wife, and was almost too beautiful to believe. Ann would contribute another granddaughter and John a grandson. My own offspring hardly expected me to be anything but a casual grandmother, and were not disappointed. Once in a while Ann or John reminded me about a birthday and sometimes I remembered on my own, but the interested parties were very nice about it.

I had to go to Alabama to see my namesake. Ann and her painlessly professorial husband were at the university where there was a famous writing course, and I seized the chance to see the new baby and do a little scouting for young talent. The new addition was good, gay, adorable, and blond. I said I would call her Tay-Two, to avoid confusion.

They were living in a pleasant apartment on the second floor of a two-storied house on a quiet, tree-lined street. A monstrously large cat, Caesar, who had started life in a Greenwich Village flat, had come south with them. Caesar was not only the biggest cat I ever knew—bigger all around and much heavier than Impo—but was a magnificently marked tiger with the world's most amiable disposition. Apparently, he thought of himself as still small enough to be stepped on, and habitually slept under something—a couch, a bed, a chair, whatever was big enough to conceal him.

In spite of distractions, I did get quite a bit accomplished and the day before I was to leave, had made an appointment with a student to come to the apartment where we could talk about his manuscript in peace and quiet. He was a gentle, pleasant chap with the strong Alabama accent I still found hard to translate across a room, so we sat on the couch with the manuscript spread out between us. The baby was asleep, Ann was being considerately quiet in the kitchen but I suppose I raised my never-inaudible voice to make some point, for I noticed that Caesar was gradually emerging from under the couch beside the young man's foot. He was yawning, he had been disturbed, but he would be nice about it, as usual.

After his great head, his huge body, inch by inch, came into view. His side brushed the youth's foot, there was a startled exclamation, a few typewritten pages fluttered from his hand to the floor and as he bent to pick them up, *all* of Caesar appeared.

The young man yelled and leaped to his feet, his eyes bugging. He pointed a shaking finger at Caesar. "Wh-wh-wha . . ." he whispered, and plunged out the door before I could speak. I heard him pound down the stairs, the outside door shook the house as it crashed shut behind him, Ann rushed in, looking alarmed, and I pulled her to the window.

We were in time to see him turn off onto the public walk, his legs working like pistons. Perhaps he was on the track team, I never found out. Before I could say, "Caesar," the shadows of the trees had swallowed him up. Caesar was sitting beside the couch, washing the sleep out of his eyes. He regarded us with mild surprise when we both collapsed on the couch and laughed until we cried. Next day, I returned the manuscript to the address the author had neatly typed on the title page. I was glad he wouldn't have to see me again, for by that time he must have heard about the Professor's big cat.

On my next trip, my namesake was already talking and, true to family tradition, once started, seldom stopped. With the most laudable grandmotherly intentions, I explained that, as I had been "Tay" for a long time, I would call her "Tay-Two" and held up two fingers, pointing one at myself, then the other at her.

The clear blue eyes sized me up. "I," she said, pointing at herself, "am Tay. You," with a finger aimed at my face, "are Tay-Too."

And Tay-Too I have been ever since.

My grandmother's first child was stillborn when she was forty years old. A dauntless woman, she bore two more and raised them successfully. I don't know how she did it. There were plenty of helping hands, it's true, but she wasn't the sort to shelve responsibilities because she was tired. Rearing children is a young woman's game requiring strength, endurance, and resiliency.

"Well," Arthur commented mildly, after I had been holding forth one evening in more or less those terms, "as I'm quite sure you don't expect to follow her example, what's all that apropos of?"

"Percy," I said bitterly.

We had been listening to music when I started talking, and he took the Brahms Quintet for Clarinet off the turntable, and stood for a moment looking at our cat. "Yeah," he said. "He's getting on, as they say. So are we. The connection seems a bit tenuous."

"Not really. Harriet and Nancy have been at me again to 'get something young to keep him interested and happy.'"

"He's happy," Arthur said shortly. He turned off the machine and sat down beside me. After a few minutes, he said, "Percy's happy, we're happy. What's wrong with you?"

"They shook me up today, I don't know why. My mother pointed out that I was just being selfish, I don't want the trouble of a young cat. And she's right, you know. I don't." Arthur made a coarse noise and I said, "Any animal with four legs and a fur coat can teach you more about the brevity and uncertainty of life than you want to know. Quite aside from the fact that I don't want the responsibility of a kitten, I just don't want to go through all this again." I picked Percy up off the floor and sat him on my lap where, at the moment, he didn't want to be. He got down. "You're an old curmudgeon," I told him. He looked at me thoughtfully, decided his right ear may have been forgotten when he took his last bath, and went to work on it with great vigor. "Give your heart to a dog to tear," I quoted. "Read 'cat' for 'dog' and the damn thing applies to our present situation."

He went over to the record cabinet. "Let's wash our mouths out with some G. & S. *Patience,* okay? It's something I find easy to run out of when Nancy and Harriet get after you."

He didn't fool me. I knew he watched Percy as anxiously as I did, and before we turned out the lights that night we had determined to take our nineteen-year-old cat to a veterinarian; we might be worrying about nothing, we told each other, so let's ask an expert.

Surprisingly, Fred Zeman who seemed to be equally indifferent to dogs and cats, knew a youngish man who had trained at Physicians and Surgeons and then decided he liked four-legged animals better than the kind with only two. We made an appointment, but when the day came Percy knew something was going on he didn't like and led us a merry chase.

"We're going to be late," I gasped as I finally got a firm grip on our ancient cat and shoved him into the carrier.

"That cat doesn't need a doctor," Arthur said, wiping his forehead. "We do. Let's stop off to see Fred."

We *were* late, and a lengthy stay in confinement didn't improve Percy's temper. When we got into the doctor's office, I said, "Better let one of us take him out. He's in a roaring rage."

"I guess I can manage," he said, and within a breath Percy was on the operating table, undergoing a swift but authoritative examination and too surprised to wriggle. The doctor rubbed him behind the ears. "You're a very fine old boy," he said approvingly, and put him gently back in the carrier.

"That's the trouble," he said. "He's very old. Even if you've got your dates mixed a little—and I find it hard to believe he's as old as you say—the fact remains. I can't find anything wrong. Except for his teeth. They should have been attended to long ago. It's too late now. I wouldn't put him through it. But perhaps I can give him a little help."

I was appalled. His teeth! That had never occurred to me. Why, Impo had been as old, maybe older, when he was the finest rat catcher since the Pied Piper of Hamelin. I stammered something of this to the doctor.

He smiled a little. "An exception," he said. "Not a very safe guide. You've been lucky, I'd say."

We didn't talk in the cab going home. Lucky! I thought of Francis. Of Talley. Even of Talleyrand. Would he have stayed with us if we had done something differently? Impo had starved to death . . . Because his teeth, because his jaw pained him? He had kept his teeth, I had seen them, but I hadn't really looked—and wouldn't have known what to look for if I had.

Arthur was trying to talk Percy out of the indignation meeting he was holding with himself over the brutality to which he had been subjected. When the cab reached our building, he knew he was nearly home and flung himself around in the carrier like a savage-hearted fury. On home territory, he came out to freedom with a bound that belied his age, glared at us, and bounced into the biggest and, incidentally, newly covered chair where he washed away the carrier, the car rides, the doctor, and us, with vicious swipes of his tongue, biting at bits of fur that had, somehow, become particularly contaminated.

For a few moments we stood and watched him helplessly. At last Arthur said, "Well, now we know. He's old. The only use he can make of his teeth is to bite hell out of his own fur. I don't know about you, but I feel as if I'd been put through a wringer." He looked at the clock. "The sun's over the yardarm. Don't you think," he said coaxingly, "don't you think we could have one, just one, martini before lunch?"

"The evening may be wettish," I said. "John and Arabel are coming for dinner. Do you think you should?"

He started for the kitchen. "Yes, I do. When the cat you love, honor, and obey acts as if you were whipping him with scorpions, it takes something with authority to restore one's faith in the goodness of mankind. I mean, of course, catkind." He stood in the doorway with the shaker in his hand. "And by the way, how did they manage to 'whip with scorpions'? Do you know?"

"No," I said. "Stupid of me. I've been on the receiving end often enough," and burst into tears. It was a dirty trick, for he had been trying so hard to laugh me out of the guilt bog. He seldom missed what I was feeling.

By the time Arabel and John rang the bell at seven, we were back in Percy's good graces and ready for a long, talky, argumentative evening with a lot to laugh at and plenty to drink and maybe Old Age wasn't leering at us just around the corner after all—not at any of us.

About five hours later, Arabel said, "John, it's twelve o'clock. We ought to go," and our doorbell rang violently. Harriet shrieked, "Arthur! Arthur! You've got to come right away . . . My place is flooded!"

She stood poised to run, her hair standing on end, her bony figure in a shabby old wrapper, her eyes wild. She clutched at Arthur. "It's awful. I don't know what to do."

Arthur ran. John ran after him. Arabel and I half carried Harriet inside our apartment, but she pulled away, crying that she must go back, and hobbled down the hall so fast Arabel and I could hardly keep up. I had the wit to leave our door off the latch for ready entrance and skidded down the hall that was damp from Harriet's bedroom slippers.

And no wonder. A young but promising Niagara was pouring into her kitchenette. The two men were gaping at it, until Arthur suddenly said something under his breath and made a dash for Harriet's fuse box. He twiddled something, and the lights went out. Harriet screamed.

John said, "What the . . ." and then, recovering himself, told Harriet, "He's right. Electricity. Wires, shorts . . ."

Harriet looked even wilder than before. John didn't know about her phobia. She felt her way to a chair, sank into it, and moaned. Arthur had vanished and now came back with a flashlight and a candlestick he had snatched off the table.

Arabel and I, who had decided it would be fun to dress up even if there would be only the four of us, sloshed around on the Oriental rug. A valuable rug, it now made me think of the bog that rimmed the Wild Life Pond. The two men were deep in a discussion about how to shut Niagara off. Since neither agreed with the other's suggestions, the flood continued.

More light on the subject might be helpful. Arabel and I went down the hall.

Taking my two pet candlesticks off the table, Arabel said, "I'm sorry for the people downstairs."

"It may not get through. Tough old concrete."

Percy saw no reason why he should be cut out of all the fun, and I had to be firm with him when we went out the door. This was one time he really wanted to go to Harriet's, so what was the matter with me? He also made it clear that one more day like this, and he'd leave. It went through my mind that he might serve as a distraction for Harriet. Arabel shut the door on his inquisitive nose. "He'd drown," she said. "We *all* may."

Arthur had telephoned the police who said they would send a couple of the boys over and would call the Fire Department.

John growled, "They won't get here until tomorrow."

"It *is* tomorrow," Arabel said brightly and got a nasty look.

"They're almost next door," I said, "and I think I hear their fairy footsteps."

Three enormous cops burst into the room. And stopped dead. I don't know what they expected or what Arthur had told them—but they hadn't expected a waterfall, or a floor that, if frozen, would be a dandy skating rink.

There are many times when I thoroughly enjoy being a woman. This was one. Neither Arabel nor I (and certainly not Harriet) had the remotest idea of how to stop a leak or a drip from a faucet. I can't speak for Arabel, but I know I had no intention of learning. There will, please God, always be men to take care of these nasty details as long as I am alive. Arabel and I hung over Harriet, ignoring the facts that our evening slippers were ruined and our long skirts looked as if we'd been dragged through mud at the tail of a horse.

Harriet pulled herself together, and welcomed the police. *They* would know what to do. John looked indignant, but Arthur knew his Harriet and hid a grin. The police shifted on their big feet and muttered to each other.

The officer in charge said, "Don't the landlord live here? Where's he at?" I explained that the Scholems were in the country for the weekend and that the superintendent went home on Saturdays and, as it was already Sunday, had undoubtedly departed. One of the men was sent down to find out. The front door had been open. "Careless," one of them said. "That's the way people get in."

Arabel and I were getting the giggles. This was partly

thanks to Harriet. She had perked up amazingly. Arthur was old hat, John (she told me later) seemed to be moody—but here were these magnificent men in blue.

With the Fire Department, the real action began. Stripped to the buff, they may not have been any bigger than the police, but in full fire-fighting regalia—rubber boots, rubber coats, helmets, the works—they might have filled the Winter Garden stage with hardly a crack showing.

Arabel whispered, "Thank God, I'm not particularly claustrophobic. Are you?"

At intervals we had tried to persuade Harriet to come back to our place, where she would at least be dry—and so would we —but she seemed riveted by the sight of disaster. I knew it would be hopeless now. To tell the truth, by this time, neither Arabel nor I could have been dragged away by teams of wild horses. Short of falling into the Johnstown Flood we could hardly get wetter anyhow.

We found ourselves left with one fireman and one policeman. I could see a reason for the fireman, he was keeping watch on Niagara, but the policeman seemed superfluous.

"I wouldn't mind stealing that Oriental," Arabel confided, "but I'm afraid it's too wet to carry."

The policeman must have heard, for he looked at her sharply. She winked at him, and he turned bright crimson.

Niagara was drying up.

Harriet suddenly moaned, "Do you realize, girls, that all the food I have in the world is soaked to a pulp? And tomorrow's Sunday, and I won't deal with that delicatessen on Third, even if they would deliver."

"Don't worry, darling," I said soothingly. "We've got plenty of the essentials."

"If they don't break a hole in the roof over *your* kitchen," she said gloomily, as several climactic bangs nearly burst our ear drums. That was indeed the climax. In a few moments, a horde of men trooped in. They told Arthur, whom they seemed to take for the man of the house, that the water tank had bust, right over the lady's kitchen, the water pressure would be low, might not be none . . .

Squelching, I ran down the hall. I would fill the tub and as many utensils as I could find before the desert took over. Telling Arabel to snatch up whatever she could find of Harriet's that would hold water—which on second thought struck me as a rather poor joke—I opened the door to find Percy alert on the ledge, not so angry as terribly, terribly hurt. Clattering like a milkmaid, Arabel followed me closely and we were able to fill the tub and most of the hardware. I gave a passing thought to the rest of the tenants, basking in the lap of ignorance, and only then remembered Miss MacDonald, next door to Harriet. Poor woman, she must be frightened half to death. We had forgotten all about her. I banged on her door. It opened promptly. Yes, she said, she had heard the noise and had gathered—through a crack in her door—what the trouble was. And thanks a lot, but she would be all right, her tub was filled and her pots and pans. She smiled pleasantly and shut the door.

It was one o'clock. The shank of the evening, Harriet proclaimed happily, and she began to get out the bottles stashed away in her handsome walnut dresser. She was bustling about, ordering Arthur and John to get out glasses, soda, ice (ours), and, laughing gaily, no water. The candles were guttering, and I went home for a fresh supply.

Percy seemed to have lost interest, or perhaps the day had tired him out, for he merely blinked at me from the couch and went back to sleep. I stopped for a moment to look at him, and thought, as I had before, we're going to go through it all again and we're such fools, again and again. I said, "No," out loud and ran from reality back to the kind of lunatic production one sees too seldom in a lifetime.

When the party had ended—and Harriet, bless her indomitable spirit, wanted it to go on forever—we climbed into bed, tired but too keyed-up to sleep, with Percy at our feet. Arthur said dreamily, "I wish W. C. Fields had been there." We began making up scenarios and laughed ourselves to sleep.

I don't know how much later, I half woke to feel Percy on my shoulder, his nose under my chin. I put my arm around him, hoping the tears that squeezed under my eyelids wouldn't bother him.

For the next two years, Percy had everything, or nearly everything, his own way. He wasn't tormented by the carrier, or a taxi ride, or a stranger in a strange place. What was the use? We had been given some vitamin stuff that was supposed to strengthen his teeth; I don't know whether it did or not, but as he rather liked it perhaps it did. When he felt in the mood to go with Arthur or me down to Nancy's, he came along. Quite often he didn't. Nancy was a little hurt but accepted the inevitable. Harriet was less easily appeased, and we put a lot of effort into trying to explain why we didn't force the issue.

"I want him to come in," she cried. "I miss him. I can't imagine why. He snubs me. He always has, but—I wonder if you'll understand this—I not only love that cat, I *respect* him."

We told her that we understood. We, also, respected him. She bounced in her chair, insisting that we didn't, we didn't at all, we were too young. For a moment, that shut us up.

Nancy, Arthur, and I were having drinks at Harriet's on a Sunday afternoon, and Nancy who had, for a wonder, said very little, suddenly spoke up. "Harriet," she said, "do you realize that Percy is years and years older, for a cat, than either you or I are (*is*, oh dear, I never know) for a woman? We both do what *we* want, as nearly as we can manage. Don't we? Why shouldn't Percy?"

I stared at my mother with surprise and pleasure. We weren't having an easy time, getting along together. Through circumstances over which she had no control, she had become my responsibility and she hated it. Her feelings had been hurt by Percy's reluctance to come downstairs with me. She had been thinking it out, and I was proud of her.

There was a moment's silence. Then Harriet said, "Arthur, freshen our drinks. For a toast to Percy, who has all the luck."

I suppose she was right. He had had the luck to live for nearly twenty-two years with people who had never tried to cramp him into a preconceived pattern. We rejoiced in his individuality, his strength of character, the special ways by which he expressed his feelings and his moods. If he was lucky, he had made his own luck. If he had had some good breaks, he himself had made the most of them.

Percy slept his life away, lying on my lap with Arthur sitting beside us, his hand on the gray and white fur, and our voices were the last sounds he heard.

✿ TWELVE ✿

Perhaps a year after Percy died, I went up to Fred Zeman for a check-up. Since the ulcer business I had made it a practice to call Fred, if he didn't call me, after Arthur's more frequent visits, and this had kept my mind—which was likely to wander off the subject—on the advisability of regular medical advice. I always enjoyed seeing Fred and this time was not surprised when he told me to stay until he was free for the day, he'd like a little chat. I wasn't apprehensive; he had given Arthur a clean bill of health only a couple of weeks before.

When the last patient had gone, he waved me into his office, called the nurse who was about to leave to bring some ice (as long as there's a doctor extant, there will be a dictator), poured a couple of drinks of Bourbon and settled back in his big chair. He began to explain why he had asked me to wait with such unnatural reluctance that I snapped at him. "I know what cerebral means and I can guess at arterio. But what's 'sclerosis' and how bad is it really?"

In layman's terms, it all meant hardening, or thickening, of the arteries of the brain. The brain could not function normally after a certain stage was reached. It might not, in this case, reach that point, miracles do happen, but . . . He went into further details while I sat and stared at him. *Arthur*.

When? He shrugged. No telling, as of now. He thought I had better be warned. It was a compliment to my good sense. No, there wasn't much to do. Drugs? Oh, yes, but there was nothing, so far, very satisfactory, nothing that really worked, for sure. He gave me another drink, kissed me as I left, and I went out into the dark.

Anyone who has read this far, will know that my one outstanding talent is the ability not to see what I don't want to see, even when It and I are eyeball to eyeball. During the following few years I was to work that talent overtime. Fred had told me the progress of the disease would probably be slow, given Arthur's temperament, and I pushed the whole thing far into the back of my mind. In effect, I forgot it for weeks, even months at a time. I noticed a certain slowing down; sometimes his clever hands fumbled over a simple job; I would catch him sleeping when I came home from the office.

Right after Percy died, we had sworn we would never again take a cat to live with us and had held to that resolution without wavering—or not much. To fill up the empty space, we went in for more sociability than usual, and then our landlord, neighbor, and friend provided a brand new line of distraction.

Business and professional people had been moving into the building for some time, but to be informed that domesticity was out, came with the shock of an explosion. There was some kind of legal stuffing in this turkey, but what it was I've forgotten if I ever knew. When we caught our breath, we couldn't blame Fred Scholem; for him, the new arrangement meant more money and less trouble.

We started looking. Let's not move out of Murray Hill, we agreed. Some problems would be solved (and others created) if Nancy were to live with us, as independently as possible. But our timing was wrong; all the large apartments were being cut up into small ones.

On a hot June Saturday, I pulled the filled shopping cart along Thirty-fourth Street, feeling as bedraggled as I looked, and for no reason whatever, thought, "Well, why not?" and walked into a new, big, "luxury" apartment house that had just opened its doors. A sign said it was air-conditioned, among other glories, and it wouldn't hurt to ask how much, and from the outside it looked pleasant, with big windows and red-brick facing.

The doorman sent me upstairs to the renting office where a perfectly groomed, pretty young woman with a blond coiffure greeted me cordially. I told her our problem, we went up a few floors, and she opened a door.

Across the length of a long room I looked out at the sort of view New Yorkers would rather have than bird song. Sky pierced by tall buildings far enough away to be appreciated. A row of old brownstones, with which I was entirely familiar from street level, came into view as I walked, in a trance, towards the nearly room-wide windows. Air conditioning. Perfect layout. The right-sized room for Nancy, with closet space galore and bathroom and doors between what would be "ours" and "hers." The rent was frightening.

We moved in July.

We did our best to persuade Harriet to let Arthur push her wheelchair around the corner and one block down Lexington to see some of the smaller apartments. She would have handy men and porters and doormen, up-to-date equipment, we would all be under the same roof, everything would be almost the same, but more comfortable.

She said, "I've lived in this apartment for forty years. I'm going to live here until I die."

The siege of Harriet Hedrick soon began. We heard only her side except for a few scraps of neighborhood gossip, most of which originated with Harriet herself. City officials, lawyers, sinisterly in the "pay of the City," Fred Scholem's lawyers—including, of course, himself—the Housing Commission, the Department of Health, the Department of Sanitation, most of her friends who took a dim view of her obstinacy, her own doctor who "turned traitor"—all were deployed against the formidable, stubborn, old woman. We were as neutral as she'd let us be; she wouldn't even come to see us. Who knew what skullduggery would take place behind her back? She was over ninety.

She had surrendered to age so far as to hire a housekeeper-nurse who slept on the sofa in the living room. She assured us, and I think it was true, that she'd intended to make this concession some time ago, and now that Fred Scholem—like everyone else—had "turned against" her, she was afraid to stay alone on the same floor. She didn't allow us to forget that we, too, had deserted.

It seemed as if she had gone clean out of her mind, but when we went to see her, which we did as often as we could, we found her bright-eyed, pink-cheeked, excitable, very full of business and bustle, keeping her lawyers up to the mark, and the nurse whispered to me that her appetite was good and she slept like a baby.

At first we had been appalled by Fred's heartlessness; it wasn't in character. Surely, as the building owner and a shrewd lawyer, he could find some way through the tangle? How could these men, presumably busy with more important affairs, waste their time trying to evict a frail, lame, nonagenarian? Her own lawyers were being paid for their trouble, but if they were half as high-powered as Harriet said, why couldn't they think up some way to rescue her?

The uproar continued for weeks, and as suddenly as it had started, it was over. Harriet had won, hands down. She bubbled with triumph, went over every detail again and again, and that carried her into the winter. And finally, we thought, we found the clue. We had been pretty slow, and we were still guessing, for Fred never admitted anything and we didn't ask.

A well-known criminal lawyer and one of the kindest of men, Fred could not help getting a kick out of baffling an opponent. Undoubtedly he would have liked Harriet out of space he could rent at a profit, but instead of giving in to her, letting her brood about her loneliness, unwelcome changes, and fears for her own safety, he staged a mock war, gave an old warhorse a last chance to gallop into battle. Whether this was true or not, it was the only explanation that satisfied us. For the Fred we knew was a gentle man.

About a year later, we sat next to him at Harriet's funeral. She had died in her sleep, in her own apartment. A friend of hers had taken charge of the "arrangements" and had allowed the mortician to smear her strongly molded cheeks and lips with red paint. I wondered if any of the people who crowded into that ghastly "chapel"—for Harriet Hedrick had had her share of fame—knew her half as well or cared for her as deeply as we three, and I doubted it very much.

Nearly four years without a cat. Or a dog. Or a nanny goat.

We were beginning to reminisce about the animals we had lived with. Arthur became nostalgic about the goat he had been given when he was a small boy. "A character," he chuckled. "She bossed the life out of me. I was eight, I guess, and she was bigger and stronger and knew exactly what she wanted, which was more than I did. She was a Christmas present from Grandma Kate and Grandfather. There was a cart, too, pretty fancy. All the other kids wanted to drive her, of course, but the minute she felt another hand on the reins, she simply sat down—harness, cart, and all. Wouldn't budge. She did a lot for my ego."

"What did she look like?"

"Sort of tan. Pretty face. Head like a slab of concrete when she butted."

There had been dogs and cats, some white mice, chickens, rabbits, the normal quota for a boy in a city where the big houses had big grounds around them and stables in back. When his parents moved into a Chicago apartment, all that ended for the boy who was an only child and, I guessed, lonelier than I had been.

After this sort of thing had continued for several evenings, off and on, I said, "Have we made a mistake? Perhaps Elsie was right when she brought us Talleyho and Talleyrand the day after Russia was killed."

"Was that how Talley came to us? Funny, I'd forgotten." He frowned. "I seem to forget damned easily nowadays."

But a kind of inertia had set in, and we let the subject drop. Until one evening Nelle came to dinner and announced that she knew the homeliest cat in New York City. He needed a home. She knew us very well and pulled out all the right stops.

She and Marcia lived in adjoining flats in a rather run-down building and late one Saturday evening had gone down to the dilapidated cellar where there was a laundry machine. They heard something crying. After a search, they found a very small, very sick kitten huddled against an exposed pipe in a hole in the wall. The super and his wife denied any knowledge of where the wretched little thing had come from, or how it got there. The girls wrapped it up and began telephoning for a veterinarian. Somehow, they got the name of one who would be available at that ungodly hour. The address was in a different and distant section of the city. Neither of them was particularly affluent, but they took a taxi and placed the kitten in the vet's hands.

He looked, and told them. "Too late, I'm afraid. Exposure, hunger, and God knows what else."

They had more charm than money, and they turned it all on. The more than half-dead kitten was restored to vigorous life. And then began their troubles. Marcia was owned by a jealous female who threatened the stranger with mayhem and certain death; Nelle had to be away for indefinite periods. In desperation, they persuaded the super's wife to feed the little stray. She fed it, logically enough, on the same food she gave her family: pastas, rich, highly flavored sauces, beans . . . He slept on a pile of filthy rags in the furnace room.

Arthur said, "Why is he 'the homeliest cat in New York'?"

"He has an extra toe on each forefoot. Silliest thing you ever saw. His feet are as big as catcher's mitts. He washes, but he looks bedraggled and no wonder, living the way he does."

A day or two later, we went uptown. The weather was sunny and the kitten was helping the super make passes at cleaning up a vacant lot next to the building. When Nelle whistled, there was a rushing sound in the dusty weeds and a small tiger leaped at her. She carried him into her apartment, where he promptly sharpened all his claws on a new wall-to-wall carpet. When dissuaded from this, he pattered from Arthur to me with flattering evidences of pleasure in making our acquaintance. His front feet were grotesque, madly disproportionate to his size. His head was broad, between finely shaped alert ears, his eyes reminded me a little of Percy's—more yellow than green or blue.

His large ears were fascinating. The tufts inside were extraordinarily thick and long, and on the tips were definite plumes of hair. (He would lose the plumes later, but not the tufts.)

Nelle was so relieved to shove the responsibility off on willing victims that she took him back to the vet for the proper shots and surgery and called to say she was about to bring him down and he would have to be kept in a dark place, and quiet, until the effects of the anesthetic wore off.

When our bell rang with an agitated jangle, we rushed to

open it. She fell inside, an irate young cat burst out of the handsome basket, looked around, and made straight for the windows. Nelle collapsed, making vague noises about "a dark place. Vet said, keep him quiet . . ." She had invested in the basket at Abercrombie's, the salesman had sworn it would hold any mere cat, and she had spent the entire trip downtown to us trying to push him into it. She was going right back to rip the hide off the salesman, that wasn't a cat, he was a monster and he belonged behind bars in a zoo and the bars would have to be strong . . .

The kitten was, in fact, still groggy, but dauntless. We put him in the bathroom where he made such a row trying to escape that we let him out for fear he would hurt himself—maybe he would find a dark quiet place if we let him alone. He had no such idea. Swaying on his enormous feet, he tottered around the living room and into the bedroom. We hurriedly shut off Nancy's rooms as a possible means of confining him in one place, more or less. He disapproved of the closed door which he reached just as we shut it, and we got a dirty look.

From the depths of a big chair, Nelle said faintly, "Don't talk to me about that yardarm. I *need* a drink. I'm supposed to be at an interview, right now." When she had gone, leaving the basket which she hoped never to see again, we in turn collapsed and laughed until our sides ached.

We named him Shadrach, because he had been rescued from a Fiery Furnace, or as near as made no difference. Nancy had other ideas, but we stood firm. This was not a character to be labeled with a cute, onomatopoetic name. Perhaps it was not the happiest thought, for the inevitable shortening came out Shad. He was another jumper, as authoritative and surefooted as Francis but less graceful. He particularly favored Nancy's room because he could go all around it without setting foot to floor. We told him firmly not to expect wall-to-wall carpeting; a scratching post had been ordered and meantime there were several upholstered chairs.

Thirty-fourth Street traffic, as viewed from the seventh floor, became almost an obsession. Except when asleep, he was quiet only when sitting on the wide window sill, staring down at cars, taxis, busses, trucks. Ears pricked forward, eyes wide, his head moved as the traffic moved. Thirty-fourth is a two-way street and heavily traveled. When a traffic cop blew his whistle at the Lexington Avenue intersection, Shadrach quivered with excitement, the sounds of a collision or an outbreak of infuriated horns sent him flying to his post no matter where he might have been. A conscientious and intelligent man named Barnes was Traffic Commissioner at the time, and we called Shadrach Mr. Barnes's volunteer assistant. Neither of them accomplished very much, I'm sorry to say.

Vanity, or instinct, or both taught him the finer points of proper grooming. It seemed unlikely that he had known a mother's care long enough to have learned from her. His origins were lost in the mysterious activities of the rapidly changing neighborhood in which he had been found. Not far from the building where he had apparently sought refuge, old houses were being torn down, block by block, unsettling not only the paying tenants but scattering the even more helpless unlisted occupants. Shadrach was among the lucky survivors. How had he lived so long? How had *we* survived so long?

Arthur threw a second-hand ping-pong ball in Shadrach's direction. Making a wide reach, he caught it neatly between his paws, in mid-air.

"This one was worth waiting for."

With sure swipes of one ridiculous foot, Shadrach turned the game into croquet or golf or pool or whatever suited his fancy. His use of his strange (although not unique) paws was endlessly interesting, for his front feet not only boasted extra toes, but were double-jointed. When, in an excess of playfulness or affection, he clamped both his forefeet around your wrist, surprising force was necessary to pry yourself loose—unless the doorbell rang or the telephone, or a fire truck, police car, or ambulance went by, in which case, naturally, he left you flat.

When we first moved into a modern apartment complete with dishwasher, even Arthur was a bit shy. Cartons of books, suitcases, and a barrel or two were still underfoot when our doorbell rang. A slender blonde smiled at me. She lived right across the hall, she said, and wondered if there was anything she could do. I gleefully seized her arm and dragged her into the kitchen where Arthur was scowling at the dishwasher. Charlotte gave a demonstration. She told us the names of the maintenance men and the doormen, which ones were most reliable, how to get hold of them, gave the building management a good reputation, and joined us in a drink. When she left we felt befriended and at home.

Neighborliness in New York has a special quality. It is ordinarily slow to show itself, usually remains casual and standoffish except in emergencies when New York nature turns human—until the fire, the accident, the death, or whatever is over when we all revert to normal. New Yorkers like it that way. But even in a big impersonal building, real friendships do develop and that happened with Charlotte and our family.

When Shadrach first joined us, Charlotte appeared one evening carrying a container of matzoth-ball soup, for which I have a passion, and of course Shadrach reached the door before I did.

She screamed. I grabbed the precious container before it fell and urged her to come in. I was a little bewildered.

Shadrach was looking up at her pleasantly, always ready to like new people and welcome guests.

"It—it's—a cat," she quavered. "I—they frighten me."

I knew her well enough by then to be firm. "You're not afraid of anything," I told her. "This is Shadrach. Shadrach, this is Charlotte. He's still very new here and very young. Please don't hurt his feelings."

Perhaps this switch in point-of-view took her by surprise. She stepped timidly over the threshold into the room, Shadrach preceding her. Conversation was rather strained, Charlotte's attention straying to the ravening beast we were harboring. We told her his story and she said faintly that he looked healthy enough now.

"I've never even touched a cat," she confessed as she was leaving.

"Well, try it," I challenged her. "Just put your finger on his head, as a starter."

She gulped, bent down, let her hand rest for the fraction of an instant on his head, and ran.

A long time later, she told us she had gone straight to the telephone, called one of her three sons and informed him of what she had done. "He didn't believe me," she added. "And then he began to laugh and said he was proud of me!"

I wouldn't go so far as to say that Charlotte ever became completely relaxed with Shadrach, and once he really scared her by hissing mildly when she accidentally rubbed him the wrong way. It was silly of him, but Charlotte was still not sufficiently feline-oriented to recognize a casual hiss as equivalent to a human's involuntary "ouch" when a comb gets caught in a tangle of hair.

Shadrach's steeplechase course around Nancy's room was closed off forever when night and day nurses came into our life. We were lucky. Each of the several knew her job, was easy to get along with and made as little trouble as possible. Shadrach had never heard horror stories about nurses in the home, but undoubtedly thought he was gathering plenty of his own. As Nancy's condition went from bad to worse, however, the sickroom lost its attraction. The odor of dissolution or perhaps an instinctive awareness of death coming close, did what nurses' discipline could not. He stayed away of his own accord.

Nancy then became the problem. She wanted Shadrach with her and blamed me for his absence. When the nurse went out on an errand or for a breath of air, I tried to get him to come with me, and went so far as to carry him. He despised being picked up, spit, scratched, wriggled, and escaped the moment I set him down near Nancy's bed. It was worse than useless, for inevitably Nancy would say, "He's cruel, like all cats. A dog wouldn't leave me." I wondered, as I had often before, why she had deprived herself for so many years. What had there been to stop her? But I couldn't ask her then, and now I shall never know the answer. She stopped breathing while she slept, and the nurse waited until early morning to call me. By the time Fred Zeman came, one of the first after-death miracles had come to pass: her face was as young and beautiful and relaxed as I remembered it from my childhood.

Uncle Charles Snedeker was dead, and so I alienated many people by rejecting the idea of any service. How could I explain? He had belonged to her youth, and to mine, and the only person who could have understood was my mother . . .

Before long we turned Nancy's room into a workroom, but Shadrach didn't like the way we arranged the furniture and snubbed us until he found the two desks had pieces of paper all over them and there were two typewriters.

"He's a literary bloke," Arthur said despairingly, after Shadrach had refused, with languishing eyes and luxurious stretching, to be ousted from the manuscript Arthur was trying to read. He had started his own literary agency, but his heart wasn't in it.

Several years before, he had reluctantly but realistically given up hope of making a new place for himself in the world that interested him. After a couple of partnerships had been tried and dissolved, he said in a unique outburst of bitterness, "I'm a lone wolf. You're the only person I can work with on equal terms. I am also a very small frog in a very big pond. Clever of me, isn't it?"

Neither of us discussed the possibility that I might give up my own work and throw in again with him. I know we both thought about it, but I, at least, knew the doctor's prognosis for Arthur and, at long last, was facing it.

So was Shadrach.

Coming home in the late afternoon or early evening, I became accustomed to finding this tableau: Arthur in the high-backed green chair, Shadrach tucked in the box Arthur had made for him under an end table, looking at him. Arthur might be half asleep or nodding over a book. Everything was quiet. I could come all the way into the room before either of them noticed. When they did, there was nothing lacking. I took to giving a wild halloo at the door. They jumped.

For how long during the day had that been going on? Finally, I told Fred Zeman. He gave me a new kind of pill. Arthur couldn't understand why he was taking them. Nor could I, really. Nothing changed for the better.

One morning Shadrach vomited several times—whitish, foamy, odd-looking stuff. I called the one person I knew whose attitude about cats was the same as ours. She gave me the name of her veterinarian. When I called him, he said, "Bring him right up."

Shadrach was too sick to object to the carrier, and we rode uptown to see Dr. J. R. Sterling for the first time. There wasn't the slightest question that he preferred animals to humans. A door closed firmly behind the doctor and our cat in the carrier. After some time, the doctor came into the waiting room; it was so early we were the only people there. He said, "Shadrach is very sick." He didn't say, "your cat." Cystitis. We didn't know then what that was. (A dim bell—Talleyho?) And he'd picked up a virus. He would stay in the hospital. Yes, of course I could call up, but no visiting; it would just upset him.

Exactly why this high-handed treatment inspired me with confidence, I don't exactly know. Possibly it was the child who knows she is to blame and welcomes righteous punishment. Possibly I recognized a kindred spirit; more than once I have been accused of arrogance and heartlessness, both of which I recklessly deny.

Two weeks later, Shadrach was pronounced ready to come home. He had narrowly escaped Talley's fate. He was already in the carrier when we picked him up and we were both too intimidated to peek. On the way home we talked to him, and he responded with all his former verve. He was entranced by what he could see of the trucks on Second Avenue. Well, he seemed to say, here I am actually in among all those lovelies I've been looking down at. Arthur took the carrier on his knee to give him a better view.

Now, coming down Second Avenue, the only way to reach the front entrance of our building is to turn on Thirty-third Street and cross Third and Lexington avenues. There's a slight rise to Park Avenue and at the corner of Park then stood one of the city's oldest and most spectacular armories, a stone edifice that consumed half a block on two streets and a full block on the avenue. Shadrach had never seen it before. He alerted as we reached it on the Thirty-third Street side, regarded it with interest as we rounded it on Park and then turned east on Thirty-fourth. He was to make that trip many times and would begin to squirm and talk as soon as we reached the old fortress. It meant Home. Whatever it is that cats have—ESP or a sixth sense—they can make gross humans feel stupid.

On the way from the taxi to the elevator, Arthur said, "Either this cat's tripled in size, or my muscles have turned to mush."

Inside our door, out of the carrier jumped a rampant young tiger. *But was he?* Was that Shadrach? Had the hospital mixed the babies up? This cat's fur was more gray than yellow. He rubbed against our legs and then made straight for his feeding plate; he had been short-changed on food, so he could eat as soon as he got home. He ate ravenously, and we watched him. When every speck of food had vanished, he turned and looked up at us. I committed the unforgivable sin. I picked him up in my arms.

He put his head against my neck, and purred. Out loud. He seldom purred and when he did it was like the sound of a waterfall very far away. Arthur put his face against Shadrach's, got a slather of kisses, said, "He's showing off," and abruptly walked into the living room.

Doctor Sterling didn't fool around. "Going to Dr. Sterling's" became a settled habit. I don't think Shadrach was a particularly amiable patient. After cleaning his teeth, the doctor looked a little shattered and remarked that next time he would administer a sedative. I asked him once about the gray tinge—which later increased—but got no satisfaction. John Terres, the naturalist, told me that after some virus infections even brilliantly feathered birds had been known to lose or change coloration. The change came gradually, and if you look closely the dark tiger markings are still visible. For a long time now he has been a rich, very dark gray with some white on the belly, throat, chin, and legs. It is a more distinctive costume than the tiger coat.

It took me a long time to put two and two together, as it frequently does, but I finally recognized the resemblance to Impo's illness after my father's death. Different cat, different people, different situations—but the same awareness of something wrong, something lost; the same blind tormented devotion.

Thanks to a doctor with wisdom and knowledge, and also probably to modern drugs, Shadrach bounded back to health like a rubber ball. I still found him curled in the box under the end table, still watchful, but the frightened tension I had tried to shut my mind to, had dissolved into a sad and loving resignation. Until he met Bridget, the Irish setter, and the mad little Welsh terrier puppy, he was becoming too sedate for his years.

Our acquaintance with Bridget began normally enough. A young man moved into an apartment near ours, bringing Bridget with him. Next to a collie—and I don't count the long-nosed, thin-headed breed—I like Irish setters. Bridget was hardly more than a puppy, gentle, friendly, lively, altogether enchanting. At the opposite end of the long impersonal hall lived a pretty girl with an infinitesimal Welsh terrier made up, apparently, of wires and absurd noises that she fondly believed were barks. Near Bridget lived a splendid basset hound named Duchess. She was no longer a puppy and had, I suspect, always been too dignified or class conscious to enter wholeheartedly into the three-ring circus that was about to start.

It began one weekend afternoon when Shadrach slid into

the public hall and announced himself at Charlotte's door. He was very fond of Charlotte and thought almost equally well of her wall-to-wall carpeting. His own home was definitely lower class with bare floors which combined, we thought, beauty and convenience. While I was trying to coax Shadrach home, a reddish whirlwind with a waving comet's tail, rushed at him in a flurry of joyful noises. Shadrach's back went up, the whirlwind skidded to a stop, got on its front knees, said "Woof" hopefully and smiled from ear to ear.

The new young man hurried to our little group. "She got out," he informed me unnecessarily. We looked down at our respective responsibilities with equal degrees of uneasiness.

"I'm not worried about Shadrach," I said, not altogether truthfully, "but if he scratches that beautiful nose . . ."

Shadrach had settled into an informal crouch. His hair lay smooth again, Bridget was panting but silent. Then the intransigent Spirit of the Welsh nation skittered through an open elevator door, yipping defiance at everything seen and unseen, braked at the unexpected confrontation of Ireland and America and poked her irreverent nose between the two.

As if a signal had been given, Shadrach took off down the long hall, with Bridget following and Welshie hell-bent behind them. Arthur came to our open door, said, "What the . . ." and began to laugh. The parade had reversed itself, Bridget now in the lead, Shadrach a close second; we could hear Welshie before she came in sight. As they reached our end of the track, they turned like bobsleds rounding a curve and shot by us. Shadrach had negotiated the curve with an ease Bridget couldn't match and was ahead, letting both dogs exhaust their energies by a cacophony of noise. Either everyone was away or our floor was tenanted by excessively timorous folk for not a door opened. Helpless with uncontrollable laughter, the human audience leaned weakly against the nearest wall.

The girl snatched up Welshie, who was wild-eyed but indomitable, the young man caught Bridget's collar, and I shoved Shadrach none too gently into home territory.

The show was repeated on other days, but not often enough to lose its charm. Once, or perhaps twice, they used our bare-floored apartment, with its long living room and hallway as an alternate course, but on his own ground Shadrach took the lead and Bridget slipped on the uncarpeted wood. Duchess was much too intelligent to compete, but now and then, on the sidelines, her heavy-set body with the mournful eyes supplied an artistic contrast to the star entertainers, who performed in the joy of their youth and vitality, and for the fun of the game. The show would have gone unnoticed in a more conventional setting—fields or lawns or sandy beaches. In the dull, drab-carpeted hall the three young animals glowed with a light that came from themselves alone.

The pace of Arthur's sickness quickened after a long period, for which I am thankful, when the disintegration of mind and body was more apparent to outsiders than to me. When the real became the unreal and the unreal the real, when the present fused with the past, places lost their meaning and people, even I, lost their identities, the inevitable finality was reached. He is far from me. If it were not for a friend, around whose head I would not be surprised to catch sight of a halo, to see him at all would be more than I could manage. It wouldn't matter to him. Sometimes he knows me and we laugh together. The timeless world in which he exists is not unhappy. There are hours when I can envy him that. He is, I am told again, "a good patient."

I moved downstairs to a smaller apartment. I took Shadrach up to Dr. Sterling's for a night and a day, Ann had come up from the South to help Margaret Carroll, who has been my right hand for years, shovel me and what was left of books and chattels into the new space. Everything was beautifully organized and, according to Hoyle, the program collapsed at unscheduled intervals, but by late afternoon everything was at last behind one door, and I went up for Shadrach. He had had a long uninterrupted stretch at home, but he remembered the turn at Thirty-third Street, and the armory, and I staggered from the taxi to the elevator hoping the carrier would not break into small pieces before I got the wild animal it contained to safety.

The new apartment was only two floors below the old one, but instead of a couple of steps between the elevator and our door, there was a long hallway to traverse. Even in the elevator he knew the difference. When I put the carrier down to catch my breath, it rocked with the fury inside. He wasn't wasting energy on vocal complaints but *we were in the wrong place—* and I was too stupid to know it.

Released, he bounded out—and stood stock still. His world had turned topsy-turvy. Then with a sure instinct, he made straight for a kitchen cupboard, pulled the door open, and crawled in. Food finally coaxed him out but furious incredulity was not assuaged. He prowled with darkest suspicion, and began to find familiar objects. They were all in the wrong places. We could have cut his disapproval with a knife.

The double bed had been made up and we were too tired to bother with the couch, so Ann and I pulled the covers around us and fell into exhausted sleep. We were awakened by an unearthly noise we could neither identify nor locate. Sitting up, I made out a dim figure in the doorway. Shadrach, of course. But no, I muttered, half aloud, he couldn't make a noise like *that*. He could, and did again. And again. It was as eerie as the cry of a bobcat on a wooded mountainside. The young Protesters who were still active might well have considered adding it to their arsenal.

"He'll quiet down," I told Ann confidently. "Now he's got it out of his system."

"I hope it hurts him as much as it does me," Ann commented crossly, and we went back to sleep.

The respite was short-lived. Something furry and the size of a young horse, pushed its way between us under the covers, and shoved. First he put his back against Ann and gave me the benefit of his considerable paws, legs, and body with his full strength behind them. It was like being pummeled by a bear. I shoved back.

He turned over with a great deal of unnecessary commotion and repeated the performance with Ann. It was a tossup whether being pummeled or used as a backstop was preferable.

Half under her breath, Ann said, "Oh, God, I wish I was home!"

I laughed, and after a moment, as if surprised, she joined in. Shadrach relaxed. Perhaps laughter was what he had been waiting for.

Nowadays, when I come home, Shadrach is waiting at the door, demanding where I've been for so long? He isn't angry, just a little hurt. That passes quickly and the criticism is familiar, common to all my tyrants. Perhaps Shadrach is more positive about it. After all, now there's just the two of us.

The time is not ripe for a further biography of Shadrach, but it's safe to say that he is the most demanding person I have ever lived with, and the most open-handed in granting rewards for good behavior. Sometimes he makes me think of the old Bosses of New York City, who extorted popularity and votes from the underprivileged by lavishing Thanksgiving baskets and jobs on the faithful. Like many of the old-fashioned

City Bosses and some of the classical tyrants, Shadrach enforces his will by personal charm.

We have a very good understanding. When I say, "Off the manuscript, Shadrach," he moves the necessary inches, usually leaving one paw resting on the paper as a kind of status symbol. Or when he thinks it's his dinner time and I say, "Not yet," he merely fixes me with eyes that remind me of Percy's until he hears, "Okay, kid, it's time now," when he leaps to the floor from wherever he has been, with sounds that clearly say, "High time, too! *Must* you be so slow?"

Some people like that kind of high-handed treatment. It's a little late to ask if I am one of them.

One long-ago summer, I accidentally struck up a sort of friendship with the ancient owner of a traveling circus. Until then the circus had meant an annual trip to Barnum & Bailey's Greatest Show on Earth at the old Madison Square Garden, and the intimacy of the tented arena drew me back night after night. The old lady, who didn't miss much, spotted me as a regular and the ticket taker said in an amused but slightly awed voice, "*She* wants to see y'," and jerked his thumb towards the glare and shadows behind the big tent. She was, I learned later, something of a legend in the circus world.

We would sit on the steps of her wagon, drinking beer and smoking cigarettes while we talked about animals and humans and audiences (she drew sharp distinctions between the last two) and love and tragedy and good times and bad times. I thought she was a hundred years old, but I doubt if she was any older than I am now.

She said one night, "Dearie, there's one kind of animal even the Good Lord hasn't ever been able to train, and that's the human." She cackled and took another cigarette from my pack. "Felines are hell to work with, but it can be done. Homo sapiens, never." She laughed again. "Didn't know I could reel off such fancy words? Live as long as I have, and you pick things up."

I suppose that's what I've been writing about—the things I've picked up.

o PLC
o BIP
2 cons. since 5/12/97
Exam 5/30/00

JSKC